The MoneyTrack Method

The MoneyTrack Method

A STEP-BY-STEP GUIDE TO INVESTING LIKE THE PROS

Pam Krueger

WILEY

John Wiley & Sons, Inc.

Published by John Wiley & Sons, Inc., Hoboken, New Jersey.
Published simultaneously in Canada.

For general information on our other products and services or for technical support, please contact our Customer Care Department within the United States at (800) 762–2974, outside the United States at (317) 572–3993 or fax (317) 572–4002.

Wiley also publishes its books in a variety of electronic formats. Some content that appears in print may not be available in electronic books. For more information about Wiley products, visit our Web site at www.wiley.com.

Library of Congress Cataloging-in-Publication Data:

Krueger, Pam
   The moneytrack method : the real person's guide to successful investing / Pam Krueger.
      p. cm.
   Includes index.
   ISBN 978-0-470-37232-6 (cloth)
   1. Investments. 2. Finance, Personal. 3. Speculation. I. Title.
   HG4521.K78 2009
   332.67'8—dc22   2008021331

Printed in the United States of America

10 9 8 7 6 5 4 3 2 1

To Harold Apfelbaum, Don Blandin, Neil Alford, Cynthia Zeiden and Katie Horgan, and the entire MoneyTrack *team, all of whom add magic to everything they touch.*

Contents

Foreword

As president and CEO of the Investor Protection Trust, I spend a great deal of time talking to people from all walks of life about investing and the "R" word: retirement. I have come to understand that regardless of differences in economic background or level of education, most of us share similar hopes and suffer the same fears about life in retirement—and I include myself in this group. With increasing responsibility being put on the shoulders of Americans to prepare for their own long-term financial security—including 20 plus years in retirement—it is crucial that all Americans know the essentials of saving and investing, and how to use that information to make wise investment choices and avoid investment fraud. We all recognize that investors need to know certain key facts and concepts, but it may be even more important to their long-term financial security that investors learn the behavioral process of investing—such as checking the background of a stockbroker or investment advisor before investing. Americans do not know what they need to about the process of investing and are often not taking even the most basic actions necessary to make good investment decisions.

Planning is a first crucial step in the process of investing. Without a plan, Americans are saving and investing blindly, and are unlikely to build a nest egg that can provide them with long-term financial security. The first step in planning is to set specific and inspiring financial goals and develop a plan to reach those goals. To quote Yogi Berra, "If you don't know where you're going, you'll end up someplace else."

The Investor Protection Trust has initiated a number of educational programs to help people understand the process of investing. I strongly believe in the power of education as a means to protect and empower all investors. Along with many other investor education initiatives, IPT supports the *MoneyTrack* national public television series because it does a great job of educating investors in an entertaining way, using humor and real life stories to illustrate important and sometimes complicated investment concepts. The program, created and co-hosted by Pam Krueger, also focuses on investment scams, helping investors recognize and avoid them as they invest for their future financial security. Let's face it—scam artists are very good at what they do. Many of them prey on people they know. The key to avoiding investment scams is to recognize them up front.

Pam Krueger brings the same practical, humorous, and down-to-earth approach to *The MoneyTrack Method* as she does to the *MoneyTrack* series. In this book, Pam has managed to distill the advice of the investment pros and present it in an entertaining fashion. The book guides readers through lessons that feature real people dealing with real financial and investment issues. We read about people who've became successful investors, as well as the people who have been victimized by investment scams. *The MoneyTrack Method* offers positive, independent, and objective advice that can be hard to find in the media these days.

I believe *The MoneyTrack Method* will help us as we strive to reach our common goal of educating and protecting investors so they make wise and safe investment decisions. I also believe the "Scam Alerts" found throughout the book will help countless readers learn to recognize and avoid investment scams. Readers will come away from this book having learned about the process of investing. They'll also know how to check out the background of a stockbroker or investment adviser as well as the investment itself.

Because of educational initiatives like the *MoneyTrack* program and *The MoneyTrack Method,* we can continue to raise the investor IQ of our nation and make it a whole lot harder for the scam artists to make a living. *The MoneyTrack Method* provides investors and potential investors with the information they need to invest wisely and safely for their future financial security.

DON M. BLANDIN
President and CEO, Investor Protection Trust

Acknowledgments

I would really like to thank Don Blandin, President and CEO of the Investor Protection Trust for developing so many outstanding programs that are helping ordinary investors make smarter investing decisions, and also for placing his faith in me by allowing me to be part of his vision. I am also grateful to all of the investing experts who've been on *MoneyTrack* Season Two, including Warren Buffett, John Bogle, Ben Stein, and many others with whom I've been fortunate enough to spend time dreaming up new ideas for turning dry investing lessons into real stories about real people. The *MoneyTrack* team at Beyond Pix and my co-host, Jack Gallagher, also deserve special recognition. (Who else would allow me to include the dog, Chloe, on a TV show about money?) Special thanks should go to Les Abromovitz who has the sharpest mind in the world of personal finance. I would also like to express my gratitude to Debbie Englander, Kelly O'Connor, and their colleagues at John Wiley & Sons, for their hard work on my behalf. Finally, Cynthia Zeiden should get all the credit she deserves for making sure *MoneyTrack* is seen on as many PBS stations as possible on this planet and any others we may discover.

CHAPTER 1

Investing 101

If you're like most people, Investing 101 is the course you knew you should sign up for but avoided taking. Even the introductory course on investing might frighten you or make you so sleepy that you shouldn't be operating heavy machinery. Nevertheless, the fact that you have avoided learning about investing doesn't stop you from complaining about how you don't have a dime put away for retirement or that your bills are piling up in that fruit bowl on your kitchen counter. Perhaps you're the type of person who whines that you don't have any money to invest, or even to buy a second fruit bowl, after paying your bills.

Investing doesn't have to be scary or complicated. On the *MoneyTrack* program that I co-host with Jack Gallagher, our motto is, "Keep it simple—and keep it real." Even when it comes to investing, we try to simplify complicated topics. Jack's role on the show is to make sure none of my advice or the advice from our experts goes over the viewer's head. You can be sure he wouldn't let this book make it into print if any of the investment topics we discuss are over anyone's head, especially his own.

Even though we feature guests such as high-energy CNBC stock expert, Jim Cramer, on our program, we take a low-key approach to money topics. There are no sound effects, except for an occasional groan in response to Jack's jokes. Since Jack is a former standup comic, he can't resist adding humor to every program. He also lightens up the educational presentations we conduct in conjunction with state securities regulators across the country. The securities

1

regulators in each state ensure that investments and financial advisers are on the up-and-up.

Aside from experts, we feature real people each week with real money issues and questions. Our goal on the program and in this book is to show you what works and what doesn't work when it comes to money and investing in the real world. As you learn about investing, you can be assured that no one is trying to sell you anything. *MoneyTrack* is sponsored by the nonprofit Investor Protection Trust, whose primary mission is to provide independent and objective information so consumers can make informed investment decisions.

Learning about investing doesn't need to be tedious or painful, and the terminology shouldn't send you to the dictionary. You'll often find that a term you've heard for years has a very simple origin. Maybe you reach for the remote at the first mention of Wall Street on the business news. The terms "Wall Street" and "The Street" are used to refer to the investment and financial community. Many brokerage firms and banks were originally located on Wall Street in lower Manhattan.

Whether you're buying or selling stocks on the New York Stock Exchange or Nasdaq, where investors buy and sell securities online, it usually boils down to a simple concept. When you buy a share of stock, you're purchasing a small piece of a company with the hope that it will be worth more someday. Even with all of the changes that have occurred over the past few hundred years, many transactions are just that simple.

The Origins of Wall Street and the New York Stock Exchange

Wall Street got its name a few hundred years ago when it used to be an area where cows grazed. A wall was built to keep the cows from escaping—hence the name *Wall Street*. I've given some thought to trying that with my dog, Chloe, a frequent guest on *MoneyTrack*.

Or maybe your eyes glaze over when you hear about the New York Stock Exchange. The New York Stock Exchange traces its roots to 1792. Twenty-four stockbrokers got together to form a private club. The club wasn't private for long, however. Well-off investors began buying and selling shares of each other's companies through the club, leading to the birth of the New York Stock Exchange. As a former stockbroker, I tip my hat to them.

Stocks are equity investments, since you own a piece of the company. In contrast, when you invest in a bond or put money in a savings account at a bank, you are a lender, not an owner. When you invest in equities, your potential rewards are greater. The historical performance of the stock market is far greater than the average return for other investments such as bonds, even though you might lose money over a shorter time frame.

OK, perhaps History 101 is even more boring to you than Investing 101, so let's fast forward to the present. Let's find an answer to this question: What do I need to know to begin investing like the pros?

Investment Basics

According to the Investor Survival Skills Survey, prepared by Opinion Research Corporation for Securities Investor Protection Corporation (SIPC) and the Investor Protection Trust (IPT) which was released on December 13, 2005, four out of five U.S. investors failed the "survival skills" test. Eighty-three percent of the participants in the survey lacked the necessary blend of basic knowledge and smart behavior to build savings into a retirement nest egg.

The results of the 2006 AARP Michigan Investor Protection Trust Survey are just as disturbing. A September 2006 survey of Michigan AARP members found that 38 percent are very concerned about being the victim of financial fraud. The participants said that if they were worried about the legality of an investment product, they would go first to their personal stockbrokers. Only 3 percent would turn to the Office of Financial and Insurance Services in Michigan.

AARP Financial conducted a survey, "The Cost of Financial Jargon: Barrier to Smart Investing?," that sheds additional light on this subject. The survey found that 30 percent of the respondents who were over age 50 made an investment they regretted, because they didn't understand it. Sixty percent said they don't read financial literature, because it is too difficult to understand. Twenty-nine percent failed to invest, or waited too long to do so, because the information they received was confusing.

Unfortunately, your own fears and lack of investment knowledge may be leading you down the wrong track. Just in case you're a member of the group that doesn't understand the basics, let's get started by explaining the distinction between saving and investing.

Saving is the process of putting away money. Investing is the process of making it grow. It's not enough to save money. To reach your financial goals, you need to invest your savings and accelerate the growth of your nest egg.

The Basics of Successful Investing

After talking with dozens of financial experts on *MoneyTrack*, we came to realize that the most basic investment advice is often the best. When you keep advice basic and simple, it's understandable and easy to follow. That's why we always try to break down the lessons from the pros into an action plan that's clear and concise. Here are five easy steps you can take to become a successful investor:

1. *Make investing a habit.* Get in the habit of investing a portion of your paycheck by contributing to a retirement savings plan through your employer. You can also arrange for a small amount to be deducted from your checking account each month and invested in a mutual fund or some other invest- ment vehicle.
2. *Establish investment goals.* Investment goals are your investment objectives, whether it's putting away money for retirement or short-term goals such as coming up with a down payment for a house. Hopefully, you'll be able to work toward several finan- cial objectives at the same time.
3. *Let time do the heavy lifting in reaching your investment objectives.* You take advantage of a concept known as the *time value of money.* If you have more time to save and invest, you are likely to end up with more money. You also utilize compounding, even if you only invest a small amount. With compounding, the money you originally invested produces earnings. You will receive additional earnings on the money you already received from the investment.
4. *Make sure your investments are diversified.* Increasing your diver- sification helps to reduce the risks that go hand-in-hand with investing. By owning a variety of assets, such as stocks, bonds, or cash investments like a savings account, you are couching your bets. It's extremely unlikely that all of these investments will perform poorly at the same time.
5. *Control the risk you are taking.* Investment temperament is your comfort level with risk. Some investors are open to taking

significant risks with their money. Others are uncomfortable with investments that present any level of risk. A certain amount of risk is necessary, however, to increase your chances of reaching your investment goals.

It is a generally accepted principle that the potential rewards are greater with riskier investments. Nevertheless, taking foolish risks won't get you any closer to reaching your financial goals.

The Risk of Not Investing

"Why should I have all that risk in the stock market?" a viewer in Boone, North Carolina, asked us. She couldn't see why investing in the stock market is a better idea than investing in CDs, which are certificates of deposit at a bank and are insured by the Federal Deposit Insurance Corporation (FDIC). You can also buy CDs through brokerage firms and credit unions. We posed her question to investment industry giant, John C. Bogle, the founder of Vanguard Investments.

Mr. Bogle responded by giving us a very practical comparison. He pointed out that if a savings account pays you 4 percent and the cost of living increases each year by 3 percent, you're only netting 1 percent each year. If you put $10,000 in that savings account, you'll end up with about $14,200 at the end of 35 years. If you put that money in the stock market and achieve a 7 percent return, your actual return is 4 percent per year after taking inflation into consideration. In 35 years, you'll have almost $40,000.

In fact, your return might be even better than 7 percent. From 1925 through 2005, the Standard & Poor's 500 Stock Index made up of large companies averaged 10.4 percent per year. Over the same time frame, the annual return for long-term government bonds was 5.5 percent.

Because you're usually losing about 3 percent per year to inflation, investments that are purportedly safe, such as CDs, are sometimes riskier than the stock market. Furthermore, capital gains from the sale of stock and dividends receive tax breaks that are not available to investors in CDs. On the flip side, however, you won't lose the original amount invested, even though the principal will be eroded by inflation.

Mr. Bogle wasn't advising our North Carolina viewer to stop investing in CDs, which certainly have a place in a diversified portfolio.

His point was that you also need stock investments to round out your portfolio and achieve the financial growth necessary to reach your goals. No matter where you put your money, the biggest mistake you can make is not saving and investing.

The Risk of Investing

With every investment, you are taking risks. If you invest in a CD at your bank that exceeds the coverage afforded by the FDIC, you might lose money if the financial institution goes belly-up. When you invest in a bond issued by a corporation, you might lose money if the company loses its ability to pay the interest owed to you or the amount to be paid back.

Within each category of investments such as stocks and bonds, there are different levels of risk. A mutual fund that invests in short-term bonds is less risky than one that invests in long-term bonds. Investing in government bonds is far less risky than buying so-called junk bonds, which are typically issued by companies that have a sub-par credit rating. Buying shares of a large and established company exposes you to much less risk than investing in the stock of a relatively new business that has few assets.

You need to be aware of the risks that are unique to each investment you are considering. Here are a few of the common risk factors:

- *Purchasing power risk.* With conservative investments in particular, you risk losing purchasing power. Because of inflation, whether it's low or high, the purchasing power of each dollar you have goes down. A savings account that pays 2 percent is a losing proposition if the inflation rate is 3 percent.
- *Volatility risk.* With many investments, their price is volatile. At any given time, the value of your investment may rise or fall. If you need to cash in your investment, you risk having to sell it when the price is low.
- *Interest rate risk.* If you see the attention paid to the Federal Reserve, you're well aware of the risk that interest rates go up and down. Fixed-income investments like bonds go up or down based on changes in the interest rate. Fluctuations in interest rates also have an impact on many other investments.
- *Market risk.* The stock market, or any market for that matter, goes through periods where prices are rising or falling. Quite

often, the general performance of the market affects the value of individual investments.

- *Company risk.* Even when the market is rising, your particular investment might be going down. A company with a dismal financial outlook will go down, even if you're in the height of a bull market where most stocks are going up.

Each company faces unique risks and challenges. For example, let's say a company makes fine fragrances for sale to upscale consumers. The company purchases its bottles and oils in France. If the value of the dollar is down against the euro, the company's costs may go up to the point where it will be difficult to make money.

A healthcare or a pharmaceutical company must cope with the risk that federal and state governments will change their policies on reimbursement. Insurance carriers may refuse to pay for a particular drug made by the company. A new drug might not receive regulatory approval from the Food & Drug Administration (FDA), or a medical study might question the value of the medication.

Companies face the risk of lawsuits leading to a drop in the value of their stock. It's also possible that a company's technology won't keep pace with other high-tech products. A weapons manufacturer may see its value fall when a new political party takes over the White House. Before investing in a company, you should consider all of the risks that it faces. Some of the best companies in the world run into temporary or even permanent problems. Consumer demand for their products may dry up or the company might be mismanaged. Fortunately, smart investors know how to reduce the risks that are an inherent element of investing.

Investment Pyramid

To understand risk, it helps to visualize an *investment pyramid* (Figure 1.1). It looks like your typical pyramid and has three sections. The base of the pyramid is made up of low-risk investments such as savings accounts and money market funds. In the middle of the pyramid, you find high-quality investments such as mutual funds and blue chip stocks. Blue chip stocks are companies that have been solid performers for years and are highly regarded by investors. The top third of the pyramid consists of speculative investments. Speculative investments are those that are quite risky,

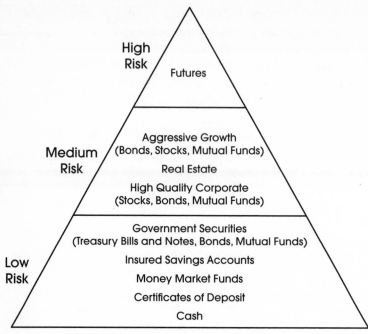

From the free Basics of Saving and Investing *guide by the Investor Protection Trust at: www.investorprotection.org*

Figure 1.1   The Investment Pyramid
Source: The Investor Protection Trust

but offer potentially higher returns. Stocks in small companies that are unproven and unprofitable are examples of speculative investments. As you move up the pyramid, your risk increases, as does your potential return.

You build your investment pyramid from the ground up. In the base of your pyramid, you keep safe and secure investments and your emergency fund. Everyone needs an emergency fund of three to six months of living expenses. This is the money that will keep your refrigerator stocked if you lose your job or need money to repair your car. Because the days of lifetime employment with one company are gone forever, you need a financial cushion in case your boss hires his nephew to handle your duties or your job disappears overseas. When Chloe acts up, I warn her that I can easily outsource her job to another dog.

But avoid investing all of your money in this layer. Shauna Kroon of Investopedia (www.investopedia.com) told us that you don't want all of your investments in the base of the pyramid. You need to take on more risk, so you have a better chance of increasing your return. Investments in the bottom third of the pyramid won't normally keep up with inflation and usually have the lowest payback.

The middle of the pyramid consists of investments that are slightly riskier but are likely to produce a higher rate of return. For example, a mutual fund that invests in stock is a good choice for the middle section of your investment pyramid. Your risk is spread among many stocks, not just one.

Some financial experts suggest that the top portion of the pyramid is your "Vegas" money. This is the money you can afford to lose without damaging your financial security. Just as you shouldn't take your rent money to gamble in Las Vegas, you should not put your financial future at risk by putting all of your savings in speculative investments.

Speculative investing does not mean throwing your money away. You should not be investing based on a stock tip from someone you just met at a party and barely know. Chances are, that person got the stock tip from someone he barely knew at a different party. Worse yet, most hot tips are cold by the time you hear them.

Billionaire investor Warren Buffett offers these straightforward rules for investing and avoiding scams. Rule #1 is, never lose money. Rule #2 is to remember Rule #1. Although never losing money isn't always possible, you can avoid losing money by resisting investment scams.

Scam Alert

Even if you're using money you can afford to lose and the base of your pyramid is stable, you should avoid the get-rich-quick schemes and scams that are designed to entice us into making a bad investment. During every *MoneyTrack* program, we expose the most common and dangerous money scams. In each chapter of this book, we will alert you to a potential scam in a special section called "Scam Alert."

Investor Scams and Traps

If you find it difficult to save and invest, the last thing you need is to turn your money over to a scam artist and never see it again. The problem is that many scams pose as legitimate investments and you're encouraged to invest by people who seem to be honest and concerned about your welfare.

Hedge funds, for example, have a reputation for being a remarkable investment opportunity. They are perceived as being reserved for the rich and famous. Hedge funds are offered by private partnerships that seek an exclusive pool of investors. The problem is that hedge funds are loosely regulated. Another potential problem is that the hedge fund manager may need to take inordinate risks with investors' money in order to achieve the high returns they are expecting.

You probably know Ben Stein, who played a teacher on *The Wonder Years* and in the movie *Ferris Bueller's Day Off.* Ben is also a lawyer, former presidential speechwriter, and the author of a number of investment books. Ben told us that hedge funds are for extremely sophisticated investors. Although you can make a lot of money, some of these hedge funds are run by crooks.

Blaine Bishop was victimized by one of those crooks. The former NFL safety was one of several players who lost big money to a slick hedge fund manager. The hedge fund manager was intelligent, sharp, and articulate, and seemed to possess considerable investment expertise.

The investment seemed to be going quite well for Bishop and other investors. The hedge fund manager sent statements indicating that the investor received a whopping 20 percent annual return. In fact, investors in the hedge fund lost big money.

The ironic aspect of hedge funds, Georgia securities regulator Kevin Moore told us, is that they started out as an investment strategy for lowering risk. Hedge funds make multiple investments that are designed to offset the risks you're taking. In theory, although one investment might lose money, others more than make up for those losses.

Kevin quipped that a better name for hedge funds is "edge funds." They look for opportunities on the edge and hope to make significant gains in highly unusual and nontraditional investments.

Blaine was one of several wealthy black athletes who fell victim to this scam. In many scams, the perpetrator targets people who share similar characteristics, interests, race, faith, or religious affiliation. Affinity fraud is a major scam that targets investors of any race, religion, or ethnicity.

Affinity Fraud

If you're an unsophisticated investor, you may tend to follow the crowd. Unfortunately, following the crowd may make you more vulnerable to *affinity fraud*. In an Investor Alert entitled *Affinity Fraud: Beware of Swindlers Who Claim Loyalty to Your Group*, the North American Securities Administrators Association (NASAA) warned investors to be aware of swindlers who claim loyalty to your group. In that alert, NASAA articulated the root cause of affinity fraud:

> *In a world of increasing complexity, many people feel the need for a short-hand way of knowing who to trust. This is especially true when it comes to investing money. Unfamiliar with how our financial markets work, too many people don't know how to thoroughly research an investment and its salesperson. So, many fall prey to affinity group fraud in which a con artist claims to be a member of the same ethnic, religious, career, or community-based group.*

Affinity fraud encompasses investment scams that prey on members who belong to an identifiable group. The perpetrators of the scam often enlist respected members of the group as a way to convince people that the investment is legitimate. Quite often, these respected members of the group are unwitting participants in the scam.

Typically, investors let their guard down because someone they know and respect is involved with the investment. Because of their affiliation with other participants, they may not investigate the investment as thoroughly as they otherwise would. Some investors assume that other members of their group conducted due diligence before investing, which may not necessarily be true.

The SEC offers this advice to minimize the risk of succumbing to affinity fraud:

- Check out everything, no matter how much you trust the person who brings the investment opportunity to your attention.
- Do not fall for any investments that guarantee returns or promise spectacular profits.
- Be skeptical of any investment opportunity that is not in writing or you are told to keep the information confidential.
- Don't be pressured or rushed into investing for fear that you will miss the so-called opportunity.

- Stay away from investments offered through unsolicited e-mails. You should forward the spam to the SEC at enforcement@sec.gov.

Until you become a seasoned investor, you should be putting your money in tried-and-true investment vehicles such as retirement savings plans through your employer and Individual Retirement Accounts (IRAs). You won't reach your financial goals by looking for shortcuts. By looking for a quick buck, you increase the odds that you'll become the target of a scam.

Other Scams to Watch out For

Some scam artists are able to gain your trust, even though they have no relationship to you. On many occasions, scams involve some variation of a Ponzi scheme. Charles Ponzi, no relation to either Potsie or Fonzie from *Happy Days,* was a well-known perpetrator of these schemes, though he was certainly not the first person to orchestrate them. In a classic Ponzi scheme, the fraudulent investment will purportedly pay huge returns. In fact, the returns, if any, come from the investments of subsequent investors, not from revenues generated by the business. Typically, later investors receive nothing as the Ponzi scheme collapses.

Ponzi probably never envisioned the types of scams that would be perpetrated today. Here are some of the crooks' favorites:

- *Spam scams.* Spam scams are quite common. You and millions of others receive an e-mail about a spectacular new investment that is basically worthless. This type of scam makes us long for the good old days when spam was limited to products that men hope they won't need until they're over age 90. Hit the delete button as quickly as possible when you receive investment-related e-mails from people you don't know.
- *Pump-and-dump schemes.* If you own a fax machine, you've probably received news about a can't-miss stock that's poised to go through the roof. In almost every case, the stock isn't worth as much as the ink and paper you lost printing the fax. These faxes are often tied to pump-and-dump schemes. The individuals who own the stock want to drive up the price so they can unload it. Once the fax campaign ends, the value of the shares will plummet.

- *Theft of personal information.* There are even scams where individuals pose as Social Security employees. They ask for personal information such as Social Security numbers and bank accounts. The purported employees claim you are entitled to extra money or that a computer glitch has wiped out your data.

Another scam made use of e-mails that appeared to be from Social Security. Recipients were advised to update their records and provide personal information. Social Security will never ask for private information via e-mail. Before providing personal information to anyone who claims to be from Social Security, you should call your local office or 800–772–1213.

You can report suspicious activity by calling Social Security's Office of Inspector General (OIG) hotline at 800–269–0271. A fraud reporting form is available online at www.socialsecurity.gov/oig.

Scam artists have also impersonated the IRS in e-mail campaigns. The IRS Web site, www.irs.gov, lists a number of fraudulent schemes. As an example, you might get an e-mail indicating that the IRS is working on a refund for you and the agency needs your personal data. If you receive an unsolicited e-mail from the IRS, you can help the agency track down the scam artists by forwarding it to phishing@irs.gov.

It's bad enough hearing from the IRS that you're being audited. It's far worse hearing from someone pretending to be from the IRS in order to steal your identity or use your personal information for fraudulent purposes.

Scams Victimizing Older Investors

Older investors are frequently the target of investment scams. These crimes are particularly heinous, because older Americans are more vulnerable. Because they may no longer be working, senior investors do not possess the ability to recover financially from a scam that wipes out some or all of their savings.

The NASAA and the SEC have warned consumers about seminars where a free meal is offered. Although the seminars are supposedly educational in nature, the sponsor of the event may pitch products that are unsuitable. These seminars often attract older investors who tend to have more time on their hands and are trying to stretch their income. The free meal is typically the bait that draws baby boomers and older Americans to the seminars. If I didn't get

Top Ten Investor Traps

In May, 2007, the Pennsylvania Securities Commission released its list of the "Top Ten Traps Facing Investors." The Commission listed those traps in alphabetical order:

1. *Affinity fraud.* With affinity fraud, con artists target religious, ethnic, professional, and cultural groups with offers of fraudulent investments. Members of the group, or individuals posing as members, gain investors' trust by playing upon the purported bond between them.

2. *Foreign exchange trading (Forex trading).* Forex scams often attract investors who are unsuited for trading international currencies.

3. *Internet fraud.* Investments of dubious value are pitched through the Internet using e-mails, instant messages, and phony Web sites. Typically, investors are spammed with unsolicited e-mails sent indiscriminately to thousands of individuals.

4. *Investment seminars.* These seminars are typically aimed at older investors and may be used to promote unsuitable investments.

5. *Oil and gas scams.* Despite seemingly endless increases in energy costs, investments in traditional and alternative energy projects may be inappropriate for small investors.

6. *Prime bank schemes.* With these schemes, investors are often promised high-yield and tax-free returns. The promoter claims they are financial instruments from elite overseas banks.

7. *Private securities offerings.* There is an exemption under the securities laws for private offerings. Because these offerings don't go through the securities registration process, they are sometimes fraudulent.

8. *Real estate investment contracts.* These investments may be securities and should be thoroughly investigated. Investing in real estate investment contracts is anything but a sure thing.

9. *Unlicensed individuals and unregistered products.* Anyone who sells securities or gives advice about buying and selling them must be licensed. Investors should also watch out for unregistered investment products. Quite often, promoters of these products claim you will receive a high return with no risk.

10. *Unsuitable sales.* Investments should be suitable for a person's age, risk tolerance, and financial situation. Too often, financial professionals recommend investments that are unsuitable for a particular investor.

to the mailbox first, my dog, Chloe, would be second in line at any seminar where a free meal is offered—right behind Jack.

According to a NASAA press release dated September 10, 2007, a recent year-long examination by members of the NASAA reached these conclusions about sales seminars offering a free lunch or dinner:

- All of the so-called seminars were sales presentations, even though they were advertised as educational workshops where no products will be sold.
- Half of the seminars made misleading or exaggerated advertising claims, such as a promise to turn $100,000 into $1 million for the attendee's heirs.
- Nearly 25 percent of them pitched potentially unsuitable products or strategies.

During follow-up sessions with attendees, salespersons frequently recommended variable or indexed annuity products, which may be unsuitable for older investors. As the old saying goes, there is no such thing as a free lunch.

Frequently, these seminars are conducted by individuals who claim to have expertise relating to older investors and retirees. They may have initials after their names that stand for a senior- or retiree-related designation. A designation like CFP (Certified Financial Planner) is extremely meaningful, because it requires extensive study and experience to obtain. In contrast, some of these senior designations require little in the way of education, training, or experience.

Designations do not necessarily reflect bona fide credentials. Titles such as "senior specialist" often serve as a way for a salesperson or adviser to gain an older person's trust. Building this trust is the first step in defrauding the older investor.

Securities regulators in Nebraska and Massachusetts have led the way by issuing rules prohibiting the use of senior designations that are not properly accredited. The Massachusetts regulation forbids the use of a credential or professional designation that indicates or implies that the agent of a broker-dealer is trained or certified to help senior investors, unless it has been accredited by an organization recognized by the secretary of the Commonwealth. The regulation defines "senior investor" as a person who is age 65 or older. On April 1, 2008,

NASAA announced a new model rule prohibiting the use of senior and retirement-related designations that are misleading.

To find out more about a particular professional designation, you can visit the Financial Industry Regulatory Authority (FINRA) Web site at apps.finra.org/datadirectory/1/prodesignations.aspx. The "Understanding Investment Professional Designations" screen allows you to learn more about designations used by financial advisors. You'll learn what educational and experience requirements must be satisfied to earn that designation.

Don't confuse the person's job title with a designation that must be earned. For example, just because someone's title is wealth manager or investment consultant doesn't mean that individual has the education and experience you expect from a financial advisor.

Before engaging anyone to assist you with your finances, you should make certain that person is licensed in your state to give advice regarding securities. You should investigate the individual's disciplinary history through your state's securities regulator. It is best to do business with someone who has long-standing ties to the community and is recommended by people you trust. Even if you have known someone for years or they come highly recommended, you still need to check out the person's background through your state securities department.

Securities Laws Violations

Many federal and state securities laws have been passed to protect investors. Unfortunately, just because there are laws prohibiting fraud is no assurance that you won't be victimized by a scam. Your best defense is to understand how some of these scams work and to keep your guard up at all times.

Scalping and *touting* violate the antifraud provisions found in Section 17(a) of the Securities Act of 1933 and Section 10(b) of the Securities Exchange Act of 1934. There have been cases where an unscrupulous publisher uses an investment newsletter as part of a scheme for manipulating the price of a stock it owns. The individuals involved in the scam tout a particular stock in the newsletter and then sell their shares after the price goes up. For example, on January 10, 2005, the SEC settled civil fraud charges against a columnist for MarketWatch.com. The columnist allegedly profited by secretly selling stocks shortly after his investment newsletter's positive recommendations caused their prices to rise.

The SEC has sued several Internet newsletter publishers who touted stocks without disclosing that they were paid to promote them. These publishers performed little, if any, independent research and lied about the success of certain prior stock picks. If an investment newsletter discusses a company and promotes it, the publication must disclose if it received compensation, as well as the nature and amount of the compensation.

Even if a newsletter is not touting stocks it owns, be wary of false and misleading statements used to promote the publication. The SEC disciplined one newsletter publisher for violating the antifraud provisions of the federal securities laws by misrepresenting the performance record of his stock recommendations and the success of his subscribers. In promoting his newsletter, the publisher falsely claimed that stocks recommended to subscribers increased an average of 135 percent over a 28-month period. He also lied and said that three of his recommended stocks increased by 660 percent, 230 percent, and 915 percent. The publisher claimed that over 1,170 of his subscribers became multimillionaires, thanks to his advice.

As our viewers on *MoneyTrack* have pointed out, if their advice is so good, why do they need to publish a newsletter? If you're a multimillionaire, one would assume you have better things to do with your time.

Skepticism is one of the best defenses you have against fraud. When you see over-the-top advertisements on television or in the newspaper, alarm bells should go off. In one full-page ad, a company advertised a free seminar to learn about software that will help you trade currency like a pro. According to the ad, you can turn a $1,000 gain into $100,000. The company extended its invitation to all types of investors, including retirees and people who have been burned by Wall Street. If you aren't skeptical when you see an ad like this and are ready to invest, get ready to be burned again.

On March 11, 2008, the SEC filed civil fraud charges against two promoters who made millions of dollars by selling a get-rich-quick stock trading system. The pair touted the trading system on infomercials and at investor workshops across the country. Victims paid as much as $40,000 for the classes, mentoring, and computer software.

The perpetrators of this fraudulent scheme told attendees about their own trading success and made bogus claims that 96.5 percent of their students were successful. In fact, neither of them had ever made money by buying and selling stocks. They did, however, make roughly $6.25 million from selling the stock trading system. Aside from the civil action alleging violations of the antifraud provisions of the federal securities laws, the pair faces a criminal indictment.

How to Avoid Investment Scams

Even if you are a risk-taker, you should approach every investment opportunity with caution. You should be building your pyramid with legitimate investments, not so-called once-in-a-lifetime opportunities. Don't allow greed to cloud your judgment.

There are many steps you can take to avoid falling for investment scams.

- Find out if the person touting this investment is registered with your state's securities agency. You should also investigate if there are any complaints against that person. Check out whether the investment is registered with your state and/or the SEC.
- Decide if this investment is consistent with your financial objectives. No financial professional should recommend any investment that is unsuitable for you in view of your goals and risk temperament. Your antennae should go up immediately if someone tells you an investment is a sure thing and guarantees that you'll make a ton of money. The marketing materials for legitimate investments disclose the risks and warn about potential losses.
- You should always understand the investment being offered to you. If the strategy or investment product cannot be explained in understandable language, you shouldn't be considering it. Don't be overwhelmed by a marketing pitch. Back away immediately from any investment that requires you to act immediately. Before investing, discuss the investment with someone you trust who has more financial expertise than yourself and has your best interests at heart.
- Make sure you understand the costs and fees related to the investment. Ask for a thorough explanation of how the person

selling the investment is compensated. Find out if the investment is liquid and what fees are incurred when you sell it.
Products like annuities may cause you to incur a tax penalty
if they are cashed in before you've reached the age of 59½.

- You need to investigate who is managing the investment and
  what that person or company's track record has been. Once
  again, your state securities regulator can point you in the
  right direction.
- You should always independently research an investment you're
  considering. Assurances and promises from the person selling
  it are not enough.

Most importantly, step away from any investment that promises
big gains with little or no risk. Every investment has risks, especially
those that are purportedly too good to be true.

MoneyTrack Method

Becoming an educated investor helps to reduce the risk that you'll
lose money on your investments. The Investor Protection Trust, www.
investorprotection.org, has a wealth of educational materials on its
Web site. Publications like *Kiplinger's Personal Finance Magazine*
also provide objective and easy-to-digest investment advice. And
I almost forgot the *MoneyTrack* Web site, www.moneytrack.org, and
our new relationship with MSN Money which offers our ScamAlerts.
OK, so I didn't actually forget, but I thought that would make the
plug more subtle.

The North American Securities Administrators Association (NASAA)
offers extremely valuable advice on its Web site, which is located
at www.nasaa.org/home/index.cfm. You'll find the name, address,
and phone number for every state securities regulator. In addition,
the SEC has published a wealth of educational materials to warn
and educate consumers about risky investments, as well as scams
to avoid. These publications are available at www.sec.gov/investor.
shtml.

Until you become a sophisticated investor and have built a
solid financial foundation, you should be sticking with traditional
investments like stock in companies that provide the products and
services you use every day. There are also well-regarded mutual

funds that have produced solid returns for investors in good times and bad. You can monitor the activities of these companies by reading the financial pages of your newspaper, instead of asking for an update from the person who cuts your hair or who gives you a free dinner at a local hotel.

Instead of investing in a company or venture that you know little or nothing about, create a diversified portfolio of investments that have been around for years. By buying different types of assets, you reduce the likelihood that all of your investments will drop in value at the same time and increase the odds that you will meet your financial goals.

One excuse people give for not investing is that it is too risky. What these folks don't realize is that they are taking on more risk by shying away from investing. By learning more about investing and how to mitigate the risks, you stand a far better chance of reaching your financial objectives. The biggest risk of all is not investing.

In the end, you don't need to get an A in Investing 101 to become a successful investor. You just need to be a little bit savvier about investing and the people who are pushing you to invest. As we always stress on *MoneyTrack,* investigate before you invest.

Even if the thought of investing makes you insecure, it's one of the best ways to achieve financial security. *The MoneyTrack* method is designed to make investing easy while keeping you from feeling uneasy.

Financial Security on $12 an Hour

*Y*ou *can achieve financial security on $12 an hour!!* Now there's a statement you expect to hear on an infomercial in the middle of the night, right after you learn about a pill that helps you lose weight while you sleep or exercise equipment that gives you washboard abs. Though most of our *MoneyTrack* viewers make more than $12 per hour, it's possible to invest like a pro even if your hourly rate is relatively low. The key is developing the right attitude and approach to investing.

I wouldn't have thought you could achieve financial security on $12 an hour until I met Mr. Earl, a gentleman who could teach us all a little bit about investing. Although his given name is Earl Crawley, his many friends in Baltimore and our television audience know him as Mr. Earl. We've talked many times on our program about the characteristics of successful investors and how investment strategies work; Earl showed us that the *MoneyTrack* method can be utilized by everyone in any income bracket.

Our *MoneyTrack* reporter, Matt Markovich, spoke with Earl at his job as a parking lot attendant. Even though he only makes $12 per hour, this likeable gentleman has achieved financial security for himself and his family. His portfolio is worth about a half million dollars. His house is paid off and he owes no credit card debt.

Earl also manages to share his good fortune with others. Charitable giving is high on his list of priorities. He gifts shares of stock to his church and has started an investment club to help others get their start as investors.

Earl is also quite generous with his financial advice. Earl told us, "Stop working so hard and let your money work for you." Throughout his life, Earl saved small, seemingly meaningless amounts, and turned them into a sizeable nest egg. His first investments were government savings bonds. Though he didn't know it, he was cementing the base of his investment pyramid. After that, he began buying blue chip stocks like IBM.

Earl took a disciplined approach to investing, and that's almost always better than putting a chunk of money in one investment at what may turn out to be an inopportune time. He also never fell for any of the get-rich-quick schemes we looked at in Chapter 1.

Dividend Reinvestment and Direct Stock Purchase Plans

A key element of the *MoneyTrack* method is to buy investments that will stand the test of time. Warren Buffett, one of the most admired investors in the world and a guest on *MoneyTrack,* has said, "If you are not willing to own a stock for 10 years, do not even think about owning it for 10 minutes." In addition, almost every expert I have talked to over the years advocates investing regularly and consistently. Furthermore, all of your earnings and dividends should be reinvested. Dividend reinvestment plans give you the opportunity to build a robust portfolio by putting your earnings to work.

Earl didn't know a thing about the *MoneyTrack* method when we first talked to him, but he took a similar approach with his investments. He understands how compounded earnings can make your investment grow faster and likes to keep stocks in his portfolio for years to come. Earl also reinvests his dividends to increase his stock holdings. This shrewd investor limits his investments to high-quality companies that pay dividends. He bought Coca-Cola stock right about the same time as Warren Buffett.

If you only own a few shares of stock, your dividends are likely to be small. Nevertheless, if you reinvest your dividends instead of cashing those small checks, it's possible to wind up with a tidy sum someday. If you pick the right investment and reinvest dividends for decades, you might be shocked by how large your nest egg can become.

Professor Pat Terrion proved our point with a quiz question he posed on our program. Pat, a professional money manager who teaches portfolio management and finance at the University of Connecticut, asked, "If you bought one share of Coca-Cola stock in 1919 for about $40 and reinvested the dividends, how much would you have today?" Here are your choices:

a. $50,000
b. $250,000
c. $4.5 million

The answer is $4.5 million.

Although that degree of success will be extremely difficult to duplicate, it usually pays to take advantage of dividend reinvestment. When you buy a share of stock, it might pay a dividend that is a portion of the earnings that are paid out to stockholders. Assuming the company offers a dividend reinvestment program, you have the opportunity to build your investment on a regular basis.

Dividend reinvestment plans go by a number of names. You might hear them referred to as a DRIP, which is an acronym for dividend reinvestment plan.

When you sign up for a dividend reinvestment plan, you agree that all of those payments will be reinvested. Your dividend check, whether it's a dollar or $100, buys more shares of stock. Each quarterly dividend buys you a bigger stake in the company.

When you reinvest dividends, your investment is compounded. The stock you originally bought pays dividends and helps you buy new shares. Those new shares also pay dividends and increase the growth of your portfolio. As Earl is fond of saying, your money is working harder for you.

It's easy to crank up a dividend reinvestment strategy. You need to own at least one share of stock, so you can begin reinvesting the dividends. There are many discount brokers through which you can purchase your first share, so you can get started.

As an example, there is an online brokerage firm that caters to small investors called ShareBuilder, www.sharebuilder.com. You can open a small account and buy the share you need to begin reinvesting dividends. In addition, ShareBuilder lets you schedule automatic investments at whatever interval you choose. You can put your investments on automatic pilot.

Once you've made your initial investment, you don't need a stockbroker to reinvest those dividend checks. The investment will take place automatically, and there will usually be a small service charge attached to each purchase. With most dividend reinvestment programs, you can also send in a check from time to time to add on to your holdings.

It's also possible to invest directly in a company and cut out the middleman. Hundreds of companies make direct stock purchase plans available to investors. These plans allow you to buy shares directly from the company without a stockbroker. Once you've purchased shares directly from the company, you can use dividend reinvestment to build your portfolio.

For example, the Walt Disney Company offers a direct stock purchase plan that enables investors to buy shares of Disney stock and reinvest cash dividends to purchase additional shares. Disney's direct stock purchase plan, as do many others, requires a minimum investment of at least $1,000. You're able to circumvent the minimum investment requirement by authorizing monthly deductions of at least $100 from your bank account to purchase stock. All cash dividends from the company are reinvested automatically to buy more shares of Disney stock. Disney, as well as most direct stock purchase plans, charges fees for enrollment in the program. You also pay a fee when you buy and sell shares of stock.

You can learn more about dividend reinvestment at these two sites:

- DRIP Advisor, www.dripadvisor.com
- DRIP Central, www.dripcentral.com

Don't let time drip away. It's one small way to get started as an investor right now.

Characteristics of Successful Investors

When I was a stockbroker, I met almost every type of investor. I found that the successful ones displayed similar characteristics. I realize now that Earl possessed many of the characteristics I saw in successful investors:

- *They engage in an information-gathering process.* Although Earl is dyslexic, he possesses an ability to listen. He talks to everyone he encounters and asks a lot of questions as part of his information-gathering process. As he works in the parking lot, he'll analyze which companies to invest in and asks questions of the people who are coming or going. He tries to find a consensus opinion about the investments he's considering. In the end, however, he thinks independently and doesn't follow the crowd.

- *They exhibit patience and don't look for shortcuts.* As a stockbroker, I had clients who were ready to sell investments after a week if they hadn't gone up in value. Unlike Earl, patience was not their strong suite. Earl, however, recognizes that you won't become wealthy overnight and you need to keep plugging away for years. Earl took extra jobs along the way, so that his daughter could attend a private Catholic school and he would have extra money to invest.

- *They are disciplined savers and investors.* Earl and others like him are good savers. They know the value of a dollar. They don't always need to drive a new car or to buy a bigger, more expensive home. To some degree, Earl's approach is like Warren Buffett's. Warren still lives in the Nebraska home he bought in the 1950s for a little more than $30,000. Living within your means is an important step toward the goal of achieving financial independence.

  Most of us throw away more money than Earl earns in an hour. We don't think twice about the small amounts we spend on gourmet coffee and Movies on Demand. We don't cut back on our cell phone usage, even though the bill is out of control—which reminds me: I'll have to get Jack to stop text-messaging me.

- *They are decisive and determined to succeed.* As we learned from Earl, it's our attitudes about investing that determine whether we'll be wealthy. If you're negative, impatient, and unmotivated, it's going to be difficult to follow the same course as Earl, even if you make much more than he does. Although you may be frightened to take that first step, you can become more sure of yourself and build your confidence.

All of us would do well to model Earl's calm, consistent, and disciplined approach to saving and investing. We need to avoid behavior that causes us to make stupid investment decisions. Each one of us is capable of developing the characteristics needed to become a successful investor.

Mind over Money

I believe in the concept of mind over money. If you make a conscious effort, you can change your behavior, particularly as it relates to investing. Our behavior affects our ability to save and invest. Although we cannot necessarily control how much we make, we can control how much we spend. And whether you make $12 an hour or $120,000 a year, you can control your investments.

Warren Buffett has said that the person with the highest IQ isn't necessarily the best investor. As long as you have ordinary intelligence, you need only to possess a temperament to control the urges that get other investors into trouble.

When it comes to saving and investing, our emotions affect our decisions and choices. Experts in behavioral finance research how our emotions and thought processes affect our investments. Some of us have a live-for-today mentality and spend more than we make, because it makes us feel good about ourselves. We rationalize that life is too short to deprive ourselves and we won't live long enough to enjoy that money. Others live in fear of the future and are afraid to spend anything.

There are many emotions, psychological issues, and behavioral traits that affect our ability to invest:

- Allowing emotions like greed and impatience to outweigh logic and rational thinking
- Rejecting data that don't coincide with what you already believe
- Following the herd mentality, where you always follow what it seems like everyone else is doing
- Fearing change
- Being overconfident
- Being competitive
- Showing unwillingness to admit mistakes
- Fearing risk, no matter how remote the risk might be

Emotions can get in the way of making smart investment decisions. If you understand your emotions and their influence on your investments, you are likely to diminish their impact on how you invest.

Scam Alert

Our behavior occasionally causes us to make stupid investment decisions. We receive a hot tip and we're so anxious to get in on the ground floor of the investment, we leave our brain at the door. Matt Kitzi, the commissioner of the Securities Division for the state of Missouri, warned our viewers about scams involving green energy alternatives. Matt and his staff shut down a fraudulent investment scam involving a car that purportedly could run on tap water.

When energy prices go through the roof, scam artists come out of the woodwork. The Securities Division for the state of Missouri has also put a stop to scam artists selling unregistered investments in oil and gas investment groups. According to a press release dated October 31, 2006, Missouri Secretary of State Robin Carnahan urged investors to be cautious when investing in oil, gas, or alternative energy ventures and call the state before putting money in these investments.

In Idaho, a company known as Genesis World Energy claimed to have invented a breakthrough fuel cell that could supply power to a household for 20 years, using only a bathtub full of water. Across the country, other companies have attracted investors using false claims that they have made energy breakthroughs.

How Gender Influences Our Behavior

On April 18, 2005, Merrill Lynch Investment Managers released a survey indicating that gender has a strong influence on investment behavior. The survey found that although women tend to know less about investing than men and don't enjoy it as much, they make fewer mistakes and don't repeat them as often. According to the survey, male investors are more likely to do the following:

- Buy a hot investment without doing any research
- Hold losing investments too long
- Ignore the tax consequences of making an investment decision

Women, according to the survey, are less knowledgeable about investing. Nevertheless, unlike men who won't ask directions when they're lost, women are more likely to turn to investment professionals for advice.

Merrill Lynch Investment Managers and Mathew Greenwald & Associates, Inc. analyzed the survey results and found that investors fall into four distinct investing personalities:

1. Measured
2. Reluctant
3. Competitive
4. Unprepared

Males were more likely than women to be competitive and measured. Women were more likely than men to be reluctant and unprepared. Nevertheless, more women than men described themselves as successful investors.

Knowing your personality type might help you to become a better investor. Competitive investors have difficulty letting go of bad investments. Reluctant investors often wait too long to begin investing. A large percentage of the reluctant investors participating in the survey said this delay was their most painful mistake.

The Paralysis of Analysis

As already noted, successful investors engage in an information-gathering process. The best investors do extensive research and analyze whatever data they can find about an investment. You need to be careful, however, that you don't run into information overload. When this happens, you learn so much that it becomes impossible to analyze all of the data. The paralysis of analysis undermines your ability to make investment decisions.

Even if you haven't done much research, it's possible to get caught up in the paralysis of analysis. You sift through articles and books about investing until you're thoroughly confused and unable to make a decision. At work, you don't sign up for your employer's retirement savings plan because you're not sure what investment option is right for you. As a result, you make the worst possible decision, which is deciding not to invest at all.

The good news is that you don't need to wrack your brain to figure out which companies to invest in. One investment option is a mutual fund that takes your money, along with capital from thousands of other investors, and puts it in the hands of professionals. The person in charge of the fund chooses which stock or other investment is best. The types of investments that will be selected are described in the fund's prospectus.

The prospectus for a mutual fund gives you the straight scoop on how your money will be invested. You'll learn about the fund's investment objective, business history, officers, operations, pending litigation, and much more.

The prospectus spells out the fund's strategy for making money. That may not necessarily occur, but you will receive enough information with which to decide if the strategy makes sense. Unfortunately, according to the SIPC/Investor Protection Trust survey mentioned in Chapter 1, only 58 percent of investors have ever read a prospectus.

Assuming you do read the prospectus, you will see that a mutual fund gives you instant diversification, although you still won't be as diversified as you need to be. True diversification comes from investing in a mixture of assets that includes different kinds of mutual funds with different investment objectives. A mutual fund's investment objective might be to invest in small companies. By investing in that fund, you will own a nice mixture of small company stocks but you will not be truly diversified. To diversify your portfolio, you might want to supplement your small company mutual fund with ones that invest in big companies, real estate, or even international stocks.

Index funds take a different approach, as we saw in a quiz question from one of our programs. An index fund is which of the following?

   a. A mutual fund that invests in index cards
   b. A fund that invests to keep up with the cost of living
   c. A portfolio of investments that are weighted the same as a stock index like the Dow Jones Industrial Average so that it will mirror the performance of that index

If you chose C, you're correct so give yourself a pat on the back.

An index fund creates a portfolio that is designed to replicate one of the many indices that are used to measure the performance of the market. An index fund contains a shopping basket filled with the same securities that make up a particular index. For example, the Wilshire 5000 Equity Index is viewed as a total market index. It measures the performance of all U.S.-headquartered equity securities that have readily available price information. The Standard & Poor's 500 Composite Index, or the S&P 500, as it is often called, tracks the largest industrial, transportation, financial, and utility stocks. In contrast, the Russell 2000 Index tracks smaller stocks.

You can find an index fund tied in with a host of indices. To name a few, there are bond indices, foreign stock indices, and even an index that tracks companies involved in clean-energy-related businesses. In fact, there are even investments tied to the S&P Global Timber & Forestry Index. That index is made up of companies that own or manage forested land and harvest the timber from it. The timber is used for wood-based products such as lumber and paper products. So now that you mention it, you may indirectly be investing in index cards. Nevertheless, you still don't get credit for answer A.

An index fund tied to one of the broad market indices tends to be a more conservative investment than one related to a more narrow index. Furthermore, an investment in an S&P 500 index fund is less risky than buying individual stocks. Because you are more diversified, you expose yourself to less risk. You're betting on a bigger chunk of the market, not just one stock.

Dollar Cost Averaging

On *MoneyTrack,* we asked which investor made $1 billion in just one day. Here's a clue: It wasn't Earl or me. It's one of the following four people:

a. Peter Lynch
b. Warren Buffett
c. George Soros
d. John Bogle

The answer is George Soros.

Most of us would be happy if our investments went up $100 in one day. Ordinary folks like Earl can be successful investors if they invest for the long haul, instead of trying to make a windfall from their investments over a short time frame. Even for financial professionals, timing the investment markets is extremely difficult.

On January 22, 2008, Comedy Central host, Steven Colbert, opened his show by going on a mock tirade about his fictional financial adviser, Gorlock, a green-faced alien from the future wearing a suit and tie. Colbert was "incensed" because Gorlock did not predict that the Dow Jones Industrial Average would drop 450 points before 10:00 in the morning. Colbert was particularly disappointed because Gorlock had come highly recommended by actor Tom Cruise. Unfortunately, not even the real stock market experts or space aliens can time the stock market and predict when it will plunge or soar to new heights.

The dollar cost averaging strategy allows you to invest systematically instead of trying to time the market. The strategy is recommended by many investment experts. When you utilize dollar cost averaging, you avoid putting too much money in a particular investment at the wrong time. For the strategy to be effective, you invest the same amount regularly, whether it's monthly or quarterly.

Let's say you have a thousand dollars you want to invest and you want to buy shares of a mutual fund. On the one hand, if you invest that thousand dollars all at once, you risk buying those shares when they're at their highest level in years or right before the price-per-share drops precipitously. On the other hand, if you invest $100 each month for ten months, you lower the risk that you'll pay too much for each share.

The dollar cost averaging strategy usually works well when you invest a fixed amount on an ongoing basis in the same investment. Suppose you want to invest $100 per month in a mutual fund that costs $10 per share. Your first $100 investment buys 10 shares of that mutual fund. If the value of each share goes down to $5, you buy 20 shares with your next investment. If the value of each share goes up to $20, your $100 investment buys 5 shares.

Over the course of time, the average price that you pay per share is likely to be favorable. You buy fewer shares when the price is high and more shares when the price is low. You don't need to guess when is the right or wrong time to invest.

To implement an effective dollar cost averaging strategy, you should continue investing through good times and bad. The strategy relies on a systematic approach, not one where you pick and choose when to invest. If you skip your regular investment because you think shares are too high, you undermine the strategy. You can't raid your principal when you're short of cash.

Automatic investment plans make it easy to implement a dollar cost averaging strategy. You can arrange for the mutual fund you've chosen to take a specified amount each month from your checking or savings account and deposit it. Because the transfer takes place automatically, you'll put your investing on cruise control and do not have to initiate the transaction yourself. One of Earl's earliest investments was a mutual fund in which he invested $25 each month.

Automatic investment plans force you to save. Money is deducted before you get your hands on it. If you agree to invest automatically, many mutual funds will waive their minimum investment. After you've initiated the paperwork, you don't need willpower to become a disciplined investor.

Aside from mutual fund investing, you can utilize dollar cost averaging to invest in individual stocks. You can schedule investments on a monthly, weekly, or biweekly basis. Assuming you keep at it, the average cost of the shares you buy tends to be lower than if you made a one-time investment of the same amount. Although there are no guarantees that your investment will go up in value if you keep investing in a bad stock year after year, the dollar cost averaging strategy keeps you from buying shares at the worst possible moment.

Even if you utilize the dollar cost averaging strategy, you still need to follow Earl's lead and thoroughly research every investment opportunity. As we always say on *MoneyTrack,* investigate before you invest, not after.

Becoming a Disciplined and Unemotional Investor

If you're like most of us who break our new year's resolutions on January 2, systematic investment programs can help you become the next Earl. Systematic investing serves another important purpose. It keeps you from trying to outguess the market. You keep investing, whether it's a bull or a bear market. A bear market is frequently defined as a 20 percent or greater decline in the stock market.

When you invest on an ongoing basis, you don't need to predict whether the market is spiraling downward or is just in the midst of a short-term correction. Automatic investing also deters you from panicking. Many investors stop investing when the market is going down. Investment professionals will tell you, however, that a down market is the best time to buy equities and the worst time to sell stocks.

Participating in dividend reinvestment programs and utilizing the dollar cost averaging strategy help investors to control their emotions. With a strategy in place that controls risk, you are in a better position to ignore upheaval in the market. You don't need to worry about whether the market is going through the roof or predict when it is ready to plummet.

After a tumultuous day on Wall Street, an equity analyst in Pittsburgh, Pennsylvania, was asked whether it was the dawning of a long-term bear market or merely a healthy short-term correction. The *Pittsburgh Post Gazette* quoted her as saying, "If I knew the difference, I'd probably own a small island called North America."

MoneyTrack Method

A key element of the *MoneyTrack* method is parking your money in a broad investment vehicle and making regular contributions to keep your nest egg growing. Whether you're Mr. Earl or an investment pro, you can never be sure which investments will go up or down. Therefore, it's imperative that you put a plan in place to invest gradually in the market. Automatic investment programs enable you to invest unemotionally and incrementally increase your holdings. Once you implement a dollar cost averaging strategy, you buy more shares when prices are lower and fewer shares when prices are higher. The average price you pay per share is more likely to be favorable over the years.

Along with shares you buy with your regular investments, dividend reinvestment plans can compound the growth of your nest egg. You build a bigger portfolio with every dividend that's reinvested.

Retirement savings plans through your employer also bring discipline to your investment strategy and reduce the emotional component. Contributions to your retirement savings plan occur every payday, so you don't need to agonize over whether it's a good time to invest.

Stop making excuses for not saving and get started now. All of us can make small cuts in our budget so we'll have funds to invest. For example, you might even take the bus to work to save on gas and parking fees. Just don't do it if you live in Baltimore, because you'll lose the opportunity to learn a great deal about investing from Earl.

CHAPTER

3

Don't Bank on an Inheritance for Financial Security

Some people expect a little help in reaching the goal of financial security. Instead of relying on themselves, they bank on receiving an inheritance to give them financial security. In reality, those unfortunate souls may find themselves with no inheritance and no plan for reaching their financial goals. Furthermore, even if they do receive an inheritance, it might not be nearly as much as they were expecting and they have no strategy for investing the money. Whether you expect to receive an inheritance or leave one to someone else, it's important that you avoid the potential problems that we learned about from the *MoneyTrack* experts.

Real life isn't like the movies. In the movies, a long-lost uncle who the star didn't know leaves a huge inheritance. Sometimes, the inheritance is a haunted house, a struggling business, or an incredible sum of money. Whatever the inheritance is, usually no one gives much thought to the person who died or how it should be invested.

In real life, inheritances are bittersweet. Someone you love usually has to die to collect that windfall. More than likely, your inheritance, if any, won't allow you to retire today or even thirty years from now. And in many families, the inheritance is a horrible painting that no one likes or a piece of jewelry that nobody wants. More than likely, you won't inherit a masterpiece or collectible that will light up the eyes of the appraisers on *Antiques Roadshow.*

Much has been written about the huge sums of money that baby boomers and their children will supposedly inherit in the coming years. There are approximately 78 million baby boomers, born from 1946 to 1964, according to a U.S. Census Bureau estimate as of July 1, 2005. The North American Securities Administrators Association (NASAA) has said that today's retirees stand to inherit over $7 trillion from their parents. Linell Smith, writing in the *Baltimore Sun* on March 11, 2007, wrote that some reports say that boomers stand to inherit $41 trillion.

Neither of these figures may turn out to be correct. There are a number of experts who believe that baby boomers won't collect the enormous windfall that was once expected to pass from one generation to the next. For example, AARP published a report in June, 2006 entitled, *In Their Dreams: What Will Boomers Inherit?*, concluding that over 80 percent of baby boomers had yet to receive an inheritance of any kind by the end of 2004. Those who had received an inheritance got a median amount of just $49,000. Over 95 percent of these inheritances were $100,000 or less.

There are various reasons for why you may not inherit a large sum of money. The person you expect to inherit money from may live past the century mark. Longer life spans, as well as rising healthcare and long-term care costs, also mean that your inheritance could be a whole lot smaller than you're expecting. Furthermore, the bulk of the inheritance you're expecting may be left to your children or your parent's new spouse. Who knows. Dad may find himself a trophy wife and start a new family, or Mom may become a "cougar," a term used to describe older women who date younger men.

If you're planning to wait for your inheritance instead of saving or investing, don't count your chickens yet. Unless you're related to Bill Gates, it's doubtful you'll receive a change-your-life inheritance. The painful truth is that an inheritance is not likely to finance your retirement. In fact, you may find yourself helping your parents make ends meet in retirement, rather than collecting an inheritance.

Therefore, you should be investing like the pros. Even if you do inherit some money or property someday, you can't go wrong by saving and investing now as if you won't receive a dime. You can't build your investment pyramid with a windfall that may never come your way. You should still be investing systematically in investments like 401(k)s and IRAs. If and when that inheritance comes, you can reevaluate your investment strategy as we will discuss in this chapter.

When it comes to inheritances, a wise person once said: "Expect nothing and you'll never be disappointed."

Preventing Battles to the Death over Your Estate

Inherited wealth comes with major baggage and can lead to family disputes. Families often wrestle with the gut-wrenching task of divvying up assets without dividing the family. When an inheritance is much less than beneficiaries are expecting and all of them feel a sense of entitlement, it is quite likely that battles over the assets will occur. Families are increasingly nontraditional with children from different parents or a spouse who is younger than the kids of the parent who died. Sometimes, the only winners are the lawyers.

We're all familiar with the protracted legal battle over J. Howard Marshall's estate. Marshall married Anna Nicole Smith, even though he was 63 years older than Anna. After J. Howard Marshall's death, his son waged a lengthy legal battle that went all the way to the U.S. Supreme Court. Before her death, few people had much sympathy for Smith and her battle to win Marshall's millions. When we filmed our *MoneyTrack* episode on inheritances, however, we heard stories that truly touched our heart and made us angry.

A woman named Sandra told us about her Aunt Audrey, who was blind. Despite that disability, Audrey began playing the piano at age four. During her sunset years, Audrey was convinced to hand over her power of attorney to two people she should never have trusted. Aside from numerous cash transfers from her Merrill Lynch account, they even took $3,500 on the day she died.

Sandra wanted little from her aunt's estate, except for some personal items that were not in the will. Sandra was devastated when she discovered those items were lost as well to the people who took advantage of her aunt.

In order to avoid a situation like Sandra's and prevent family squabbles, you need a will and/or other legal documents, such as a trust. A sizable percentage of the population doesn't even have a will, let alone the other documents they might need. For instance, an AARP survey found that 41 percent of Americans who are 45 or older do not have a will. Not having a will can cause unnecessary court costs, delays, and legal fees. And as unpleasant as the thought of dying is, everyone needs to think about estate planning in case you die prematurely or not so prematurely. Before we go further, let's look at some of the important legal terms that you should know about so that you can ensure your money and investments do not get exploited by scam artists.

Legal Documents You Can't Live or Die Without

A *will* is the legal document that transfers your property at death. A will stipulates how your property is to be distributed. A properly drafted will appoints an executor who is in charge of distributing your estate pursuant to your estate plan. Although it's preferable that legal documents be drafted by a licensed attorney, you can find a simple will form on Web sites such as Nolo.com.

Each state institutes formal requirements for creating a valid will. You must sign the will and your signature must be witnessed. Holographic wills are handwritten without witnesses, but they are not valid in every state.

You are much better off to dot the i's and cross the t's when preparing a will. A properly drafted self-proving will is less likely to cause problems down the road. Self-proving wills save time and effort if witnesses are deceased or can't be located.

If you have children who are minors or a relative with special needs, your will should appoint a guardian and an alternative guardian in case the primary person isn't willing or able to take on this responsibility. Otherwise, a court may appoint a guardian who isn't necessarily the person you would have chosen to raise your children or take care of the individual with special needs.

Probate is the process where the will is authenticated and property is distributed. The procedure varies from state to state and can take many months if all of the legal paperwork is not in order.

As part of the estate planning process, a trust might be established. *Trusts* are used to assure a quicker and more efficient distribution of property. They also help to protect a family's privacy.

Some trusts are extremely complicated, while others are relatively straightforward. Whereas some trusts are established during your lifetime, others are created by your will. A living trust is created during your lifetime and you still maintain control over the property in it. There are also irrevocable trusts, which cannot be changed after they are created.

A trustee manages any money or property you leave in a trust. The trustee ensures that the terms of a trust are enforced and beneficiaries are kept apprised. Among other purposes, trusts are a good way to keep irresponsible children from spending their entire inheritance or to pass wealth to ensuing generations in a tax-efficient manner. I could even set up a trust to take care of my dog, Chloe, if I pass before her. I could make Jack the trustee, assuming he won't steal Chloe's dog biscuits.

Wills and trusts allow you to effectuate your wishes, even if they seem a bit odd to the rest of us. For example, hotel baroness Leona Helmsley left a $12 million trust fund to her beloved Maltese. The dog, who answers to the name of Trouble, will be buried next to Helmsley in her mausoleum. Though Trouble made out under Helmsley's will, two of her grandchildren received nothing. She did, however, leave millions to her brother, who will care for Trouble. I think it goes without saying that it's not too much trouble caring for a dog that has millions.

Hoping for the Best and Planning for the Worst

On *MoneyTrack*, we continually urge our viewers to take control of their financial affairs. In addition to financial planning, you must ensure that your legal affairs are in order. That means you must plan for the best and worst times in your life.

Although planning for retirement may give you pleasure, it's not much fun to plan for a time when you must depend on others for care. There are a number of other legal documents that are necessary in case you become incapacitated during your lifetime. An *advance directive* is a set of written instructions that express the types of medical treatment you want or don't want.

A living will is one type of advance directive. The living will provides specific directions to healthcare providers regarding what type of medical care you do or don't want in case you lose the ability to articulate your wishes. A living will tells physicians whether you want to stay alive, even though you have no hope of recovery.

Your advance directive may contain a durable healthcare power of attorney in which you name an agent who will make medical decisions on your behalf. A durable healthcare power of attorney gives a trusted individual the right to make medical decisions on your behalf.

Some people avoid signing advance directives and healthcare powers of attorney because they're afraid their agent will pull the plug prematurely. These advance directives only apply if you have an end-stage medical condition or permanent unconsciousness.

Before it's too late, you should choose the person you trust with life and death decisions. Appointing a healthcare agent puts your healthcare decisions in the hands of someone you trust. Otherwise, the decision might be made by someone who is thinking about your inheritance, not you. The agent you appoint will not be responsible for your medical bills, so don't be reluctant to appoint a loved one for fear that the person will be stuck paying costs not covered by insurance.

You also might need a power of attorney so someone can make financial decisions on your behalf. As we saw during our filming of Aunt Audrey's sad story, however, you should exercise the utmost care before turning over this authority to anyone. Sadly, even a close friend or relative may take advantage of you.

Will It or Won't It?

Wills do not always achieve the purposes for which they were created. Wills do not control the disposition of property titled in a certain way. For example, a jointly held bank account is transferred at death to your co-owner, not the beneficiaries named in your will. A bank or brokerage account is often structured as payable on death (POD) or transferred on death (TOD) to named beneficiaries. The assets might, depending upon the wording, be transferred first to a co-owner, who has the authority to change the beneficiaries.

A will doesn't affect real estate owned by you and someone else who has a right of survivorship. Suppose your father remarries and owns his home with his second wife. Even if your father's will leaves his share of the house to you, all rights go to his second wife.

Wills do not change the beneficiaries named on a life insurance policy. Worse yet, those beneficiaries may not be up to date. If a loved one fails to update her beneficiaries, the proceeds of the policy might go to a divorced spouse or whoever was named at the time.

Unlike a trust, wills have no effect before you die. Even though you are named as an heir to a fortune in a will today, the person can change the will tomorrow and you're out of luck. A divorce, a death in the family, or other significant changes in your life should prompt a change in your will. For example, when you move to another state, it is a good idea to seek out legal advice and have a new will drafted. Your new state of residence may have different rules for drafting a valid will. In addition, states often have their own inheritance tax statutes.

Even if you have a trust, you'll still need a will. The will distributes property that may have been overlooked in creating the trust or newly acquired assets. If assets are not transferred to the trust, they are distributed via the will. Your trust and your will may name different beneficiaries.

If a person dies without a will, assets are distributed according to the laws of intestacy, which depend on the state you're in. These state intestacy laws are often based on traditional family relationships. Someone who has lived with the deceased for years may not be entitled to any portion of the estate. Ultimately, without a will, the wishes of the deceased may not be fulfilled.

Killer Living Trusts

In areas of the country where the population is older, you'll see numerous ads for living trusts. Most of these ads make you think that no older person should be without a living trust. Mary Beth Franklin of *Kiplinger's Personal Finance Magazine* warned us that although living trusts can be a valuable estate planning tool, they may not be the panacea that they're billed as by a persuasive salesperson.

With all the hype surrounding living trusts, here are a few things you might not be told:

- *The cost of a living trust may be significantly more than a simple will.* Although it will save on probate down the road, the up-front cost might be considerable. You must also title all of your assets in the name of the living trust, and that may be expensive.
- *Because a living trust is revocable, the assets contained therein are still part of your estate.* A creditor can come after those assets to collect bills. In addition, many older persons mistakenly believe the assets in a living trust won't disqualify them for Medicaid if they need to rely on that program to pay for long-term care.

- *Although living trusts are often touted as a way to quickly and privately distribute your estate, this isn't always the case.* Since you still need a will to dispose of property not included within the living trust, the process may not be as quick or private as your heirs hope it will be. That will must be probated. Furthermore, some of your personal information will become public, such as when your house is sold by the trustee of the living trust. In addition, a poorly drafted living trust can result in legal problems for your heirs, just as a sloppily written will can lead to court disputes.

To avoid potential problems, you should engage the services of a competent attorney who has considerable experience in the estate planning area.

Watch out for seminars that deal with living trusts but the promoters have a different agenda. As we will see in Chapter 4, con artists sometimes use living trusts to introduce themselves to older investors. They might charge a modest fee for preparing the documents. Their goal, however, is to soften you up with the hope of selling you unsuitable financial products or to entice you into questionable investment opportunities.

Finding an Attorney to Draft Your Living Trust

Living trusts and estate planning documents should be drafted by a licensed attorney with expertise in this area. Many state bars operate certification programs to set standards for lawyers who practice in certain specialties. In those states, you can find an attorney who is certified in a particular area such as wills, trusts, and estates.

You can also ask friends, relatives, and business associates for recommendations. Make sure they used the lawyer for estate planning and not an unrelated matter like a landlord-tenant dispute. You might also check with your county's bar association to see if it offers a lawyer referral service.

Another resource is a national directory of attorneys called Martindale-Hubbell. It gives you details regarding the lawyer's educational background, and ratings are available for some firms. This resource is available in most public libraries and online at www.martindale.com.

Some states allow you to investigate whether any disciplinary actions have been taken against an attorney or if clients have filed complaints against the lawyer. The bar association in your county can point you to any public records that might be available. Once you've found some good candidates, call and ask for an estimate of the fees and whether there is a charge for an initial consultation. The written fee agreement should spell out the charges.

Avoiding Family Feuds

Discussing the inevitable now is the best way to avoid problems down the road. According to Les Kotzer, an estate planning lawyer and the coauthor of *The Family Fight: Planning to Avoid It,* children should be encouraging their parents to address inheritance issues. Les believes that the key to avoiding disputes over an inheritance is for parents and children to communicate, even though those conversations are sometimes uncomfortable. Children don't want to be perceived as being greedy or giving the impression that they are looking forward to their inheritance.

Parents may also avoid bringing up the subject. On the *MoneyTrack* program, Les told us that many parents come from a generation that didn't like to discuss these issues. Les believes that having these discussions is extremely important. Otherwise, there may be painful surprises when a parent dies.

Just as it's important to have a frank discussion with your kids about sex at a young age, it is imperative that families discuss wills and estate planning before it is too late. A parent or grandparent may lose cognitive function or could lack the capacity to make or change a will. It behooves parents and their children to sit down as soon as possible to discuss this uncomfortable subject.

Many families wrestle with whether to divide the estate evenly among the children or give more to the child who needs the money most. Even though a child may not necessarily need the money as badly as a sibling, uneven distributions may lead to hard feelings. The child who is shortchanged may resent that a sister or brother is "rewarded" for not working as hard or making bad choices.

Another contentious issue is whether a child with several children should receive more than a brother or sister who has no kids. If a great deal of money is left to grandchildren, the child who doesn't have kids may question the fairness of the distribution. All of these issues should be discussed with the hope that the will's beneficiaries will feel they have been treated fairly. In the end, however, parents can leave their money to whomever they wish, including charity, or spend every dime. In the end, when families fight over money, nobody wins except the lawyers. Will contests are often lengthy and costly disputes.

In Les's book, that he wrote with Barry Fish, the estate-planning attorney points out several situations that may result in disputes. Suppose a father in his will leaves his baseball card collection to his son. The baseball card collection was appraised years ago for $5,000 and he leaves $5,000 in cash to his daughter. A dispute may arise if the baseball card collection is worth $20,000 at the time the father dies, yet his daughter only receives $5,000.

Les is no fan of do-it-yourself wills, because they often use imprecise language. A will that leaves all of a woman's antiques to her daughter may create a controversy. It may not be clear which property bequeathed is actually an antique.

One possibility is for children to use events in their own lives, such as enrolling in their 401(k) plan at work, as an opportunity to ask about their parents' retirement savings plans. Kids can talk about software they're using to organize their assets and might ask if their parents would like to try it out with their paperwork. If there is an event in the news like the Terri Schiavo court case, ask your parents' opinions and whether they have a living will. When you prepare your own will, as well you should, it's the perfect excuse to ask your parents about theirs and where it's kept.

When you ask your parents about these sensitive matters, remember that it's a discussion, not an inquisition. Frank discussions about estate planning can help family members understand their parents' thought processes. Even if you don't necessarily agree, it's one positive step toward understanding why the estate is being distributed in a particular way. These conversations can help parents avoid leaving a legacy of hate among their children.

Estate and Inheritance Taxes

Estate planning is particularly difficult, because the federal estate tax exemption is a moving target. Nevertheless, estate planning is important even for families with relatively small estates.

In 2008, there is no federal estate tax unless your estate is valued at $2 million or more. For extremely large estates, the highest federal estate tax in 2008 is 45 percent.

In 2009, the estate tax exemption rises to $3,500,000. In 2010, no estate taxes are owed, no matter how much property you leave to your heirs. In 2011, unless Congress acts, the estate tax exemption is scheduled to go back to $1 million.

Your taxable estate may be much larger than you think. The value of all of the following are added up to determine if the estate owes federal taxes:

- Stocks, bonds, real estate, interest in a business, and cash
- Personal property
- Your share of jointly owned property and accounts
- Retirement savings plans, profit sharing plans, and IRAs
- Property you have given away but retain a lifetime interest
- Gifts that don't take effect until you die
- Half of any community property owned by you
- Life insurance policies unless ownership was transferred irrevocably to a trust or another person
- Annuities

Even though a CD or bank account goes directly to a beneficiary at the time of death, it is still part of the deceased's taxable estate. Property transferred in anticipation of death may also be viewed as part of your taxable estate. Although the property transferred may be subject to tax, this doesn't affect the recipient's entitlement to keep it.

No estate taxes are owed if property is left to a surviving spouse, assuming that person is a U.S. citizen. Your family might still be in need of estate planning, even if you are planning to leave all of your assets to your spouse. If you have a large estate, it might make sense to leave some of your property directly to your children to take full advantage of your estate tax exemption. Your spouse can then use his or her exemption to pass on the remainder of the assets.

You can also take advantage of the annual gift tax exclusion. You are permitted to give away as much as $12,000 per year to anyone and to as many people as you choose without reporting those gifts. As we will see in Chapter 14, a parent or grandparent can make a lump sum contribution of up to $60,000 per beneficiary to a Section 529 college savings plan. To make a contribution of that size, you are permitted to use five years of the annual gift tax exclusion all in one year. Once this occurs, however, the annual exclusion cannot be used again for the same beneficiary until the five-year period has passed. If the gift-giver dies within five years, some of the money may be viewed as part of the deceased's taxable estate.

As already noted, the revocable living trust helps your estate to avoid probate. Because the trust is revocable, however, the assets remain in your taxable estate. Only an irrevocable trust can remove assets from the decedent's taxable estate.

State Inheritance and Death Taxes

Even though you may not owe federal estate taxes, the state where you live in may tax an inheritance. It is important to check with an attorney in that state to see what taxes may be owed. Many retirees decide where to live based on how inheritances are taxed in that state.

Jan Warner, an elder law attorney, and Jan Collins wrote about the confusion regarding these taxes on February 12, 2008, in the *Pittsburgh Post-Gazette*:

> *It's easy to get confused when talking about the various taxes that may affect the assets of an estate. In fact, estate, inheritance and death taxes are often used interchangeably, although they are quite different. The estate tax is one levied by the U.S. government on estates that exceed certain asset levels and is paid by the personal representative of the estate. Depending on where the deceased person lived, the state government may also levy an estate tax.*

According to Warner and Collins, some states levy an inheritance tax, which is paid by the person receiving the inheritance. In these states, beneficiaries are required to pay a percentage of what they receive. Smaller inheritances may be exempted. Inheritance taxes may be owed, even though there is no estate tax. Their Web site can be found at www.nextsteps.net.

The Risk of Needing Long-Term Care

You may not need to worry about estate planning or estate taxes if you or your spouse needs long-term care. Long-term care expenses have the potential to exhaust the assets of average-sized estates. If you need long-term care for an extended period, the issues of estate planning and estate taxes may be moot.

Statistically, the odds of your needing long-term care are high. According to a February 2008 report issued by the Center for Retirement Research at Boston College, more than two-thirds of those over age 65 will need long-term care at some point in their lives. Forty percent of that group will need care for two years or longer.

No matter how old you are, you face the risk of needing long-term care. Although the average nursing home stay is about 2½ years, you or a loved one might need care for far longer. For example, people who suffer from Alzheimer's disease might require care for years, and the expense can wipe out even a large estate.

Even if you are wealthy, long-term care expenses can take a big chunk out your estate. Most long-term care is viewed as custodial in nature, not curative, and isn't covered by Medicare or Medicare supplemental policies. If you have few assets and a low income, you may qualify for Medicaid, which is a federal program administered by the states. Generally, although there are exceptions, Medicaid won't pay for long-term care until your other assets are exhausted.

Long-term care costs are rising steadily. According to the 2007 MetLife Mature Market Institute survey, the national average daily rate for a private room in a nursing home is $213, or $77,745 annually. A semi-private room in a nursing home costs an average of $189 per day, or $68,985. Be grateful if you don't live in Alaska, because that state has the highest average daily rate for a private room, $510.

Assisted living is less expensive, because the resident requires less assistance with the activities of daily living. The average monthly base rate, according to MetLife, is $2,969 or $35,628 annually. In Washington, D.C., however, residents of assisted living facilities pay an average of $5,031 per month. There are usually additional charges for dementia care. With nursing home care or assisted living, residents are sometimes charged separately for certain services. Even if you receive care at home, services are quite expensive.

What Long-Term Care Policies Cover

Despite these risks, many folks avoid buying long-term care insurance. Their excuse is that they would rather die than go into a nursing home.

In fact, a long-term care policy can help you stay out of a nursing home. A comprehensive long-term care policy will pay for care in a variety of settings, not just a nursing home. A good long-term care policy should cover nursing home expenses, assisted living, home health care, adult daycare, and even homemaker services. Many policies pay for house modifications like a wheelchair ramp, so the person who needs care can live at home for as long as possible.

Each policy has conditions that must be satisfied before any benefits are paid. Usually, it must be demonstrated that you are unable to perform two or more activities of daily living, such as bathing or feeding yourself, or have a cognitive impairment.

The consensus among experts is that you should decide whether you want to buy a long-term care policy by age sixty. As you get older, the price becomes prohibitive, since the premium is based in part on your age at the date you apply for a policy. You also risk that your health will deteriorate and you won't be eligible to buy long-term care insurance.

According to the American Association for Long-Term Care Insurance, the average premium for a 55-year-old is $1,075 per year. The average premium at age 65 is $1,923 per year. Couples can get a significant discount if they both purchase policies. There are even a few companies that offer shared-benefit policies where spouses can tap into the same pool of money to pay for long-term care expenses.

The premium for a long-term care policy is based on factors such as the daily benefit purchased, duration of the benefits, your health, and your age when the policy is bought. The premium stays the same for the life of your policy, unless a rate increase is granted by your state insurance department for all policyholders in the same classification as you. Sometimes, the rate hike will be significant. If you buy a tax-qualified policy, some of your premium may be deductible and your benefits may be tax-free.

Cutting the Cost of a Long-Term Care Policy

Although long-term care insurance may be expensive, there are ways to cut the cost of a policy.

- *Avoid the bells and whistles.* You don't need to buy all of the extras that the agent is pushing. One important option to consider is an inflation rider. This helps your policy's benefits keep pace with the escalating cost of long-term care.

- *Extend the elimination period.* To cut the cost of a long-term care policy, you should consider a longer elimination period, which is the waiting period for benefits to begin. Agreeing to wait longer for benefits to begin reduces your premium. It's much like raising the deductible on your car insurance to save money. Another option is to buy a policy that pays benefits for a shorter time frame or with a lower daily benefit.

- *Buy a group policy.* Group long-term care insurance is usually less expensive than an individual policy. Group policies often offer basic coverage with fewer options at a cheaper price. Many employers are now offering long-term care policies as an employee benefit, although the company won't necessarily pay any of the premium. You can pay for the policy using payroll deduction. You may be able to cover a parent or in-law at the lower group policy premium.

- *Look for investments that also provide long-term care coverage.* If you're in the market for an annuity to generate income in retirement, you might find one that also provides coverage for long-term care expenses. There are also life insurance policies that you can buy, or may even own now, that permit tapping the death benefit to pay for long-term care expenses.

You must also take the time to compare prices from company to company in order to find the best price on the coverage you need.

Evaluating a Long-Term Care Policy

Before buying long-term care insurance, you thoroughly need to investigate the company offering the coverage and compare the policies offered by several carriers. Don't rely on the assurances of the agent selling you the policy.

It's extremely important to check the financial strength of the company that stands behind the policy and look at its commitment to selling long-term care insurance. Try to find a company that has been selling long-term care policies for a long time. Otherwise, you may wind up with a policy issued by a company that will lose interest in these policies and stop writing them. You could find yourself hunting for coverage at a much older age and you won't necessarily be a very desirable risk to insure.

The insurance company must supply an outline of coverage that will help you compare policies. In addition, the National Association of Insurance Commissioners (NAIC) offers a consumer guide and worksheets so you can compare policies. The publication is called "A Shopper's Guide to Long-Term Care Insurance" and can be found at: www.naic.org/store_pub_consumer.htm.

Check with your state's insurance department for help in evaluating the company and the policy. Ask if there are complaints against the company and if it has a history of requesting rate increases every few years. Check out the agent, too.

Some people recognize the risk of needing long-term care but haven't done anything about it. The 2008 Retirement Confidence Survey conducted by the Employee Benefit Research Institute (EBRI) and Mathew Greenwald & Associates found that 54 percent of workers and retirees surveyed are not confident about having enough money for long-term care expenses. However, according to a February, 2008 report from the Center for Retirement Research at Boston College, about 90 percent of elderly households do not have any type of long-term care insurance. Based upon these statistics, a sizable number of retirees and their families will find themselves in a very difficult position if the risk of needing long-term care becomes a reality.

Investing Your Inheritance

Assuming you do get an inheritance someday, what should you do with the money? Although it's difficult to generalize when your inheritance might be anywhere from a thousand dollars to six figures or more, the *MoneyTrack* method offers several strategies for investing your inheritance money.

If you do inherit *change-your-life money*, the last thing you should do is change your life right away. Don't quit your job in a huff or start giving lavish gifts and money to friends and family members. Remember, these gifts are irrevocable, and you may be sorry afterward, especially if the recipient blows the money instead of investing it. Accordingly, we recommend giving yourself a cooling-off period before investing, lending, or spending the money. During this time, it might be wise to put the inheritance in a money market fund until you develop an investment strategy.

It may become public knowledge that you've come into a large sum of money. You may begin to get phone calls from financial professionals who have heard about your windfall. They might even pressure you to take action now, and that action invariably starts with hiring them. Put their name on a list and tell them you will be deciding whether you need an adviser in 90 days. If they call before the 90 days is up, take them off of your list.

How you invest an inheritance depends on many factors, including your dreams and long-term goals. For example, you may dream of changing careers or opening a business. If you dream of early retirement from your current job, you might use some or all of the inheritance to move toward that objective. If you aspire to travel the globe, your inheritance may cover those expenses, but you still need to consider how you'll make a living when you get back. Short-term thinking will not help you formulate a strategy for investing your inheritance.

Remember that your inheritance may not go as far as you think it will. It might be compared to someone who dreams of making $100,000 and finally does, but doesn't realize you still must set priorities and can't buy everything in sight. Similarly, even if you inherit a large sum of money, you must still prioritize. Furthermore, although you may now be able to afford the initial cost of a dream, you must still pay for ongoing expenses. As an example, you may have enough to buy your dream house, but you still need to pay the taxes and other bills that come each month.

Your strategy also depends on your current financial situation. If you haven't saved a dime for retirement, your first priority is funding to the max all retirement savings plans for which you're eligible. You may even wish to look at using your inheritance to fund an annuity that guarantees an income for you and a spouse or life partner.

If your finances are in order, you should still carefully consider your long-term goals in order to develop an investment strategy. You may wish to put more money in aggressive investments that have the potential to produce higher investment returns. Nevertheless, this doesn't mean you should be viewing your inheritance as your

"Vegas" money, as we discussed in Chapter 1. An inheritance should reinforce your investment pyramid, not topple it over.

Depending on the size of your inheritance, you might have enough to live your dream right now. In that case, your investment strategy should be focused on preserving your brand new nest egg and generating income. Even if you're able to retire tomorrow, however, you must still plan for the years ahead to ensure that your income needs will be met. That means you need to keep some money in the stock market to keep pace with inflation.

As you develop your strategy for investing the money, you must look at your current portfolio and your asset allocation. Asset allocation is the process of dividing your nest egg into a diversified mixture of asset classes, such as stocks, bonds, and cash investments such as money market funds. Your asset allocation should be based on your investment objectives, risk temperament, and time horizon, which is when you expect to need the money. If you find you have too much money invested in one particular asset class such as stocks, it's time to rebalance and shift more of your funds to a different investment like bonds. Rather than shifting assets, you might use some of your inheritance to bolster the asset classes in which you are underinvested.

It is a good idea to avoid investing your windfall all at once. When you invest a large sum, you risk leaping into the market at a very bad time. One alternative is to invest 10 percent at a clip in investments you've researched extremely well.

You may decide to pay down debt with some of the money. This is a particularly good idea if you have high-interest credit card loans. As we will see in Chapter 15, the issue isn't as clear-cut if you are thinking about paying off your mortgage with some or all of your inheritance. Depending on the terms, it may be smart to let your mortgage ride and invest your inheritance. A compromise position is to put some of your inheritance toward prepaying your mortgage and invest the rest.

Honoring the Memory of Your Benefactor

You may wish to honor the memory of your loved one by using some of the inheritance to benefit one of that person's favorite charities. Aside from writing a check to charity, another option is a donor-advised fund. According to the American Endowment Foundation,

Scam Alert

You won't have to worry about how to invest your inheritance if your benefactor is scammed. Scams can ruin your retirement and can pass along your inheritance to a crook.

Ruth Mitchell, a retired professional skater and coach, trusted the wrong person. She and her husband, Len, dreamed of a leisurely retirement until their CPA and close personal friend, Barry Corkin, stole their $100,000 nest egg. Corkin lured nearly 40 of his so-called friends and clients into a phony real estate bond scheme that was, ironically, called Guardian Investments. Corkin promised investors a 7 to 8 percent return each year. For 11 years, he kept the scam alive by sending investors "dividend" checks. In reality, they were receiving their own money back, as well as doctored-up statements. The IRS eventually caught on to Corkin's scheme that had netted him $11 million.

Today, Ruth gives skating lessons to help ease their financial shortfall. Len works on architectural projects in his garage workshop. They hope to receive roughly 30 percent of their money back after Corkin's assets are liquidated. Corkin was sentenced to just over seven years in prison for fraud and tax evasion.

If they're lucky, the Mitchells will receive a fraction of the money they lost to Corkin. Ironically, not only did their CPA steal a huge sum of money from them, the Mitchells also paid taxes for 11 years on the so-called income they were receiving from their investment with Corkin. In reality, they were only receiving their own money back from the investment, which isn't taxable.

www.aefonline.org, donor-advised funds are vehicles "that provide simple, flexible, efficient ways to manage your charitable giving. You and your family can enjoy immediate and maximum tax advantages, make grants on a flexible time table, build your charitable legacy, and increase your philanthropic funds for future grant making."

Generally, contributions to a donor-advised fund are deductible. You can also donate securities that have gone up in price and are permitted to deduct their fair market value on your current tax return. This donation also helps you to avoid paying capital gains taxes on the sale of those securities. In most cases, donations remove assets from your taxable estate.

You can draw on the assets in the donor-advised fund in order to make grant recommendations to a public charity, usually in the amount of $100 or more. In the interim, your account balance grows tax-free.

Another way to honor the memory of your benefactor is to use your inheritance in a way that would make that person smile. If the person leaving you an inheritance believed strongly in higher education, use the money to pay your child's tuition—or your own, for that matter. If your benefactor built his or her fortune by investing in mutual funds, maybe you should continue that tradition. The person leaving you money may have made many sacrifices over the years that resulted in your good fortune. It's doubtful that your benefactor would be pleased if you frittered the money away.

Unless you are left a fortune by your Uncle Mortie who was a riverboat gambler, it's unlikely that your benefactor wanted you to blow the money in a high-stakes card game or on a new wardrobe from Paris that will be out of style by next year. And even Uncle Mortie might turn over in his grave if you use his inheritance to buy a gas-guzzler like a Hummer or Lamborghini. As I recall, Uncle Mortie cared about the impact of fossil fuels on the environment.

MoneyTrack Method

If you're waiting for an inheritance to fund your retirement or make you financially independent, you're asking for trouble. To achieve financial security, you need to begin investing now rather than waiting for a windfall from a relative who may like his dog more than you. The planning process involves much more than just saving and investing money. It means making plans to address the legal, health, insurance and tax issues that come with being mortal.

You probably need an estate plan, even if you're not wealthy. Mary Beth Franklin told us that having a simple will isn't enough for most families. Although most Americans won't need an elaborate trust, estate planning can benefit even middle-class families.

Wills and trusts can't just be filed away in a dusty drawer—or even a clean one, if you're a better housekeeper than I am. You should always make sure they're updated as your circumstances change, such as the birth of a grandchild or a divorce. The person you're leaving money to might be the last human being on earth you want to inherit your estate.

It's imperative that you regularly update the beneficiaries on your retirement savings plans, bank accounts, and life insurance policies. You might have forgotten to change them and are leaving money to a former spouse or a life partner who turned out not be your life partner. Remember that these beneficiary designations take precedence over your will.

Estate planning is tied in with retirement planning. With both processes, you're preparing an inventory of your assets and liabilities. You're also gathering information regarding all of your retirement savings plans, as well as any insurance policies you might have. As you plan for what you hope will be a long and satisfying retirement, you must also determine how you want your assets distributed during your lifetime or upon death.

Potential heirs to a fortune should never bank on that money to fund their retirement or some other financial goal. The estate may be dissipated because of an extended illness or financial reversals. The parent may remarry or choose someone else to receive the bulk of the estate.

You need to shop around for an attorney to handle your estate planning, rather than just picking one out of the phonebook. It is also imperative that you shop around for the best price on long-term care insurance and find yourself a reputable carrier from which to buy a policy. The insurance company that insures your home, car, or life is probably not the carrier to write your long-term care policy. Many major insurance companies do not sell long-term care policies.

Long-term care policies are sometimes marketed by agents as estate insurance. Children are encouraged to pay the premiums for a policy that covers their parents. This strategy helps to diminish the risk that the parents' estate will be eaten away by long-term care costs. It also cuts the risk that children will bear the full burden of caring for aging parents.

Going through life with the expectation of an inheritance is not a financial plan. An inheritance is a gift from a loved one that might enhance your lifestyle, not finance it. It's not your birthright. And more than likely, it won't fund your retirement, so you'd better start planning now for the day you retire.

CHAPTER

4

Retirement Reality Check

If there's one element of the *MoneyTrack* method that you can't ignore, it's that planning is everything. In the course of our travels while filming *MoneyTrack* and talking to investors across the country, we discovered that some people spend more time planning vacations than planning for retirement. Without thorough planning, you're in for a rude awakening when you retire. As part of the planning process, it's important that you get real about how much you need to save and invest for retirement.

After considerable planning, we spent one episode of *MoneyTrack* on Cape Cod in New Seabury. We chose that location because one out of every four Cape Cod residents is retired. It's always been one of those exquisite resort communities that attracts retirees. No matter where you live in retirement, whether it's Cape Cod or Cape Coral, Florida, you'll need to watch your spending to make sure you don't run out of money.

As mentioned in Chapter 3, the first wave of 78 million baby boomers is on the cusp of retirement. Boomers, the nickname for the segment of the population born between 1946 and 1964, should be planning seriously for the day they retire. With hopefully 20, 30, or even 40 years or more of life ahead of them, a key issue facing them is how much it will cost to live in retirement.

Maybe you're not worried about outliving your money, but perhaps you should. As comedian Jackie Mason joked, "I have enough money for the rest of my life—as long as I don't buy anything." As we all know, living the good life costs real money. Therefore, when it comes to retirement planning, you need to get real about how much it will cost.

Wake Up and Smell the Coffee

Before she died, advice columnist Ann Landers frequently advised readers to wake up and smell the coffee. As you plan for retirement, you need to heed her advice. You need to be much more realistic about how well you're doing as you plan for retirement.

According to the 2007 Retirement Confidence Survey conducted by the Employee Benefit Research Institute (EBRI), about 60 percent of folks age forty-five and older have less than $100,000 in retirement savings. Almost half of the workers surveyed have saved less than $25,000, not including their house. Seven in 10 members of that group say they have less than $10,000 in savings. Remarkably, despite these unsettling statistics, 70 percent of the respondents are somewhat or very confident that they will live comfortably in retirement.

EBRI's survey also indicates that less than half of baby boomers have planned seriously for retirement. Most of them have not tried to calculate how much they need to save and invest. No one can have confidence that they will thrive financially in retirement unless they've crunched the numbers.

Unless you really want to become anxious, make sure that coffee is decaf as you consider some of the factors that affect your ability to retire:

- *Longer life expectancies:* To plan appropriately for your retirement, you need to accept that longer life expectancies mean you'll need more money in retirement. After you stop working, your nest egg has to last a lot longer than it once did. Not that any of us is complaining about longer life expectancies; it just means you need to put away more money for retirement and keep it growing for an extended period.
- *Rising cost of healthcare:* Advances in medical science are helping us to live longer. We're paying a price, however, because healthcare costs are escalating rapidly. The rising cost of healthcare necessitates that we save even more for retirement. The cost of long-term care is also skyrocketing. As we saw in Chapter 3, the average cost of a year in a nursing home is approaching $80,000. Another grim reality is that many corporations are scaling back healthcare benefits for retirees, as well as current employees, and passing along more of the cost to them.

- *Providing for children and parents:* Baby boomers in particular are viewed as members of the "sandwich generation." Because their parents have longer life expectancies, many baby boomers are caring for them. At the same time, they face high tuition bills and the expense of raising children or even grandchildren. In many cases, these children come back home after college and graduate school until they get on their feet. Being pulled in multiple directions keeps baby boomers from putting away enough to finance their own retirement.

- *Disappearance of the traditional pension:* Whether you're a baby boomer, a member of generation X, generation Y, or some other group with a nickname that only makes sense to the marketing gurus, you've come to realize that there is no pension in your future. The ball's in your court when it comes to saving and investing for retirement.

- *Inflation:* Chances are, your morning coffee will cost you more as you approach retirement. More than likely, you'll also be paying much more for gas, groceries, and a dozen other necessities as the years go by. Even if the value of your house goes down during a slumping real estate market, your home-related expenses will continue to go up. You'll be paying more for utilities and repairs. It's a good bet that you'll be paying much more for homeowners insurance, especially if you live in the hurricane belt. The cost to maintain your home is likely to go up unless you're still able to cut the grass and paint your house as you get older.

When we whine about getting older, someone will invariably wisecrack that it beats the alternative. Although there are many obstacles in the road as you engage in retirement planning, it certainly beats the alternative, which is not planning at all.

Making Your Savings Last as Long as You Do

Even the experts neglect to address certain issues as they plan for retirement. To prepare successfully for retirement, you need to be certain that you cover all of the bases.

Stan Hinden, author of *How to Retire Happy,* wrote a book on retirement planning but found he still had a lot to learn. Stan learned that although he had written two newspaper columns each week on the stock market and mutual funds, he really didn't know enough about other aspects of retirement. Stan confessed to us on *MoneyTrack* that he knew nothing about Medicare, Medigap policies, Social Security, long-term care insurance, pensions, and nine other things.

Back in the day, financial planners used to analogize retirement planning to a three-legged stool. One leg of the stool was your Social Security income. The second leg was your savings. The third leg was your pension. Today, however, the days of the traditional pension are gone. Most of us will be relying on a two-legged stool. The danger is that if we use that wobbly stool to look in our cupboards, we'll find they're bare and we're likely to take a hard fall.

There are two types of pensions: the defined benefit plan and the defined contribution plan.

The Defined Benefit Plan

The *defined benefit plan* is the technical name for the traditional pension that was much more common years ago. Today few workers receive a traditional pension and must rely on the income generated from their investments during retirement. In lieu of traditional pensions, employers typically offer defined contribution plans.

According to EBRI's 2007 Retirement Confidence Survey, a high number of respondents mistakenly believe they will receive a pension from a defined benefit plan. Based on the declining number of defined benefit plans, many workers do not fully understand the employee benefits they are getting through their employer. They may not realize yet that there is no pension in their future.

If you are entitled to a pension, that benefit is protected to some degree. The Pension Benefit Guaranty Corporation (PBGC) insures most defined benefit plans up to $51,750 for plans that end in 2008. You can find out more information by visiting its Web site at www.pbgc.gov. PBGC does not insure defined contribution plans such as 401(k)s.

Defined Contribution Plans

Defined contribution plans are the typical employee benefits offered by employers. The amount you accumulate for retirement depends on how much you save and how well your investments perform. With a typical defined contribution plan such as a 401(k) retirement savings account, you are permitted to put away a percentage of your paycheck before taxes are deducted. Employers usually match some or all of your contribution up to a specified amount.

401(k) retirement savings accounts, as well as similar defined contribution plans, make it possible for you to put away money before it is taxed and before you can spend it. The specified contribution is deducted each pay period. The money is invested in a tax-sheltered savings account, along with your employer's contributions. Your employer may contribute 50 cents or more for each dollar you save up to a certain amount.

Funds invested in a 401(k) grow more quickly, because your nest egg is not depleted by taxes. You pay taxes when the money is withdrawn, hopefully when you're retired and are in a lower tax bracket. Although there are ways to withdraw from your account without a penalty, it is best to allow the money to grow until you're ready to retire. You will owe taxes on your withdrawals, since you never paid taxes at the time those contributions were withdrawn from your paycheck.

There are a variety of other defined contribution plans that may not be offered by your employer, such as Roth 401(k) plans. In a Roth 401(k) plan, you pay taxes on your contributions, but your withdrawals someday will be tax-free if you follow all of the rules. We'll look at other plans in Chapter 7.

Making the Best of Your Investment Options

It's not enough to enroll in a 401(k) or some other qualified retirement savings plan. You also need to pick the investment that's right for you from the options that are offered by your employer.

Cartoonist Gary Markstein of the *Milwaukee Journal-Sentinel* captured the concerns of 401(k) participants after a huge drop in the stock market. In the cartoon, a wife asked her husband about how bad their financial situation is after the stock market plunged. The husband replied, "I think our 401(k) is a 201(k)."

The sponsors of 401(k) retirement savings plans owe a legal duty to offer a mixture of investment options. The options typically range from very conservative to risky. Here are a few of the options that are typically offered:

- *Balanced funds* offer a mix of equity investments like stocks and fixed-income investments like bonds. Balanced funds usually appeal to investors who are looking for a healthy blend of safety and income, but with the potential for capital appreciation.
- *Stable value funds* attempt to provide a stable rate of return on your investment with little risk. The stable value fund invests in guaranteed investment contracts (GICs) that pay a fixed

interest rate for a specified period of time. These GICs are issued by insurance companies and the interest rate changes at designated intervals.

- *Money market funds* usually invest in U.S. Treasury-backed securities and corporate securities that offer higher yields but carry some risk.

- *International and global funds* look for investments throughout the world. They may limit their investment, however, to a particular region or hemisphere. Emerging market funds typically invest in the financial markets of countries whose economies are expected to grow significantly. Investing in foreign countries poses unique risks, such as currency exchange rate fluctuations and the possibility of political upheaval in those nations. Depending on the fund manager's strategies, some international and global funds are riskier than others.

- *Bond funds* are viewed as fixed-income investments. The fund manager buys the types of bonds described in the prospectus. The bonds owned by the fund pay different interest rates and mature at various times. If interest rates go up, the value of bonds tend to go down. If interest rates drop, the value of bonds tend to go up. The risk associated with each bond fund depends on the fund manager's strategies for making money. If a fund invests in bonds issued by companies with questionable credit ratings, the risks are greater. The term "high-yield bond fund" is a euphemism for junk bonds. Although junk bonds pay a high interest rate, it's more likely the issuer won't pay back the interest or the face value of the bond when it comes due.

- *Growth funds* include a variety of different objectives. There are aggressive growth funds that invest in newer companies or even initial public offerings (IPOs) that have the potential to grow rapidly. These companies are unlikely to pay dividends, since their focus is on expansion. There are also growth funds that have a moderate or conservative bent. You also might be given the option of investing in a growth-and-income fund, which usually invests in dividend-paying stocks and income-producing securities such as bonds. With growth funds and other actively managed funds, there is a risk that the manager's investment strategies will not achieve their desired objectives.

- *Index funds* invest in a shopping basket filled with stocks, bonds, or some other investment. An index fund tries to replicate the securities that make up a particular index such as the S&P 500. When you hear on the news that the S&P 500 rose that day, the index fund tied to it goes up too. Conversely, if the index goes down, your index fund goes down with it.

- *Lifestyle or life-cycle funds,* also known as target date retirement funds, contain a mix of investments that are usually suitable for someone who plans to retire on an estimated date. You don't need to know the exact date, just the approximate year. Funds are available for the person retiring in 5 years, as well as for those employees who plan to retire in 40 years. Investments in the fund become more conservative as you get closer to the target date. These funds are designed to maximize the growth of your investment until a specified retirement year.

- *Company stock* is often the worst choice you can make with your 401(k) retirement savings plan. You're putting too many of your eggs in one basket, and that's a recipe for disaster. No matter how prosperous your employer is now and no matter how well its stock is performing, there are no guarantees that this success will go on indefinitely. When that happens, the value of your stock may go down. Furthermore, the risk of losing your job is usually greater. You might find yourself without a job and with a 401(k) that's diminished greatly in value.

If you can't decide which of the investment options is best for you, choose the one that gives you the most diversified portfolio. Another possibility is to split your investment among two or more funds. Almost any choice you make is better than not investing at all.

Getting Started before It's Too Late

Although the *MoneyTrack* method works best when you start young, it's tough convincing young people that they need to begin investing for retirement now. Stan Hinden admitted that when he was young, the last thing he thought about was retirement. He was too busy working hard to make ends meet and support his family.

Thanks to the Pension Protection Act of 2006, many companies are encouraging employees to contribute to 401(k)s and other retirement savings accounts. A major goal of the PPA was to increase employee participation in retirement savings plans. In passing the law, Congress realized that automatic enrollment in 401(k)s or similar defined contribution plans will have a significant impact on participation. Studies show that automatic enrollment in 401(k) plans increases participation rates from 66 percent to 92 percent.

The Pension Protection Act eliminated the barriers to automatically enrolling employees. The law also permits employers to increase their employees' contributions each year. Nevertheless, employees who are automatically enrolled may still "opt out" of the plan. They may also turn down automatic increases in the amount they are contributing to the plan. Although they are automatically enrolled in the plan, participants must be given the opportunity to direct where their contributions are invested. If they fail to do so, the employer may invest the money in one of the investment alternatives selected for automatic enrollees.

Where's My Social Security Check?

Age 65 may be the new 55, but it's not the year when you can collect full Social Security benefits. Your full retirement age is based on your date of birth and might be as old as 67. Table 4.1 shows the age break down.

According to EBRI's 2007 survey, many workers are unaware of these increases in the eligibility age for Social Security benefits. Only

Table 4.1   Full Retirement Age

Year of Birth*	Full Retirement Age
1937 or earlier	65
1938	65 and 2 months
1939	65 and 4 months
1940	65 and 6 months
1941	65 and 8 months
1942	65 and 10 months
1943–1954	66
1955	66 and 2 months
1956	66 and 4 months
1957	66 and 6 months
1958	66 and 8 months
1959	66 and 10 months
1960 and later	67

*If you were born on January 1st of any year, your full retirement age is based on the previous year.

a small minority of workers are aware of the age at which they can collect full retirement benefits from Social Security without a reduction for taking benefits early.

Even if your full retirement age is 67, you are still permitted to begin receiving benefits at age 62, but your payment will be reduced permanently by about 30 percent. If your full retirement age is younger than 67, the percentage varies according to the year of your birth. For example, let's say that Sam was born in 1951 and his full retirement age is 66. If Sam elects to begin collecting at age 62, he will only receive 75 percent of his full retirement benefit.

Conversely, you can hold off from collecting benefits until past your full retirement age. If you delay taking benefits beyond your full retirement age, your monthly benefit will be increased, but only so far. You will stop receiving credit for delaying receipt of Social Security benefits at age 70. Therefore, if you delay receipt of Social Security benefits until age 72, you won't receive a larger check than you would have gotten had you begun benefits at age 70.

Most of us plan to take our Social Security benefits before age 70. There are a number of factors that influence whether you should take your Social Security benefits before your full retirement age. If you take your benefits early, you will receive them for a longer time frame. If you live long enough, however, you will reach a point when you start losing money by having taken your benefits early. To help you make your decision, Social Security's Web site provides a calculator that illustrates where your break-even point is. It can be found at www.socialsecurity.gov/OACT/quickcalc/when2retire.html. Another Web site that can help you decide when to begin taking your benefits can be found at www.analyzenow.com.

If you don't expect to live to a ripe old age, it may be best to take benefits earlier rather than later. At age 62, you may wish to begin enjoying the benefits you've worked so hard to earn. If you plan to work part-time in retirement, however, you need to be extremely careful until you reach your full retirement age. Until that time, you will lose one dollar in Social Security benefits for every two dollars you earn that exceeds the earnings cap. In 2008, that earnings cap is $13,560.

In 2007, according to AARP, the average monthly benefit for retired workers was $1,044. According to EBRI, Social Security benefits account for about 40 percent of the average income for people who are age 65 or older. The top monthly benefit in 2008 is $2,185.

Your retirement benefit is calculated using your highest 35 years of earnings. If you don't have 35 years of earnings, Social Security will use zero to calculate your benefit in years where you did not earn any money. Years where you earned little or no income will have a negative impact on your benefits.

Retiring early can reduce your Social Security benefit, even if you don't begin collecting until your full retirement age. The 35 years of earnings used in Social Security's calculation are likely to be less than if you worked until your full retirement age. Typically, workers receive the highest earnings of their career in the years leading up to retirement.

The best place to learn more about your Social Security benefit is at www.ssa.gov/retire2/. The toll free number is 800–772–1213 (TTY 800–325–0778).

When to Pull the Plug

At the end of a particularly hard day at work, most of us are ready to pull the plug and retire. Even if you're more than ready to retire, however, you still need to determine when is the right time to call it quits. On our *MoneyTrack* program, we asked best-selling author David Bach for his thoughts on this subject. David is CEO of Finish Rich Media and the author of *Start Late Finish Rich*. When considering retirement, David suggests that you ask yourself the following questions:

- What are you going to do on that first day of retirement?
- What are you going to do during that first year of retirement?
- What will you be doing three years from today?
- Where will you be living?

From there, you work backward and begin focusing on how much that lifestyle will cost. This is a mental exercise that should begin one or two years before you stop working, not the day before.

Today's retirees are more active than ever. They're traveling and staying active for years longer than one might expect. Unfortunately, the cost of an active lifestyle may cut into their retirement savings. At one time, the rule of thumb was that retirees spend 70 to 80 percent of their pre-retirement income. In reality, however, many retirees come to realize that they are actually spending more after retiring.

David has found that retirees spend much more than normal during the first two years of retirement. By the third year, spending tends to return to normal.

Overspending can put a major dent in your retirement savings. A *MoneyTrack* viewer in Chicago had what appeared to be a sizable nest egg of $230,000 in retirement accounts. His money was invested in stock and bond mutual funds. He expected to withdraw 10 percent from the accounts each year. Even though his investments were growing about 7 to 8 percent per year, that rate of withdrawal was way too high.

David suggested that the viewer withdraw less than 5 percent each year. If your return is 7 to 8 percent, your money keeps growing, even in the face of inflation. If you crunch the numbers, you'll see that this particular viewer will only be able to withdraw about $12,000 per year without cutting into his principal. Even with Social Security benefits, the viewer won't reach the $40,000 he needs to live on this year.

David told us about a couple with a $600,000 house who retired and bought a cheaper home in Arizona for $200,000. The couple was able to use the money they made by trading down to fund their retirement. That strategy works well if your home has gone up significantly in value and you're debt-free.

But let's say you're in your fifties and haven't saved for retirement. David advised that you need to double-down on your retirement savings and put the maximum amount away. You should pay yourself first, as we discussed earlier, and pay yourself first faster by supersizing your contributions. People over the age of 50 are permitted to make larger contributions to their IRA accounts and 401(k) retirement savings plans.

In 2008, you can contribute up to $15,500 into a 401(k) retirement savings plan. If you are age 50 or older, you can contribute an extra $5,000 to the plan. Although the IRS allows you to make these catch-up contributions, not all plans permit them.

In 2008 and 2009, you are permitted to contribute a maximum of $5,000 to an IRA. If you're over age 50, you can put away an extra $1,000 for a total of $6,000.

Working or Hardly Working in Retirement

The idea of working in retirement sounds like an inherent contradiction. Traditionally, folks retired and stopped working. Today, it is quite common for people to keep working after they retire, and here are a few reasons why they do:

- *Healthcare costs are escalating.* Stan Hinden took a part-time job, because he underestimated what his medical bills would be after he retired. A woman in Boynton Beach, Florida, still works part-time, because her employer pays for a health insurance policy to supplement Medicare.

- *They didn't save enough.* In some cases, a retiree's nest egg won't generate nearly enough income to pay for the person's lifestyle, even if it's modest. And as the cost of insurance, utilities, gas, and groceries go up, the income from the retiree's investments aren't keeping pace with inflation.
- *Social Security benefits aren't enough to live on.* For average wage-earners, benefits only cover about 40 percent of their pre-retirement income. Furthermore, as I mentioned earlier, fewer people have traditional pensions that pay a set amount each month.
- *They enjoy working and miss the social interaction of the workplace.* A number of retirees work out of boredom and to keep their minds active. Whether at paying jobs or as volunteers, they enjoy being with people and making a contribution.

A great many aging baby boomers view retirement as the perfect time to pursue a second career. They can open a business or find their dream job. Another option is finding work that is more meaningful. Marc Freedman wrote about those opportunities in his book *Encore: Finding Work That Matters in the Second Half of Life.*

Work helps to give retirees a sense of purpose, but that doesn't mean you should stay at the same old job. Web sites like My Next Phase, www.mynextphase.com, help you decide how you want to spend the rest of your life. My Plan After 50, www.myplanafter50. com, is another Web site that can help you navigate your way to a meaningful retirement. My Plan After 50 lists eight essential elements you need to work on in order to enjoy a vibrant life after age 50:

1. Social
2. Health
3. Purpose
4. Resilience
5. Relaxation
6. Financial
7. Family
8. Work

Though you may not have control over all of those elements, they play an important role in whether you will enjoy a happy and meaningful retirement.

Although nearly 80 percent of near-retirees plan to work in retirement, it doesn't always come to pass. Retirees may not like working at a job that pays far less than they made during their pre-retirement career. Older workers might resent taking orders from someone 40 or 50 years younger than they are. Even if you want to work, there may not be a demand for your skill set in the area where you're living or your talents are too specialized.

Before you retire, update your skills. In most areas, there are night school classes offered that can help you improve your computer skills. You might also take continuing education courses that can broaden your area of expertise. As the population ages, you will see more job-hunting Web sites aimed at older folks. If you're interested, take a look at RetirementJobs.com, DinosaurExchange.com, RetiredBrains.com, Seniors4Hire.org, or SeniorJobBank.com.

All of the talk about running short of money in retirement scared my *MoneyTrack* co-host, Jack Gallagher. He's worried he'll be flipping burgers to supplement his income during retirement. I assured him he has too much personality for that and he'll be working the register.

Too Much Money Can Be a Problem

We should all have this problem: Suppose you already have too much income in retirement and don't need any more but you're required to make IRA withdrawals. One *MoneyTrack* viewer found himself with this predicament. He wrote to us to ask about the rules requiring mandatory withdrawal from your IRA at age 70.

To answer this question, you need to understand the difference between a traditional IRA and a Roth IRA. If you qualify for a traditional IRA, you get a tax break now. Your contribution reduces your current income. Although your money grows in a tax-deferred account until your retirement age, all withdrawals someday are taxable.

Because some people don't need the income, they want to leave it untouched in the IRA. With traditional IRAs, however, you must begin making withdrawals at age 70½, even if you don't need the money. You are required to take mandatory minimum annual distributions based on your life expectancy. The amount withdrawn is taxable.

Typically, when employees retire, they transfer their 401(k) retirement savings account to a traditional IRA. Whether you transfer your 401(k) to a traditional IRA or leave the money there, distributions must begin at age 70½.

The good news is that you can push off your first minimum annual distribution until April 1 of the following year. The bad news is that you must take your second annual distribution during that same year. As a result, you may find yourself in a higher tax bracket. Therefore, it's not always a good idea to delay the first distribution.

Many financial experts endorse the Roth IRA. With Roth IRAs, you do not get an immediate tax break. If you follow the rules, however, you can make tax-free withdrawals someday. That means your earnings grown tax-free over many years and are compounded. Ultimately, you can withdraw all of those earnings without paying a dime of federal income taxes.

Roth IRAs permit you to withdraw your contributions at any time, regardless of your age and when you contributed. To withdraw earnings tax-free and without a penalty, the account must be open for at least five years and you must be at least age 59½. There are other events that permit penalty- and tax-free withdrawals of up to $10,000, such as death, disability, or a first-time home purchase.

Another great feature is that with Roth IRAs, you are not required to take minimum annual distributions at age 70½. If you die, however, your beneficiaries must begin taking withdrawals.

You can convert a traditional IRA to a Roth IRA, but you must pay taxes at the time of conversion. Beginning in 2010, you can convert your traditional IRA to a Roth IRA, regardless of your income. Until then, you can convert a traditional IRA to a Roth IRA only if your adjusted gross income is no more than $100,000.

An accountant can run the numbers to see if that's a better option than leaving the money in a traditional IRA and taking minimum annual distributions. It may also make sense to convert your 401(k) retirement savings plan to a Roth IRA.

Because of the Pension Protection Act, you can now convert funds in a 401(k) to a Roth IRA. Until that change in the law occurred, you were required to roll over your 401(k) into a traditional IRA and then make the conversion to a Roth IRA. According to IRA expert Ed Slott, you don't need to roll over all of your 401(k) into a Roth IRA. You can roll over the remainder into a traditional IRA and there are no immediate taxes on that portion of your 401(k). It's only when you convert your assets to a Roth IRA that the IRS wants its share of tax-sheltered account. You can find answers to almost all of your IRA questions on his Web site, irahelp.com/consumers.php.

Finding Money to Invest

I like to tell Jack that when he retires, he can make extra money by buying a metal detector to comb the beach for coins. Finding money to invest shouldn't require you to buy a metal detector. There are plenty of ways to find money to invest and you won't need to wear suntan lotion. David Bach has written about the latte and the double latte factor. You find money every day for Starbucks but you can't seem to save $5. Instead of blowing money on premium coffee drinks, it's time to save instead.

Saving on gourmet coffee may get easier now that McDonald's is competing with Starbucks. Many McDonald's are offering high-end coffee drinks at lower prices to chip away at Starbucks' dominance. And when you're old enough, McDonald's will give you your coffee with a senior discount.

In almost everyone's budget, there are expenditures that can be curtailed, whether it's a muffin the size of Rhode Island, bottled water, or cable television channels you never watch. If you and

Scam Alert

The 78 million baby boomers seem to have a target on their back. They are in the crosshairs of scam artists who call themselves "senior specialists" or "elder experts." Jeffrey Gordon Butler and his company, Senior Information Services, were accused of bilking 129 senior citizens out of $10 million. Butler orchestrated a classic Ponzi scheme, paying dividends to existing investors from money collected from new investors.

According to the February 23, 2006, edition of the *OC Register*, Butler helped senior citizens with their wills and living trusts. He then told them about an investment opportunity paying 12 percent per year. The Orange County District Attorney's Office filed 853 felony charges against Butler. His wife was charged with tax evasion. The *OC Register* offered these tips to prevent fraud:

- Just say "no" to anyone who presses you for an immediate decision.
- Avoid investments you don't understand.
- Seek advice from family members or an objective professional before investing.
- Ask tough questions and don't be afraid or embarrassed to report fraud.

Many of these investors lost their life savings to Butler.

your spouse or life partner can each find an extra $10 per day to put away, you can invest almost $7,500 during the year. In 10 years, you might find yourself with an extra $100,000 for retirement.

To see how small savings add up, use one of the many calculators that are available on the Internet. Some great online calculators can be found at www.Dinkytown.net. You should also take a look at www.choosetosave.org/ballpark/. This simple, easy-to-complete worksheet allows you to estimate how much you need to save to fund a comfortable retirement.

MoneyTrack Method

The sooner you begin planning for retirement, the better off you'll be. Otherwise, your retirement, if it ever comes to pass, will be a reality you won't even want to imagine.

It takes decades to build a retirement nest egg, so you need to get started now. The younger you are when you start, the easier it will be. A year or two before you retire, make a realistic estimate of how much it will cost to retire. You can decide if you need to continue working for a while longer. Another possibility is working part-time in retirement, assuming job opportunities are available.

Pin down how much your retirement lifestyle will cost. Once you determine your anticipated rate of spending, calculate if that's feasible based on a reasonable rate of withdrawal from your retirement nest egg. The last thing you want is to withdraw too much and run out of money. You'll run out of money much quicker if you become the target of a scam artist.

If you want to retire sooner and not later, you should be contributing the maximum amount allowed to your 401(k) and IRA. Higher contributions are permitted if you are age 50 or older. Even if you can't afford to contribute the maximum, make every effort to contribute something each year to your retirement savings accounts. Although there are ways to tap retirement savings plans before age 59½, they're not a piggybank to draw from when you're short on cash.

For anyone who doesn't get around to saving and investing for retirement, there is a fallback plan. On *MoneyTrack*, we asked Kato Kaelin, O.J. Simpson's one-time house guest, how he was preparing for retirement. Kato's advice was simple: "Hang around people who are wealthy." It's doubtful that Kato's tongue-in-cheek advice is the right solution for most of us.

CHAPTER 5

Taking Control of Your Investments Online

It's difficult to implement any aspect of the *MoneyTrack* method if you don't have control over your finances and investments. No matter how busy you are, you can and must be in control of your investments in order to reach your financial goals. Before you make excuses for why it's impossible for you to do so, it might help to hear about how a young man in Orange County, California, took control of his investments online.

If you're not familiar with Orange County, or the OC as it's known, it's filled with multimillion-dollar homes in lushly landscaped gated communities. Even the dogs are high end. Some pet lovers own designer poodles, which are called labradoodles. Amidst that wealth, a college student searched for the perfect parking lot where he could bed down for the night.

On *MoneyTrack*, we met a college student who was living in his truck to get his finances in order. When we filmed his story, Andy Bussell was so deep in debt that he decided to live in his truck. Among other bills, Andy was having trouble paying off $11,000 in credit card debt. When the episode was filmed, Andy had already lived in his truck for over 18 months and was a full-time student at California State University in Fullerton.

Andy explained his financial strategy to us. The film student used the $800 he would have spent on rent to pay off his credit card debt. He belonged to a rock-climbing gym and showered there. He ate at school or bought food that doesn't require cooking. The tech-savvy 27-year-old relied on free Internet access.

Perhaps Andy will one day hit in big in the entertainment industry. Maybe he'll achieve the success of someone else who lived in his car at one point in his life. It's been reported that Actor Jim Carrey's family went through hard times when he was growing up and was forced to live in their car for awhile. Even though Andy may never make $20 million a film, he still can become financially secure.

Until he's making big money in the movie biz, Andy should be investing some of the money he saves by living in his car. By investing $150 per month for eight years, Andy can build a nest egg that will grow automatically, even if he stops investing at that point.

If your money is invested in an IRA or 401(k) retirement savings plan, the account will grow and compound without paying taxes each year. Your money grows much more quickly in a tax-sheltered account.

Living a High-Tech Lifestyle Even If You Live in a Truck

As you travel the freeways at high rates of speed, you'll see high-tech drivers multitasking with BlackBerrys and cell phones. At the same time, they're eating and grooming themselves. Occasionally, they even watch the road. We're in an age where you can lead a high-tech lifestyle, even if you live in a truck.

When it comes to finances and investing, a computer puts financial data at your fingertips. It can help you to keep your life organized and give you access to your finances in the click of a mouse. You can pay bills, buy stocks, or even find the home of your dreams.

A computer can also give crooks access to your finances in the click of a mouse. Even if you have a computer that cost more than your truck, you still need to know where to invest and how to protect yourself from people whose business plan is to take your money.

CBS Marketwatch columnist and author Paul Farrell provided advice to Andy to guide him on the road to becoming a millionaire. Paul wrote *The Lazy Person's Guide to Investing* and advocates low-maintenance investment plans. For Andy, Paul suggested that he consider the Coffeehouse Portfolio that was originated by a former broker, Bill Schultheiss. Schultheiss described the approach in his book, *The Coffeehouse Investor*.

To create your own Coffeehouse Portfolio, you invest in seven low-cost index funds. These index funds invest in a mixture of stocks and bonds. In the original Coffeehouse Portfolio, seven Vanguard index funds were used because of their extremely low costs, but you aren't limited to that financial services firm. Other companies offer low-cost index funds that use the same investment strategy. It's akin to using a different brand of coffee.

Here is how you can create a coffeehouse portfolio using Vanguard funds:

1. *Vanguard S&P 500.* This index fund tracks Standard & Poor's five hundred largest companies. The index is known as the S&P 500.
2. *Vanguard Large-Cap Value.* This fund matches the returns of a value index consisting of large companies. Generally, value stocks are those securities that seem underpriced when compared to their earnings, book value, and other measures. Fortunately, you don't need to know how to calculate these ratios. The fund manager does that.
3. *Vanguard Small-Cap Index.* This fund tracks the Russell 2000 small-cap index.
4. *Vanguard Small-Cap Value.* This fund seeks to replicate the performance of the MSCI Barra index. The index consists of small company stocks whose share prices seem relatively low in view of their anticipated earnings per share, book value, cash flow, sales, and dividends.
5. *Vanguard International.* This investment is tied to international stocks. To be truly diversified, your portfolio should include international stocks.
6. *Vanguard REIT Stock Index.* This index fund seeks to provide a high level of income and modest capital appreciation by tracking the performance of a benchmark index that measures the performance of publicly traded equity REITs. A REIT is the acronym that stands for a real estate investment trust. As we will see in Chapter 9, REITs invest in real estate, such as shopping centers, or loans secured by real estate.
7. *Vanguard Total Bond Market Index.* This fund seeks to track the performance of a broad, market-weighted bond index. A bond index fund adds a different asset class to your portfolio.

With these seven investments, you've created a diversified portfolio that should serve you well in years to come.

An even simpler approach is the so-called Couch Potato Portfolio, which was created by financial columnist and author Scott Burns. This approach uses only two index funds, which can be purchased from a low-cost mutual fund company. For example, you could invest in the Vanguard 500 Index Fund, which tracks the S&P 500 index. To finish off your Couch Potato Portfolio, the remaining 50 percent of your money can be invested in the Vanguard Total Bond Market Index Fund. This index fund matches the performance of the Lehman U.S. Aggregate Bond Index and also has a very low expense ratio.

Since creating his original Couch Potato Portfolio, Burns has tweaked his formula but it remains quite simple. He substituted the Vanguard Total Stock Market Index Fund for the index fund that tracks the S&P 500. He also has suggested a 75/25 Couch Potato for younger investors that puts more money in the stock market rather than bonds.

No-Brainer Portfolio

Many novice investors are stymied by the paralysis of analysis. They get so caught up in analyzing where to put their money, they don't invest at all. Many investment pros have suggested strategies that help you avoid overthinking where to put your money.

Dr. William Bernstein, the author of *The Four Pillars of Investing*, has created the No-Brainer Portfolio made up of four index funds.

1. (25%) Vanguard 500 Index
2. (25%) Vanguard Small-Cap Index
3. (25%) Vanguard European Stock Index
4. (25%) Vanguard Total Bond Market Index

Bernstein has also suggested an investment strategy called the Coward's Portfolio. Your portfolio is a mixture of up to 10 index funds. You put anywhere from 5 to 20 percent of your investment nest egg in a mixture of up to 10 index funds in amounts from 5 to 20 percent. If your mixture is correct, it should add up to 100 percent.

Larry Swedroe, an investment book author and principal of an advisory firm, offered another easy-to-create stock portfolio. He recommended that you own at least four index funds focusing on large stocks in general, large value stocks, small stocks in general, and small value stocks. Swedroe has also suggested that you consider adding an index fund that tracks real estate investment trusts.

Dogs of the Dow

If you would like to take a more aggressive approach to investing by buying and selling individual stocks, a popular investment strategy developed in the 1990s was the Dogs of the Dow. According to Jack Hough, author of *Your Next Great Stock: How to Screen the Market for Tomorrow's Top Performers,* the strategy still has many proponents.

You start by analyzing the 30 stocks that make up the Dow Jones Industrial Average. You select the 10 companies that have the highest dividend yields. You invest in those 10 stocks and then hold them for a year. You repeat the process a year from now.

According to Hough, the Dogs beat the Dow by three percentage points per year until 1995. Although the dogs achieved impressive results in 2006, the strategy hasn't matched the overall performance of the Dow since 1995. As a result, the strategy has been updated and you're advised to look at a measure called "net payout yield."

To utilize this new Dogs of the Dow strategy, you look at the Dow Jones Industrial Average or any investment index. Once each year, you select the 10 companies with the highest net payout yields. You can find these stocks by visiting Hough's Web site at YourNextGreatStock.com, www.YourNextGreatStock.com.

There is no guarantee that any of these strategies are right for you. They are offered to show you that there is no need to overthink the investment process. There are simple approaches that can work for you as a starting point. With all of these portfolios, you can tweak the basic formula to suit your purposes and change course later on.

Controlling the Cost of Investing by Educating Yourself

Whether it's through books like this one or online education, you can be a home-schooled investor. Being a home-schooled investor can cut your expenses significantly. If you develop the knowledge and ability to pick your own investments, you can control your expenses and that will increase your rate of return over the years. The only problem with being a home-schooled investor is that it's very lonely at the prom and you can't count on any graduation gifts.

When you're able to make your own investment decisions, you can use a discount broker to execute stock trades. You won't need a full service broker to provide advice. Using a discount broker to trade stocks is much less expensive.

Taking a Load off Your Investing

You can also invest in no-load mutual funds directly from an investment company. No-load funds do not charge any front-end or back-end fees to buy and sell your shares.

If you buy funds through a broker, make certain you fully understand the fees that will be charged. In contrast to no-load mutual funds, there are funds that charge a load or sales commission. At the risk of oversimplifying, there are three common share classes among load funds.

- *A Class shares* charge a front-end load and may impose a small 12b-1 fee. 12b-1 fees are used by a mutual fund to pay for sales, marketing, advertising, and distribution expenses. According to the Investment Company Institute (ICI), more than 70 percent of funds assess a 12b-1 fee. A fund may not be referred to as no-load if its 12b-1 fee is greater than 0.25 percent.
- *B Class shares* usually come with a large 12b-1 fee and a contingent deferred sales charge if shares are redeemed within a certain number of years. The deferred sales charge declines each year until it eventually disappears. A deferred sales charge is a fancy name for a back-end load.
- *C Class shares* are often referred to as "level load" funds. The heavy 12b-1 fee is paid annually for as long as the shareholder owns the fund. Typically, the fee is 1 percent of the value of the investor's account.

Although there are other share classes among load funds such as Class F and Class Y, Classes A, B, and C are the most common. With B and C shares, 100 percent of your initial investment goes into your account, which helps the investment grow faster. Nevertheless, higher 12b-1 fees reduce your rate of return.

The SEC has begun to scrutinize 12b-1 fee practices, and regulatory changes are expected. SEC chairman Christopher Cox has pointed out that $11 billion in 12b-1 fees are used primarily to compensate brokers and pay for administrative expenses for existing fund shareholders. Some industry veterans believe that the SEC may repeal the rule permitting 12b-1 fees, since they are no longer being used for their original purpose of marketing mutual funds. In a speech to the Mutual Fund Directors Forum in April 2007, Chairman Cox said that 12b-1 fees have become a "substitute for front-end loads."

Low-Cost Ways to Becoming a Smarter Investor

There are many low-cost ways to gather information about investing and to become a smarter investor. As you sift through that information, however, make certain that the person or company providing it is telling you the whole story and isn't just trying to sell you a financial product.

If you're looking for a structured educational setting, many communities offer night school classes dealing with the basics of investing and personal finance. The cost is usually quite low. Quite often, however, the person teaching the course is a financial services professional. Watch out for signs that the person is pushing certain financial products too hard with the hope that you'll come to him or her to buy one of the investments recommended.

A good way for novice investors to learn is by joining an investment club. Amateur investors get together and choose investments for the group to consider.

The American Association of Individual Investors (AAII) is a nonprofit organization that can provide you with a wealth of information. The organization's goal is to "arm individual investors with the education and tools they need to build wealth." The organization offers very helpful advice that can add to your knowledge of stocks, financial planning and retirement funding. The Web address is www.aaii.com/.

Organizations are cropping up to give women the tools they need to achieve financial freedom. Women often face more difficult financial issues, because they typically spend less time in the work force and live longer than men. According to the Women's Institute for a Secure Retirement (WISER), Social Security is the only source of income for 25 percent of unmarried women. WISER's Web site is www.womensretirement.org. Another organization trying to educate women on financial matters is New York-based Savvy Ladies, www.savvyladies.com.

The U.S. government has a Web site that is sponsored by the U.S. Financial Literacy and Education Commission. MyMoney.gov, www.mymoney.gov is committed to teaching Americans about the basics of financial education. As mentioned in Chapter 1, the Investor Protection Trust Web site, www.investorprotection.org, strives to provide independent and objective information to consumers, so they can make informed investment decisions.

And just so you won't have to flip the pages back to Chapter 1, I'll mention the *MoneyTrack* Web site again, www.moneytrack.org. Please don't thank me. I'm a giver, especially when it comes to giving plugs for our series and Web site.

Resolving to Take Control of Your Finances

A survey conducted by Country Insurance and Financial Services of Bloomington, Illinois, found that only 17 percent of Americans mentioned money-related issues in their 2008 resolutions. Our goal at *MoneyTrack* is for everyone to make money-related resolutions and keep them. According to the survey, Americans' resolutions focused mainly on exercising more often and spending more time with family. Here's a thought, and I'm just spit-balling here, you can resolve to watch *MoneyTrack* with your family and multitask by doing a few sit-ups.

Just like resolving to go on a diet, many people resolve to take control of their finances and don't follow through. They pledge to improve their financial security, pay down debt, and make smarter money decisions, but it doesn't happen in most cases. Worse yet, many people don't even discuss their finances on a regular basis.

Here are a few resolutions that can help any one take control of their finances:

- *Resolve to curb your impulse buying.* Stop and think about how many hours you have to work to pay for an item. If you start thinking about purchases in terms of hours worked and not cost, you'll gain a different perspective on whether you want to purchase an item. You also might find that your spending adds up to more hours than you're working. That means you're spending more than you make.

- *Resolve to distinguish between your wants and needs.* You need to pay your rent or buy groceries. You don't need a new TV; you want it. You may want a new car, but you don't necessarily need it.

- *Resolve to start contributing to a retirement savings plan.* If you already make a contribution, resolve to increase it. Before the ink is dry on this resolution, which doesn't make much sense if you typed it on your computer, walk down to your human resource department and seal the deal.

- *Resolve to pay your credit card balance in full each month.* If you can't pay off the entire balance, make sure you that you pay more than the minimum amount owed. Otherwise, you'll be making those payments for years longer than necessary. According to the editors of *Consumer Reports,* if you pay only the minimum amount due each month, it will take 22 years and two months to pay off a $5,000 debt on a credit card that has an interest rate of 15 percent.

- *Resolve to pay off your credit card bills and other bills before the due date.* Late payments show up on your credit report. Furthermore, making late payments on your auto insurance bill can result in your policy being canceled. Once your policy is canceled, you will be viewed as a substandard risk, even if your driving record is perfect. You might need to buy insurance through a company that writes a more costly substandard policy or your state's assigned risk plan which is likely to be more expensive than what you're paying now.

Your credit report is available from www.annualcreditreport.com. Under federal law, you have the right to receive a free copy of your credit report once every 12 months. Although your annual credit report is free, you must pay to receive your credit score. Your credit score uses a complex mathematical formula that evaluates the information contained in your credit report. Lenders use that credit score to determine if you qualify for a credit card or loan.

You will also see clever commercials for www.FreeCreditReport. com. This company gives you your credit report and your score, but you must sign up for its credit monitoring service. Although the trial membership is free, you will be billed $14.95 per month if you don't cancel within 30 days.

Taking control of your finances is likely to make you feel like Scrooge at the holidays. Terry Savage, a registered investment adviser and personal finance author in Chicago, told *Investment News* that it's important to overcome emotional spending habits around the holidays. The $2,000 that you spend on a gift might mean so much more if it were invested in an index fund that tracks a particular market, such as the S&P 500. That $2,000 might be worth $45,000 in 30 years. If that $2,000 were invested every year, you might have $450,000 someday.

Whose Identity Is It Anyway?

Many people resist putting their finances online because of fears about identity theft. According to David Horowitz, a leading consumer advocate, 8.4 million Americans were the victims of identity theft. In the January 2008 edition of the *Costco Connection,* Horowitz wrote that identity theft is the number-one crime in the United States and is spreading across the globe.

Identity theft leaves its victims with damaged credit reports that are extremely difficult to repair. Congress is working on legislation that will make it easier for federal prosecutors to combat cybercrime and identity theft.

At the risk of making you paranoid, rip up or shred any personal information you're throwing away. Don't hand over your credit card to just anyone. Check your bank account and credit card balances frequently to make certain no one is using them without your authorization.

You need to protect your Social Security number. Wherever possible, avoid giving it out. Don't carry your Social Security number around in your wallet or write it on a check unless it's absolutely necessary.

Keep your personal information in a safe place. If you have roommates or workers in your house, make certain your personal data are locked up.

Watch out for signs that someone may be using your identity. You may receive a denial of credit for no apparent reason or a bill for products you didn't order. You might even begin receiving calls or letters regarding purchases you didn't make.

According to the Federal Trade Commission (FTC), identity theft commonly occurs in the following ways:

- *Dumpster diving.* Someone rummages through your discarded bills and paperwork, looking for personal information.
- *Skimming.* Thieves use a special electronic storage device when processing your transaction in order to steal your credit card number.
- *Phishing.* The thief poses as a merchant or financial institution in order to get you to reveal your personal information.
- *Changing your address.* An unscrupulous individual diverts your billing statements by completing a change of address form.
- *Old-fashioned stealing.* The identity thief steals your wallet or purse or takes mail from your mailbox.

To report identity theft, you can call 877-ID-THEFT (438–4338). You can report the theft online at www.ftc.gov/idtheft. Obviously, you should also call the police, your bank, and your credit card company if you suspect someone is using your identity. You should also report the incident to the three major credit bureaus:

- Experian: 888–397–3742
- Equifax: 800–525–6285
- TransUnion: 800–680–7289

You can subscribe to cyber scam alerts by going to www.fbi.gov and clicking E-mail Updates. You can report suspicious e-mail and file a complaint by visiting www.ic3.gov. This complaint center is a partnership between the FBI and the National White Collar Crime Center.

Guidance for Online Investors

If you've ever seen folks working on their laptop computer at Starbucks or Panera Bread, you may wonder what they're working on. If the person has a tie, you might think the computer user is working on a presentation or a business project. You might guess that an attractive man or woman without a ring is on Match.com. If the person is younger and a bit of a geek, you might presume he's designing a Web site or buying Star Trek memorabilia on eBay. For all you know, however, the individual sipping coffee might be trading stocks online.

Scam Alert

In May of 2005, a North Carolina real estate consultant learned the hard way about identity theft. George Rodriguez logged on to his computer and found he was selling his stock in Dell, Home Depot, and a number of other companies. The not-so-funny twist was that George had not logged on to his online trading account. Someone had hacked into his account and changed the routing number to a different bank. Identity thieves had instructed Ameritrade to send the proceeds of the stock sales to a bank in Texas, not George's account with Wachovia in North Carolina.

George confessed that he didn't use all of the security tools available to fight online raids on your personal accounts. Here are some possibilities recommended by the Nebraska Department of Banking and Finance:

- Make sure the site you're using is encrypted. The Web address should read https, not http. Look for a padlock icon on your toolbar.
- Use an unusual password, not one that is easily figured out, such as your mother's maiden name. It also prevents Mom from hacking into your account.
- Log off the Internet when you're not using it.
- Avoid checking your financial records at an airport or on a computer at the library.
- Keep your computer's security features and software up to date.

Luckily for George, he found out quickly that someone was accessing his account and Ameritrade reversed the phony trades.

To avoid George's situation, inspect all of those statements you receive from your brokerage firm and make sure all of the transactions are yours. Read them right away as George did, and contact the brokerage firm immediately if there is a discrepancy.

Nebraska securities regulators have also warned online investors about hack attacks. The scam begins with a hacker obtaining an investor's password and user name. After liquidating the investor's online account, the hacker uses the funds to buy a stock where few shares are traded. The hacker already owns shares of that stock and then sells them when the price goes up. The hacker's goal is to execute a pump-and-dump scheme.

According to a J.D. Power and Associates study, about 56 percent of investors who trade securities online describe themselves as being self-directed. Only 38 percent admitted to getting some professional advice. Six percent responded that they received all of their advice from an adviser.

These online traders tend to take more risks than other investors. Fourteen percent described themselves as aggressive traders. Online investors were found to be more active traders. Eleven percent made 60 or more transactions each year. Unless you're an old-hand at investing online, you need to be cautious.

Tips for Online Investors

The North American Securities Administrators Association, Inc. (NASAA) offers many tips for online investors:

1. *Understand that most likely you are not linked directly to the market through your home computer, and that the click of your mouse does not instantly execute trades or cancel orders.*
2. *Determine if the stock quotes and account updates you receive are real-time or delayed.*
3. *Check the online broker's ability to get the best price for investors. Most brokerage firms provide this information on their Web site.*
4. *Receive information from the firm to substantiate any advertised claims concerning the ease and speed of online trading.*
5. *Obtain information about entering and canceling orders (market, limit, and stop loss), and the details and risks of margin accounts (borrowing to buy stocks).*
6. *Get information from the firm about significant Web site outages, delays, and other interruptions that may affect your ability to execute trades. Make sure that the firm has an alternative way to execute trades.*
7. *Review the firm's privacy and security policies. Determine if your name will be used for mailing lists or other promotional activities by the firm or any other party.*
8. *Receive clear information about sales commissions, transaction fees, and conditions that apply to any advertised discount on commissions.*
9. *Know how to contact a customer service representative if problems occur. Request prompt attention and fair consideration. Be sure to keep good records to substantiate any problems that may occur.*
10. *Contact your local securities division to verify the registration status and disciplinary history (if any) of the online brokerage firm, or to file a complaint, if appropriate.*

NASAA also warns that short-term trading in an online account is tempting and extremely dangerous. Attempting to profit from rapidly changing market prices is a very risky strategy. NASAA's Investor Alert can be found at www.nasaa.org/Investor_Education/Investor_Alerts___Tips/1254.cfm#.

Watch out for the Newsletters, Too

Securities regulators have also expressed concern about online investment newsletters. Although some online newsletters offer legitimate investment information, others are used for fraudulent purposes. As we saw in Chapter 1, some of the activities to watch out for are these:

- *Touting:* The newsletter publisher is paid to tout or recommend a stock.
- *Scalping:* Although the publication claims to be independently researching a stock, the publisher already owns a great many shares and is attempting to drive up the price. As a result of the hype, the price goes up and the publisher makes a huge profit.
- *Bulletin boards:* Online bulletin boards give investors a forum to share information. Some of the messages may be hype to pump up the value of a company's stock. Sometimes information is posted to jolt the price of the stock temporarily, so a day trader can reap the benefits.
- *E-mail spam:* A company will send out thousands of e-mails targeting investors. Spam is a great deal cheaper than cold-calling potential investors.

Even if a newsletter is legitimate, however, there is no guarantee that the publisher can pick investments better than Chloe, my dog.

The *Hurlbert Financial Digest,* www.marketwatch.com/hurlbert, tracks the performance of investment newsletters. Writing in the February 15, 2008, issue of *Bottom Line Personal,* Mark Hurlbert observed that the price of a newsletter has nothing to do with its performance. High-priced newsletters pick winners and losers with the same accuracy as low-priced ones. Hurlbert's publication gives you accurate information regarding a newsletter's track record. You shouldn't necessarily rely on a publication's hype about its ability to pick investments. Securities regulators have sanctioned several publications for inflating these statistics.

You should also exercise caution when approached by firms offering auto-trading in conjunction with investment newsletters. If you sign up for an account, every recommendation in the newsletter is implemented automatically. When recommendations are made, your account will make the trade automatically without you deciding if it's a good idea or not.

MoneyTrack Method

If someone living in a truck can get his finances on track and improve his financial situation, you can do so as well. All it takes is having the willpower to save and invest and to keep your hands off the money until you're ready to retire. You can use software and the Internet to get your finances organized and put your investments on automatic pilot. Make certain, however, that you're using all of the available security measures to protect yourself from viruses and spyware.

Being online has a down side as well. You'll be approached with all types of financial scams. Watch out for e-mails asking for personal information that is purportedly for verification purposes. If a solicitation uses words like "guarantee," "high return," "quick profits," "inside information," or "double your money," you should be far more skeptical about the sender. If you don't know the person sending the e-mail, delete it.

Although online banking can simplify your life, complications occasionally arise. In Ron Burley's column in the July & August, 2008 issue of *AARP* Magazine, a woman complained that the bank transferred $8,200 to her cable company instead of $82, the actual amount owed. Until Burley intervened, neither the bank nor the cable company would correct the mistake. With online banking, a misplaced decimal point can wipe out your account.

It doesn't take a whole lot of money to build real wealth over your lifetime, as long as you know how to invest wisely and stick with a systematic investment program. You also need to control your debt, which is frequently caused by excessive discretionary spending. Your debt burden affects the most important decisions you'll make in life, including buying a home, having children, and saving for retirement.

You need to decide if you are going to be an online investor or an online trader. Day traders and frequent traders hope to profit from a rapidly changing market. They are not buying stocks to build a portfolio that will hopefully grow over the years. Their goal is to turn over that portfolio on an ongoing basis. Spurred on by advertisements saying they can quit their day job or trading tips that guarantee success, these online traders are taking enormous risks. They may suffer losses caused by inaccurate information, market volatility, and delays in executing trades.

Before trading online and making risky trades, make sure you're not all hat and no cattle, as the saying goes. You may say you're willing to take risks with the hope of reaping greater rewards, but it's far different when aggressive trading leaves you with half of your nest egg. Although there is usually a correlation between risk and return, this principle applies to long-term investments and isn't applicable to situations where you're trying to make a windfall on a virtually worthless security.

As we will see in Chapter 6, you should be listening to the advice of the investment pros, not the gurus who claim you'll become instantly wealthy with trades they recommend. Although being able to make trades with the click of a mouse is convenient, it can also entice you to make foolish investment decisions.

CHAPTER

6

Investing Like the Pros, Not the Gurus

If you play your cards right, investing is a far cry from gambling. One important goal of *MoneyTrack* is to help you to become an investor, not a gambler who happens to play the stock market instead of the ponies. An important element of the *MoneyTrack* method is to give you advice from the pros, not some investment guru who claims to have a fool-proof system for making money.

Its Not Just a Game

As we filmed *MoneyTrack*, we came to realize that too many people believe that investing is the same as gambling. We spoke to gamblers at a horse racing track and watched how they attempted to pick winners. Many people that we spoke with had no rational basis whatsoever for their choices. One woman put money on a horse because her name was Suzie and the horse's name was Sue.

Some people turn investing into gambling, because they have no rational basis for investing. Instead of researching a stock or mutual fund before investing, they're ready to invest with only a modicum of information. Sadly, they could research investments in less time than it takes to drive to the nearest racetrack. Instead of viewing investing as a slow and steady process, we keep meeting people who view it as a mad race to riches.

Just as Suzie picked horses on a hunch or gut feeling, many investors do the same thing. The pros will tell you that hot tips and hunches are usually losers at the race track and in the stock market. The good news, however, is that investors don't need to put their money on the right horse to succeed and become financially independent.

Despite the differences, there are a few principles of investing you can learn from watching horse racing fans place their bets at the track:

- *Check out prior performance.* The first lesson you can learn is that it pays to look at prior performance of an investment just as you review how horses have done in previous races. In both cases, however, past performance is no guarantee of future success.
- *Spread your money around.* You shouldn't bet all of your money on one horse. With investing, you need to build a diversified portfolio. You're spreading your money around, not risking your nest egg on one nag who couldn't beat Mr. Ed and will break your heart.
- *No one has a fool-proof system.* With both gambling and investing, you will meet people who think they have a system that guarantees they'll win. On too many occasions, there are major flaws in these so-called fool-proof systems. In the investment world, you'll encounter people who are selling their system for picking stocks. In too many cases, you waste your money on purchasing the system and you lose money on the stocks you buy as a result of using it.
- *Even the handicappers and gurus aren't always right.* Many betters pay close attention to handicappers who possess significant expertise regarding horses and who has the best chance of winning. Similarly, the stock market has its own gurus who claim they know which stocks are worth owning. They also claim to know a great deal about when to buy and when to sell your stocks. Unfortunately, however, not even the best gurus can predict stock market winners with absolute reliability. Instead of relying on someone who claims to be a guru, you can follow the recommendations of many investment pros who recommend that you stick with index funds tied to the market as a whole.
- *Check out the jockey.* Whether you're betting on a horse or a company that just hit the stock exchange, you need to do your homework. Just as your chances are better with a jockey who has ridden winners before, you need to research who runs this company and what that person's track record is. When

you invest in a mutual fund, it's also important that you know who's jockeying the fund toward its investment objectives.

As horse racing aficionados will tell you, all of the research in the world doesn't mean you'll ride home a winner. Even a well-researched investment can also be a loser. Nevertheless, if you aren't going to do research before investing, you are just a gambler who is betting on stocks, not horses.

Nationally-syndicated columnist, Charles A. Jaffe, made a very important distinction between betting on horses and mutual fund investing in an article published on May 4, 2008 in the *Philadelphia Inquirer*. According to Jaffe, unlike horse racing, investing in mutual funds is a lifelong marathon and not a short sprint.

Sorting through the Gurus' Advice

From the moment we wake up each morning, we're bombarded with investment advice. If you're smart, you'll make a conscious effort to sift through this advice and decide if any of it has value.

Whether it's on the radio, television or in a financial publication, there is always a guru who is all-knowing about investments. You can watch a guru like Jim Cramer and he'll tell you with absolute conviction which stocks to buy and sell. Unfortunately, no matter who the guru is, there are no guarantees that the person's investment advice is right. On March 11, 2008, which was about a week before the value of Bear Stearns stock plummeted precipitously and the company was bailed out by the Federal Reserve, Jim emphatically told a viewer that the company was fine and investors should hang onto their shares.

Whether it's Jim Cramer or some other stock-picking guru, business writer Mark Hilbert told us that it's quite often a losing proposition. You would do better by putting money in an investment that tracks the S&P 500 index, which consists of large company stocks. According to Mark, even if Jim or another guru picks a winner, the typical investor doesn't know when to unload the investment. Unlike a horse race, most investors must stick with their pick for a longer time frame than it takes to go from the starting gate to the finish line.

One problem with investing based on tips from a guru or a financial publication is that the recommendations are old news by the time you hear the advice. If the guru is extremely popular, the investment might already be up in price by the time you buy it. You're usually investing at a stock's peak instead of when it's down in value. Even if you're sitting at the computer and are logged on to an online broker, you're not necessarily going to buy a recommended stock before it's gone up in value. Furthermore, there are no guarantees that the stock will keep moving in an upward direction.

When Jim appeared on our program, he gave us some great advice on how to use his tips or recommendations from any investment expert. Jim told us that viewers should not invest based on his recommendations until they're put their finances on solid ground. You can do this by funding your 401(k) and IRA. You should also buy a house first and pay down your credit card debt. Investments based on Jim's recommendations should be limited to your discretionary funds.

Don't Gamble with Your Investments

Larry Swedroe, a noted author of investment books, as well as a principal and director of a registered investment advisory firm, believes people have difficulty distinguishing between gambling and investing. They go to Vegas expecting to lose but chalk it up to the price of entertainment. When they return home, they're willing to gamble money on investments if they have fun doing it. Investing, according to Swedroe, was never meant to be entertaining. Investing is about giving yourself the best chance to reach your goals while taking the least amount of risk.

In a November 27, 2006, posting on SeekingAlpha.com, (seekingalpha.com/article/21272-jim-cramer-s-mad-money-effect-a-winning-strategy), Swedroe wrote about the entertainment value of Jim Cramer's program. He took note of a study conducted by three Ph.D. candidates at Northwestern's Kellogg School of Management. They found that after Jim recommends a stock, its value soars. The profits turn out to be illusory, however. The run-up in price is reversed in full within 12 trading days.

In his article, Swedroe wrote that investors should ignore the "noise" coming from gurus like Jim. Investing should be focused on giving yourself the greatest chance to achieve your goals. Swedroe recommended building a globally diversified portfolio and having the discipline to stick with it.

Trying to time the market may be fun, but it's closer to being gambling than investing. Gambling on stocks because you heard the recommendation on TV may prove to be far more expensive than paying for cable or a satellite dish.

Jim also advised our viewers to avoid being greedy. If a stock goes up 40 percent in a month, it may be time to sell. If a stock goes down, it may be wise to buy more shares in stages and accumulate a larger position. Before buying more shares, however, it is important that the same good reasons for investing in the stock still exist. The CNBC guru suggested that investors spend an hour each week researching each of their holdings.

Remember that the title of Jim's show is *Mad Money*. If Jim's entertaining personality isn't enough and you must invest, you should be investing only your mad money in stocks that Jim recommends. You shouldn't be building the base of your investment pyramid with stocks recommended by any guru. The most important lesson you can learn from the program is how a guru like Jim evaluates which stocks to buy.

Why Aren't They Sitting on the Beach Somewhere?

One of our viewers, Sherry, joined us from McCafferty's Coffee House on the outskirts of Seattle, Washington. Sherry asked a question that should make you wonder about every guru. Sherry asked why these so-called gurus, if they're so smart, aren't retired and relaxing on a big yacht. John Bogle answered that question with one of his own. "Who says they're that good?" John asked.

John observed that you really don't know if their track record is any good. John is aware of a few academic studies showing that gurus often produce mediocre investment returns. After you take the cost of investing into account and taxes, you may not make nearly as much money as you're expecting.

As John told us, the secret to investing is that there is no secret. There are just the relentless rules of humble arithmetic. John advised investors to do the following:

- Get your emotions out of the picture.
- Get your expenses out of the picture.
- Invest in the stock market as a whole and not in individual securities.

Most of us will come out ahead if we spread our money and our risk over the entire market. It's like betting on every horse in the race, or stock in this case. If you do, you can be sure that you'll own at least a small amount of Google or whatever the next hot stock is.

Once you buy into the stock market, plan to keep your holdings for a long time frame.

In answer to Sherry's question, I suspect that some of these gurus make more money selling their books and newsletters than they do in the stock market. Nevertheless, there are true investment pros who've made a fortune but enjoy the thrill of investing. Warren Buffett, for example, is still very active, but gives billions away to charity. He's even passing his investment advice on to a new generation, as we will see in Chapter 13.

Steve Forbes, publisher of *Forbes* magazine, said it best: "You make more money selling the advice than following it."

Passive versus Active Investing: What's Right for You?

For years, investment gurus have debated the merits of active versus passive investment strategies. Active investment strategies are built on the premise that stock market professionals can produce a higher rate of return than the market in general. The investment managers of actively managed mutual funds attempt to build a portfolio that will outperform the index to which it is being compared. Indices are composed of many securities.

Advocates of active investing believe there are experts who are capable of identifying the best investments. Their goal is to buy and sell securities on an ongoing basis, rather than just investing in an index consisting of many stocks, bonds or some other holding. Unfortunately, there are no guarantees that the person in charge of your actively managed fund will have the magic touch, even if he or she has done well in the past.

Passive investment strategies have the goal of matching a particular index. Instead of trying to pick stocks that will do better than the index, passive investors are satisfied with keeping pace with the market as a whole. Advocates of passive investing take the position that few experts can reap higher returns than the market in general. They believe it is better to invest in a fund that attempts to match the performance of a particular index, such as the S&P 500. Passive investors believe that in the long run, it is better to achieve an average gain instead of looking for companies and mutual funds that will hopefully go through the roof but may wind up in the basement of the stock exchange.

Passive investment strategies tend to be less expensive than active investing where securities are bought and sold based on market conditions. After the portfolio is created, there are fewer trades except as they are necessary to match the particular index. The cost of investment advice is also lower with a passive strategy. Little research is necessary, because the fund simply recreates the same mix of securities that are contained in a particular index. Passive investing tends to be tax-efficient, because there is little turnover in the fund's portfolio.

According to John Waggoner's article in *USA Today* on January 7, 2008, index funds clobbered actively managed funds over the past two decades. During the past decade, however, actively managed funds performed better than index funds. The average diversified U.S. stock fund gained roughly 6.7 percent over the past 10 years. During that same time frame, the S&P 500 rose about 5.9 percent each year, assuming you reinvested dividends.

Waggoner wrote that this improvement in the performance of actively managed funds can be attributed to the success of small company stocks. Because small company stocks performed so well over the past 10 years, the average actively managed stock fund went up by a larger percentage than the S&P 500, which is made up of large companies.

Whether you're investing in an actively managed fund or an index fund, you still must decide which one is a good fit for you and your family. Much depends on your investment objective, whether its growth, income, or some other goal. Almost everyone needs to own several quality funds so your portfolio is diversified to weather different economic conditions.

The ABCs of ETFs

Exchange-traded funds (ETFs) are used by many passive investors to create a diversified portfolio that will match the performance of a particular index. Although ETFs are traded like stocks, they resemble an index fund in many ways. ETFs are sometimes used by active investors to create a diversified portfolio and offset some of the risk that comes with investing in individual securities.

Though it looks like a stock, an ETF is actually a mixture of securities. With a single trade, you buy and sell all of the securities encompassed by that share of an ETF. With the purchase of an ETF, you are actually buying a very tiny piece of a vast number of stocks, bonds, or whatever investment the ETF is based on. Here are some reasons why ETFs are so popular:

- *ETFs add great diversity to your portfolio.* Each share of an ETF is like having a shopping basket filled with stocks or some other type of security.
- *ETFs offer low expense ratios.* Because they are not actively managed, ETFs have expense ratios that may be even lower than index funds. Expense ratios range from a little less than 0.1 percent to 0.5 percent. In comparison, actively managed domestic stock funds charge an average of 1.4 percent.
- *ETFs invest in a vast array of securities.* You can use ETFs to invest in almost every type of security. For example, you can buy an ETF that invests in every stock in the U.S. stock market. There are ETFs that invest exclusively in financial stocks, utilities, foreign countries, or just about any niche you prefer.

Unlike a no-load mutual fund, which has no front-end or back-end commission and can be traded without a charge, you must pay a brokerage fee to buy and sell an ETF. This commission can cut into your profits, especially if you're investing only a small amount each month. Nonetheless, ETFs tend to have extremely low operating expenses that don't drag down the value.

Because they are traded like stocks, you can buy or sell an ETF at any time. In contrast, an index fund's value is determined once each day at 4:00 and all transactions are officially executed at that time.

A survey of 1,400 independent investment advisers conducted by Schwab Institutional found that 75 percent of investment advisers use ETFs in creating portfolios for new clients. Since investment advisers possess a considerable amount of expertise, it may be a good idea to follow their lead. Just because investment advisers buy and sell ETFs in building their clients' portfolios, however, they may be using them much differently than most investors. Investment advisers rely on their instincts, expertise, and research to pick when is the best time to buy or sell those ETFs. If they feel a certain sector of the economy is going to do well, they might invest clients' money in an ETF comprising those stocks. At the same time, they might sell an ETF consisting of stocks from a different sector that looks bleak to them.

In contrast, investors using the *MoneyTrack* method will be holding onto ETFs for the long-term, rather than buying and selling them in response to market conditions. ETFs give investors a way to diversify and build wealth steadily over the years. Systematic investing is the antithesis of gambling.

ETFs—Tied to the Size of the Company Invested In

Some ETFs are tied to indices based on a company's market capitalization. Market capitalization refers to the aggregate value of a stock. To arrive at this figure, you multiply the number of shares outstanding by their current price per share. If a company has 10 million shares outstanding and each share is worth $40, the market capitalization is $400 million.

Typically, market capitalization is broken down into three categories:

1. *Large cap:* The market capitalization is $5 billion or greater.
2. *Mid-cap:* The market capitalization is usually $1 billion to $5 billion.
3. *Small cap:* The market capitalization is less than $1 billion.

The company in our example would be a small-cap stock, because its market capitalization is $400 million.

These distinctions are not written in stone and you will see different break points utilized. As an example, an article on Forbes.com titled, "The 100 Best Mid-Cap Stocks In America," defined a mid-cap as having a market capitalization of between $1 billion and $4 billion.

Don't be surprised if you see different categories somewhere else such as the following:

1. *Large cap:* $5 billion or greater
2. *Mid-cap:* $500 million to $5 billion
3. *Small cap:* $100 million to $500 million

It you're a typical investor, however, the most important thing is for you to understand the basic distinction between large cap, mid-cap, and small cap stocks.

As the companies you invest in get smaller, your risk increases. Micro-cap stocks are quite risky. The Motley Fool, www.fool.com, defines a micro-cap company as one having a market capitalization of $100 million or less. In other publications, a micro-cap stock will be defined as having a market capitalization of less than $250 million.

The first ETF was the SPDR, which stands for Standard & Poor's Depositary Receipt. *Spiders,* as they're called, track the value of an index such as the S&P 500, which consists of large company stocks. There are also spiders that track the S&P MidCap 400 stocks, as well as other indices. Other companies offer ETFs under their own brand names such as VIPERs and i-Shares.

ETFs tied to broader indices are geared to more conservative investors. The SPDR Dow Jones Wilshire Total Market Index tracks almost all of the publicly traded stocks in the U.S. The ETF allocates more money to stocks that have higher market capitalizations. According to Eleanor Laise's February 3, 2008, article in the *Wall Street Journal Online,* investors are taking more risks when they invest in a narrowly focused ETF.

You can find ETFs that track small-cap, mid-cap, and large-cap stocks. For example, the iShares S&P 1500 Index invests in 600 small-cap, 400 mid-cap, and 500 large-cap stocks. There are also ETFs tied to much-narrower indexes and sectors of the economy, such as consumer staples. Staples are the items you buy regardless of economic conditions, like groceries and toothpaste.

ETFs—Tied to Different Styles of Investing

Buying ETFs also makes it possible to add different styles of investing to your portfolio. For instance, if you want some of your portfolio to utilize a value approach to investing, you can invest in the iShares Russell 1000 Value Index. Those shares seek investment results that correspond to the performance of U.S. large-cap value stocks. Value investors look for stocks that appeared to be undervalued based on their current price.

One measure used to determine value is a company's price-earnings ratio, or P-E ratio, as it is frequently called. The ratio is calculated by dividing the stock's price by its earnings. If a stock is selling for $20 and each share earned a dollar last year, the P-E ratio would be 20. Remember that earnings are different from dividends and a company's P-E ratio may change every day as the price of the stock goes up and down. The P-E ratio will also change if the dividend goes up or down.

A value investor might look at the P-E ratio of a market sector such as financial stocks. For example, if the investor sees that financials in the S&P 500 are trading at an average P-E ratio of 15, she might then look at the P-E ratio of the entire S&P 500. Let's say the S&P 500 price/earnings multiple at that point in time is 20. The value investor might conclude that financial stocks are undervalued and that sector might look attractive to her. She might also decide to invest in a financial stock that has an even lower P-E ratio than 15.

Obviously, a value investor will look at other factors besides a company's P-E ratio. Although the P-E-ratio looks good, there may be a number of reasons why the stock isn't much of a bargain.

You can also buy shares tied to a growth stock index. Growth investors look for stocks that they expect to grow substantially over the years. They are far less concerned about earnings and dividends. Their goal is capital appreciation. To achieve that capital appreciation, they believe a company should be reinvesting earnings rather than paying out dividends to stockholders.

When you invest in ETFs, your purchases aren't limited to stocks indices. You can find ETFs that are tied to a multitude of indices, such as a fixed-income index. There are even ETFs that invest in gold if you would like to add that asset to your portfolio. An indirect way to invest in gold, silver, and platinum, is to buy an ETF tied to the Dow Jones Precious Metals Index. That index measures the performance of U.S.-traded companies engaged in the exploration and production of gold, silver, and precious metals. There are even ETFs tied to vaccines, nuclear energy, and luxury goods.

Like index funds, you won't get the highest return from ETFs, but you will build a portfolio with considerable diversity. You won't get that diversity, however, from buying one or two ETFs tied to a certain index. For example, buying an ETF filled with stock in large companies isn't enough. You also should be investing part of your wealth in ETFs that buy stock in small companies, as well as other asset classes such as bonds.

You can find data regarding the performance of ETFs at www.morningstar.com. There are nearly 700 ETFs tracked by Morningstar. According to Laise's article, 270 new ETFs were launched in 2007. IndexUniverse.com can also provide a wealth of information related to ETFs and index funds.

Day Trading for Fun, Profit, and Losses

Day trading is investing on steroids and is akin to gambling, especially if you're an amateur investor. During its heyday, many investors thought they could quit their day job and make money at their computer with very little effort. Just as real estate investors got burned by flipping properties, it's not as easy as it looks to make money while sitting at the computer in your underwear.

Day traders trade frequently over the Internet with the goal of profiting from rapidly changing prices. Whereas most successful investors buy stocks for the long-term, day traders may only hold them for a few minutes. True day traders don't hold any stocks overnight.

Short-term capital gains do not receive the same favorable tax treatment as long-term capital gains. Gains on the sale of stocks that you've held for a year or longer are taxed at a lower rate on your federal income tax return. There are even some states that tax long-term capital gains at a lower rate than short-term capital gains.

The SEC and state securities regulators have warned investors about the risks of day trading. The SEC warns:

- *You may suffer severe financial losses.* You should only invest money you can afford to lose.
- *It is inaccurate to view day trading as investing.* You are hoping to ride the momentum of a stock and exploit short-term fluctuations in price.
- *Day trading is expensive.* Even if a day trader guesses right regarding a stock, the gain must be more than the cost of the commissions for buying and selling securities in order for the person to make a profit.
- *Many day traders borrow money to buy or sell stocks.* This increases the likelihood that the day trader will go in the hole.

As is the case with any form of speculative investing, you should only wager money you can afford to lose.

Although day trading might make an interesting hobby, it's a tough way to make a living. You must stay on top of the stocks you're looking to buy and hold so you're ready to seize whatever opportunity arises. If you're depending upon your profits to put bread on the table, it's a very intense way to make money. If you want to make a go of it, you should be wary of newsletters and Web sites that cater to day traders. Making money in day trading is not nearly as easy as some companies make it look.

Warren Buffett does not believe hyperactive trading is a good way to make money in the stock market. He has been quoted as saying,

"We believe that according the name 'investors' to institutions that trade actively is like calling someone who repeatedly engages in one-night stands a romantic."

Scam Alert

Even the rich and famous fall victim to scam artists. Celebrities like Giovanni Ribisi, Jeffrey Tambor, and Peter Coyote were duped by Reed E. Slatkin. Slatkin used his clout as a minister of the Church of Scientology to con fellow members into investing in a young Scientologist's Internet business. Slatkin's operation conned investors out of millions. He stole $10 million from one man on his deathbed and another $2 million from a paraplegic.

According to a press release issued by the SEC on September 4, 2003, Slatkin was sentenced to 14 years in prison after pleading guilty to criminal charges relating to a massive Ponzi scheme. In March 2002, Slatkin pleaded guilty to 15 felony charges, including mail fraud, conspiracy to obstruct justice, and money laundering. During a 15-year period, Slatkin fraudulently solicited almost $600 million from approximately 800 investors.

As part of his plea agreement, Slatkin admitted that he attempted to obstruct the SEC's investigation using false account statements and fabricated correspondence. He also lied to the SEC under oath about the success of his investments.

Scam artists will cloak themselves in the mantle of any religion. In Boca Raton, Florida, a stockbroker promised double-digit returns to fellow members of his congregation. Instead, he caused them to lose millions of dollars by investing their money in extremely risky and volatile securities. The broker also, according to an article by Dan Christensen in the *Miami Herald*, covered his tracks by falsifying reports. Some of the broker's victims included his rabbi, widows, elderly clients, and even a Holocaust survivor that he met at a scholarship fundraiser.

The key to avoiding scams is to check out all of the parties involved, even if they're friends of yours or members of the same church or synagogue. The foundation for affinity fraud is built on people being less suspicious of persons they know or who share similar interests. Call your state securities regulator to find out about any investment adviser's background before giving the person any money. Never invest based on rumors, whims, or someone's urgent recommendations.

Improving Your Odds as an Investor

When you invest for the long haul, your odds of success improve. Nevertheless, there will be periods where you'll hate to check your investments online or anywhere for that matter. According to Jonathan Clements' article, in "Five Good Reasons Stocks Are Attractive Despite Downdraft," in the January 23, 2008, issue of the *Wall Street Journal*, the odds of a multiyear losing streak in the stock market are quite low. According to Clements's article, which relies on Ibbotson Associates' data, we have only seen four multiyear losing streaks since 1925:

- 1929–1932
- 1939–1941
- 1973–1974
- 2000–2002

The years 2000 to 2002 were far more than a standard bear market. The S&P 500 fell 49 percent from its peak in March 2000 until it hit rock bottom in October 2002.

In a *Law & Order* rerun, detectives Lennie Briscoe and Mike Logan were investigating a homicide where they suspected the murder was committed by a man whose mother was the victim of a scam. Briscoe told Logan that he has his money in three banks and two different mutual funds, so he won't lose everything to a con man. It was shocking that Briscoe had any money after his divorces and his numerous complaints about trying to live on a detective's salary. Nevertheless, Briscoe was also teaching us a lesson about asset allocation.

Asset allocation is the process of dividing your money among various assets such as stocks, bonds, and cash investments like savings accounts. The strategy operates from the assumption that certain investments will do well during different economic climates. It's unlikely that all of your investments will perform badly at the same time.

Asset allocation encourages you to be thoroughly diversified. It's more than just having savings accounts in different banks as Briscoe recommended. You're splitting your nest egg among asset classes such as stocks, fixed-income investments like bonds, real estate, and cash. These asset classes have subcategories as well. In the fixed-income investment category, you can achieve a higher degree of diversification by putting money in municipal bonds, government bonds, and corporate bonds.

Many financial pros believe that how you allocate your assets is more important than what investments you choose. Putting an asset allocation plan in place gives you the opportunity to generate favorable investment returns over the long haul.

It is also important that you rebalance your investment portfolio on a regular basis. The process of reallocating your assets is known as *rebalancing*. By reallocating your investments routinely, you are less likely to react emotionally to changes in the market. Your goal is to stick with the mix of investments that is right for your age, objectives, and risk temperament. If stocks go up in value, for example, your portfolio may be overweighted in equity investments. Therefore, you should reallocate your portfolio so you have the ideal mix of stocks, bonds, and other assets. This may seem counterintuitive, because you're selling some of the best-performing assets in your portfolio.

Despite the frightening ups and downs of the market, a portion of your portfolio should still be in stocks. The standard asset allocation rule of thumb suggests that you should subtract your age from the number 100 to calculate how much of your money should be in stocks. For example, if you're age 60, 40 percent of your assets should be in stock, since 100 minus 60 is 40. If you're age 30, 70 percent of your assets should be invested in the stock market, since 100 minus 30 equals 70.

A rule of thumb is a very unscientific method for determining how your assets should be allocated. It also doesn't tell you how to diversify each of your asset classes. Nonetheless, you should be taking steps to ensure that your portfolio includes a variety of investments in the various asset classes.

MoneyTrack Method

A core principle of the *MoneyTrack* method is that although investment gurus say they can pick stock market winners, you shouldn't rely on their advice. You're much better off if you listen to true investment professionals who recommend investing for the long haul rather than trying to time the market or pick a stock that will have a quick payoff.

Although ETFs trade like stocks, they give you exposure to an index comprising many securities. One strategy we recommend on *MoneyTrack* is systematically investing in different ETFs that are composed of small, medium, and large companies. You can also buy ETFs that utilize different styles of investing to diversify your investment nest egg. In addition, you can invest in ETFs in order to add different asset classes to your portfolio.

The bulk of your money should be invested in a portfolio that is consistent with your age, risk tolerance, time horizon, and investment objectives. Instead of trying to pick the right horse in the race to financial security, you can cut your risks by spreading your money over the entire stock market. To achieve true diversity, you should split your investment among various asset classes and subclasses.

Stock trading is much more of a gamble if you're betting on a huge investment return over a short time frame. Your time horizon is when you expect to need the money you're investing. It would be foolish to invest money that you need a year from now for a down payment, wedding, or some other financial objective. Your odds of success improve if you commit to investing in the stock market over a long time frame.

From time to time, you'll hear an infomercial or radio commercial for a revolutionary trading system that can help you make a fortune in the stock market. In one radio ad, someone who used the company's system and software talked about what a "rush" it was to trade stocks, which makes it seem that you're gambling not investing. Be wary of any investor education company that leads you to believe you'll be able to quit your day job and trade stocks for a living. Buying and selling stocks and options isn't a can't-miss strategy to achieve instant wealth, just as "flipping" properties didn't make people instant millionaires as the infomercials claimed.

Many stock traders are like compulsive gamblers. When they lose money on an investment, they try to double down and take bigger risks in an attempt to break even. In the end, however, they often lose twice as much. Sometimes, too, they'll refuse to sell a stock, even as it goes down with no hope for recovery. They rationalize that they haven't lost any money until they sell the stock.

Stock market gurus will come and go, so you're better off sticking with a strategy that will guide you through good times and bad. A time-tested strategy is to invest in the stock market as a whole, not individual securities. With your fun money, you can take a shot at buying individual stocks that some guru recommends.

Too many people make the mistake of thinking they'll make a killing in the stock market and will then shore up their finances by paying off credit card debt or buying a house. That approach is putting the cart before the horse. You're not ready to invest in individual stocks until you have your debt under control and you've put money in an emergency fund in case you lose your job or suffer a financial setback. And for goodness sake, don't take your emergency fund to the track.

There's no harm in watching programs like Jim Cramer's *Mad Money* or the various business programs that are filled with useful information. Make sure you're watching real business news and not an infomercial, which is paid programming. Start reading the business pages and the columnists who write about investing. Check out the *MoneyTrack* Web site from time to time and take a few minutes to learn something new about investing. Make a daily trip to MSN Money for *MoneyTrack* videos, as well as a wealth of investment advice from a great many experts.

If you work at it, you might one day be an investment guru or at least a novice investment guru. Aside from books, financial shows, and the Internet, you can learn a great deal by reading the business section of the newspaper every day. Watch how the news affects stocks you own and don't own. In time, you might be the person your friends and relatives go to for an objective opinion about an investment they're considering.

As we will see in Chapter 14, you can encourage your children to learn more about investing, so they can become investment pros at a relatively young age. It certainly beats taking them to the race track and teaching them how to bet on the ponies.

CHAPTER 7

Me, Inc.

There are some people who go through life with an attitude, "It's all about me." When it comes to investing and securing your financial future, it truly is all about you. It's imperative that you maximize the value of your employee benefits, as well as the investment opportunities available through your employment. Using the principles of the *MoneyTrack* method, you can make the most of your financial resources and create a brighter future for yourself, as well as your family.

My co-host on *MoneyTrack*, Jack Gallagher, used to be a teacher. Jack has often said that his employee benefits were far more important than any $2,000 per year raise he might receive. Jack is one of the fortunate few who will receive a traditional pension. Today, you cannot count on getting the kind of pension plan through work that your dad received. More than likely, your benefits in retirement will be based on how much you saved and how well your investments perform over the years.

Salary Isn't the Only Thing that Matters

Most Americans work for someone else. When they accept a position or change jobs, company benefits are a key consideration. Here are some of the benefits that draw talented workers to a company:

- 401(k) retirement savings plan, especially those that offer matching contributions from the employer and a relatively short vesting period

- Medical and dental benefits
- Vacation
- Sick pay
- Disability insurance
- Flexible work schedule
- Pleasant work environment
- Tuition reimbursement

MoneyTrack reporter N'Deye Walton interviewed Paul Thompson, a Ford factory worker who thought he would receive a nice pension after nearly thirty years of loyal service. Ford laid him off just ten months shy of his thirtieth anniversary. As a result, he did not qualify for a full pension that's nearly $3,000 per month and includes free healthcare.

N'Deye also interviewed an assemblyline worker for General Motors who found, too, that the benefits he relied on didn't come to pass. Over the years, Leroy McKnight had turned down other jobs to stay with GM in anticipation of a good pension and free healthcare in retirement. In the end, however, Leroy found that the company's promises wouldn't be upheld. He is thinking about changing careers and working as a stockbroker, the kind of job he turned down years ago.

If You Don't Take Care of Yourself . . .

As the old saying goes, if you don't take care of yourself, no one else will. It used to be that employers took care of their employees, as well as their families, from cradle to grave. Now, ten years or more with a company is considered to be a good run. Most large corporations are far more worried about their shareholders than their employees.

Guaranteed pensions are becoming a relic of days gone by. Instead you'll find that most employers now offer retirement savings plans where you take responsibility for funding your sunset years. Nevertheless, a 401(k) may be the most important employee benefit you receive through your job.

The 401(k) retirement savings plan takes its name from the provision of the Internal Revenue Code that gave birth to this tax-sheltered savings account. When you sign up for the 401(k) plan offered by your employer, the contribution you specify is automatically deducted from your paycheck each payday. Your contribution reduces your current taxes and makes it less difficult to save. When you're retired and are presumably in a lower tax bracket, you pay taxes on your withdrawals. Depending on where you live, contributions to a 401(k) may reduce your state income taxes.

Typically, employers match a portion of or all of your contribution, thus giving you an incentive to save. Many employers contribute fifty cents or more for each dollar you contribute up to a maximum amount. Your employer's contributions vest after you've been with the company for a specified period of time. *Vesting* means you've reached the milestone when you qualify to keep contributions made on your behalf by the company. If you decide not to participate in your employer's 401(k) plan, you're passing up free money and a terrific tax break.

Because 401(k)s are so important to your long-term financial well-being, many companies now enroll employees automatically in their plan. It is up to you to opt out of the plan if you do not want to participate. Some employers increase your contribution automatically, unless you indicate otherwise. Opting out of your employer's retirement savings plan or rejecting automatic contribution increases is a mistake that will haunt you for years to come.

If you leave your place of employment, you will have three options:

1. Transfer your account to your new employer's 401(k).
2. Transfer your funds to an Individual Retirement Account (IRA).
3. Take the money and pay taxes on it.

The process of transferring your funds from the plan to an IRA is known as a *rollover*. A rollover would be right up Chloe's alley if she participated in a 401(k) and could actually do tricks like rolling over. Chloe's one and only trick is to walk in front of the camera while we're trying to film *MoneyTrack*, and frankly, it's getting old.

The worst decision you can make is to take the money you've put away in a retirement savings plan as a taxable distribution. In most cases, you will pay income taxes and a 10 percent premature distribution penalty. More importantly, you will lose the ability to keep that money working for you in a tax-sheltered account for the next 10, 20, 30, or 40 years. Depending on your age, you might be losing $100,000 or more in lost earnings. At age 70, you might still be regretting your decision.

Although the 401(k) plan is the most common, your employer may offer a comparable retirement savings account that operates in a similar fashion. 403(b) accounts are usually offered to public school employees, as well as folks who work for tax-exempt organizations. As we will see, smaller businesses also offer tax-sheltered retirement plans that can help employees reach their financial goals.

Some employers have begun offering a Roth 401(k). The plan resembles the Roth IRA in that your contributions don't reduce the taxes in your paycheck. Assuming you follow the rules, when you make withdrawals, your distributions are tax-free. All of the earnings you make over the years are also tax-free, which makes it more appealing than your typical 401(k). Even if your employer only offers a traditional 401(k), however, it's imperative that you participate. You may be able to participate, even if you work part-time for a company.

Crunching the Numbers

Of 157 million working Americans, 78.6 million work for companies or unions that sponsor a pension or retirement plan. According to EBRI's *Campaign 2008: Facts on Benefits Issues,* the participation rate for full-time working women in a retirement plan is roughly 54 percent. About 51 percent of men participate.

One of the best motivational tools to encourage people to participate in a 401(k) is to crunch the numbers. We asked one of our guests, Stephen Butler, for help. Steve is the president of Pension Dynamics, but we like to call him Mister 401(k).

One of our viewers was putting away about $12,500 each year in his 401(k). If that viewer allows the earnings to compound and earns an average of 8 percent per year, he'll have about $1.4 million in thirty years.

As you review your employer's plan, look at what fees are being charged. You shouldn't be paying more than 1 percent in fees on the investments in your 401(k) account. One of our viewers, John Fuchs of Pennsylvania, found that his plan was also charging employees 0.5 percent of the assets for a pension consultant, plus other expenses.

Fees and expenses limit your investment success. In an article published by Steve on September 11, 2006, that can be found on his Web site, www.pensiondynamics.com, he referred to a report issued by Boston College's Center for Retirement Research. The report observed that a 1 percent difference in annual return cuts or increases your retirement nest egg by 20 percent. Therefore, cutting the fees on your investment by 1 percent can increase the size of your nest egg by 20 percent, because of the effects of compounding.

Although you may not have as much control over the expenses associated with your company's 401(k) retirement savings plan, you can certainly curtail the cost of other investments in your portfolio. Exchange-traded funds (ETFs) and index funds usually have the lowest fees.

Health Insurance Check-Ups

According to the Census Bureau, 47 million individuals had no health insurance of any kind in 2006. Although the cost of health insurance is rising steadily, you don't want to be among them. A devastating illness can wipe out your nest egg and will severely hurt your chances of achieving your financial objectives.

In addition to the millions of people who are uninsured, there are many more who possess inadequate health insurance. Their policies only offer limited coverage for medical problems. Some of these policies have deductibles of $7,500 or more. To avoid being financially devastated by an illness, there are people who rely on an excess medical policy that doesn't make payment until the insured has run up at least $25,000 or more in medical bills.

Because of these statistics, it is easy to see why health insurance is one of the most important employee benefits. Your employer typically chips in a portion of your premium. As healthcare costs have escalated, however, many companies have cut back on their contributions and more of the costs are passed along to employees. Even retirees have found that their former employers are scaling back healthcare benefits.

EBRI's 2008 Retirement Confidence Survey indicates that health costs have become a big concern for retirees. Nearly half (44 percent) of the retirees surveyed said they spent more than they expected on health care expenses. More than half (54 percent) of them reported that they were now more concerned about their financial future than they were immediately after retirement.

Flexible Spending Accounts

Flexible spending accounts are part of many employee benefits packages. An employee may set aside money in this account to pay for qualified expenses such as medical bills. Money set aside is not subject to payroll taxes. The employee can then use the money to pay for medical expenses not covered by insurance.

Many employees shy away from flexible spending accounts, because they contain use-it-or-lose-it provisions. This means that if you don't use the money in the flexible spending account by the end of the year, it goes to waste. Some plans offer a grace period of several months, so you have extra time to use any money that's left over. As a practical matter, as long as you don't put far too much money in a flexible spending account, you're unlikely to lose any of it. You can always get a new pair of glasses or an extra teeth cleaning to ensure that the money in the account doesn't get squandered.

Health Savings Accounts (HSA)

Health savings accounts (HSAs) were created as a way to combat the high cost of insurance. HSAs can cut your taxes and help you save money on insurance. A health insurance plan with a high deductible costs significantly less than coverage with lower deductibles. You can use some of those savings to fund your HSA. You might then use the account to pay medical bills that aren't covered by your health insurance plan.

Contributions to an HSA, whether from your employer or yourself, are deposited in an account that is similar to an IRA. Earnings and contributions grow without being taxed. Withdrawals to pay for qualified medical expenses are tax-free. Other withdrawals trigger penalties and taxes.

To be eligible to open an HSA, you must be covered by a high-deductible health plan or not covered at all. In 2008, the deductible must be at least $1,100 for an individual and $2,200 for a family to qualify.

You can contribute up to $2,900 in 2008 if you're an individual and $5,800 per family. An extra contribution of $900 is permitted if you're age 55 or older.

COBRA and HIPAA

If you leave your place of employment, make sure you understand your rights under COBRA, the Consolidated Omnibus Budget Reconciliation Act. COBRA permits workers and their families to continue their group health benefits for a period of time by paying the entire insurance premium, plus a service charge. You are not entitled to your former employer's contribution, if any, to the cost of the coverage. COBRA eases the pain of a voluntary or involuntary job loss that leaves you without coverage. COBRA may also be available where coverage is affected due to a death, divorce, or reduction in hours.

The Health Insurance Portability and Accountability Act of 1996 (HIPAA) protects group health plan participants who switch jobs and their beneficiaries. HIPAA limits exclusions for preexisting conditions. The law also prohibits discrimination against employees and dependents based on their health status. You are permitted, in certain circumstances, to enroll in a new plan. HIPAA might also give you the opportunity to purchase individual coverage if there is no group health plan available at your new job.

As we saw in Chapter 4, it's imperative that you understand what your health insurance benefits are and whether they will continue after you retire. Find out if your group health plan covers retirees and what the cost is projected to be. In certain situations, employers are permitted to renege on health insurance benefits owed to retirees.

Typically, your group health plan becomes secondary to the coverage you get through Medicare. If your employer's coverage is not available to supplement Medicare, you should consider buying a supplemental policy. Remember that even though you can collect Social Security benefits as early as age 62, Medicare will not cover you until age 65 unless you're disabled.

Benefits You Don't Get through Your Employer

Even though employee benefits are extremely important, you may still need additional protection. Many companies only offer short-term disability insurance. At a young age, you are far more likely to become disabled than die. Losing the ability to work and earn an income will devastate most families. It also impacts your ability to put away money for retirement. It's important to purchase a policy that pays disability benefits if they are needed for an extended period.

A number of companies provide life insurance to employees at no cost, but it may not be enough. Young families, in particular, may need large amounts of life insurance in case the primary bread-winner dies. Companies also offer additional life insurance to employees at a group rate, but it often pays to shop around for a better deal. Group life insurance that you purchase through work isn't necessarily cheaper, because the insurance company's premium is based on the health and demographics of everyone at the company who is buying insurance. You may be paying a higher premium because other employees aren't as good an insurance risk as you are.

Individual term life insurance policies are relatively inexpensive. You can shop around for the best price through companies such as AccuQuote or BestQuote. If you're healthy and relatively young, you can usually get a huge policy for a modest premium.

You may receive life insurance offers through the mail. Generally, these policies are rather expensive, because unhealthy people are more likely to respond to these offers. The premium reflects the fact that many of the people insured might have difficulty qualifying for an individual life insurance policy.

Long-term care insurance is another policy that is usually not available through your employer. As you age, the odds increase that you or a loved one will be unable to perform the activities of daily

Scam Alert

Although it's rare, you'll find situations where someone is stealing from your 401(k) plan. Janessa Dabler worked her way up from Silicon Valley secretary to executive vice president of a $5-million-in-sales software company. She was also the trustee of the company's pension plan. On the surface, Dabler had a big heart and even created an animal rescue foundation.

She began spending employees' 401(k) savings on herself and drained the company's coffers. Eventually, however, her scam was discovered. Dabler was convicted of stealing her employees' retirement savings. In a larger company, there is considerably more oversight of the business' retirement savings plans.

The Department of Labor states that there are a number of red flags that might alert you to fraud involving your 401(k):

- Are statements consistently late?
- Are contributions coming out of your paycheck but not appearing on your 401(k) statement?
- Are the markets going up but your balances are going down?
- Are there unexplained drops in your account balance?

Your employer is required to provide you with yearly reports on your 401(k) plan. If you suspect there are problems with your retirement savings plan, you should contact the U.S. Department of Labor, www.dol.gov.

living such as bathing or walking. Long-term care is not normally covered by your standard health insurance policy. Even Medicare only provides limited coverage for long-term care expenses. Many people who don't have long-term care insurance must rely on Medicaid, a federal program administered by the states that pay benefits if your income is low and you have few assets.

Opening and Closing Your Own Business

Rather than investing in the stock market, some people like the idea of investing in their own business. On the one hand, if you possess the entrepreneurial spirit, make good decisions, and are willing to work long hours, you can open a successful business. On the other hand, if you don't expect to work hard and listen to the wrong people, you'll soon be closing your own business with a lot less money than when you started.

Maybe you've seen the ads for incredible business opportunities that only require you to work a few hours each day yet you'll make big bucks. Usually, the ads say that you don't need any special skills. Lately, there have been a number of seminars advertised that will show you how to make $10,000 plus per month selling merchandise on eBay. The ads push all the right buttons, such as the ability to work from home and avoid commuting forever.

Well, don't quit your day job yet. So-called work-at-home opportunities have been popular scams for decades. Opening a business is difficult and requires a number of different skills. Owning and operating a business is not for everyone. You need to fully understand all of the potential advantages and disadvantages that come with working for yourself.

If the business is profitable, you might be able to write off your health insurance premiums. You might also be able to deduct some of your travel expenses if you must make business trips to a particular destination or are attending a seminar.

Assuming a business will be profitable is a big assumption. When buying an existing business or opening a new one, you are putting your financial well-being at risk. Most businesses require a great deal of capital to get started and keep going during the lean years when the business is just getting off the ground.

Buying a franchise is also no guarantee of success. You should consult with a franchise attorney before signing any agreement.

You'll also need an accountant to review the franchiser's audited financial statements. In addition, you should conduct your own research by contacting current and former franchise owners. If you're older and nearing retirement age, you should be particularly careful because you may destroy a lifetime's worth of savings by funneling money into the franchise.

Opening a small business while you're still working for someone else is an excellent way to make the transition to retirement. You can test the water to see if you'd like to spend more time on this business after retiring. Ideally, the business will incorporate activities you enjoy and it won't just be a job. You can also bolster your retirement savings by contributing to a business-related retirement savings account.

When people think about changing jobs or opening their open business, a major concern is losing their benefits. Paying for your own benefits, as well your employees' perks, is a major expenditure. The cost of these benefits should be factored into your decision as to whether to open a new business and how much money you'll need to launch it.

Retirement Plans for the Self-Employed

When you own your own business, you need to create your own perks. The good news is that there are a number of retirement savings plans that can be utilized by small businesses. The SEP-IRA is the popular name for the simplified employee pension individual retirement account. With the SEP-IRA, the employer makes all of the contributions and employees are not permitted to contribute to the plan. It's often used by businesses where the owner is the only employee. In 2008, the contribution limit of the SEP-IRA is the lesser of 25 percent of net income, or a maximum contribution of $46,000.

If your business has employees who have been with you for at least three years, they are also entitled to participate in the SEP-IRA and receive the same contribution that you make for yourself. Although the business owner may wish to contribute a great deal of money to the firm's SEP-IRA, this means he or she will be required to make the same contribution on behalf of a qualified employee. This is a trade-off that doesn't sit well with many business owners.

The savings incentive match plan for employees is known by most people as a SIMPLE-IRA. The SIMPLE-IRA is available to companies that have less than one hundred employees. All qualified employees must be permitted to make contributions.

If the business has a SIMPLE-IRA, the employer must make a matching contribution for each participant. The employer can opt to match employees' contributions on a dollar-for-dollar basis up to 3 percent of their salary or contribute 2 percent of each qualified employee's wages, whether that person contributes to the plan or not.

Another possibility is an individual 401(k), or a solo 401(k) as it is sometimes called. The individual 401(k) is very similar to traditional 401(k)s, except there are far fewer administrative requirements. Nevertheless, an individual 401(k) is more complicated to administer and maintain than a SEP-IRA or a SIMPLE-IRA. With an individual 401(k), you are permitted to take out a loan from the plan.

Before choosing which plan to establish, you should have a lengthy discussion with your accountant. The plans differ as to how much money you can put away. These caps may mean little to you, however, if all of the money you make will be plowed back into the business.

Taxing Your Knowledge about Taxes

Unless you have this overwhelming desire to give more money to the government, it's time to think about yourself. Paying more attention to taxes helps you keep more of the money you save and earn. Tax planning can help you make the most of your money now and for years to come.

Throughout this book, we've looked at tax-advantaged ways to save and invest for retirement. Compounding works its magic when it is unimpeded by taxes. Although there are exceptions, most retirement savings plans require that you wait until age 59½ to access your money without restriction. Withdrawing money prior to that age may subject you to a premature withdrawal penalty of 10 percent, not to mention a significant loss in compounded earnings.

In theory, you will wait until you're retired before withdrawing funds from an IRA, 401(k), or some other tax-sheltered plan. Presumably, you will be in a lower tax bracket at that time. Nevertheless, if your investments do extremely well, and we should all have this problem, you may be in a higher tax bracket after retiring.

Whether you're investing for retirement or some other investment goal, you must always keep your eye on the tax implications.

No matter how old we get, we all love to complain about taxes. Once your children are grown, you'll probably complain that you're paying property taxes to educate someone else's kids. After you begin collecting Social Security, you'll complain that your benefits are taxed.

"Say what?" you're probably asking. "You have to pay taxes on Social Security benefits?" Although I hate to be the bearer of bad news, the truth is that your benefits are taxable if you make too much.

Married couples who file joint returns may be subject to taxes on their Social Security benefits if their adjusted gross income is more than $32,000. All other filers may owe taxes on their benefits if their adjusted gross income is more than $25,000.

To keep your taxes down now and when you receive Social Security benefits, you should work to become a tax-efficient investor. More often than not, you are better off maximizing your contributions to tax-sheltered retirement accounts before putting money in taxable accounts. Obviously, if your employer adds money to that tax-sheltered retirement account, it sweetens the deal.

You also need to consider the tax implications as you make withdrawals from your accounts. Generally, you should try to keep money in tax-sheltered accounts for as long as possible. If you need cash to live on in retirement, it's best to take it first from accounts that have already been taxed.

An investment that causes you to pay the most taxes is better suited for a tax-sheltered retirement account. For instance, the interest on bonds is taxed at your current rate, which might be as high as 35 percent. That's much higher than the 15 percent rate that is usually paid on most stock dividends and capital gains. Therefore, you're usually better off keeping taxable bonds or bond funds in a tax-sheltered account. As we will discuss in Chapter 9, a real estate investment trust (REIT) often generates income that is taxed at a higher rate and might fit better in a tax-sheltered account.

Although the tax consequences of holding certain investments are important, they should not necessarily dictate how you invest. Taxes should, however, be a consideration. For example, index funds tend to produce a lower amount of capital gains, because there is less turnover than in an actively managed account. Therefore, an index fund might be better suited for a taxable account. To take another example, it would not be wise to put tax-free municipal bonds in a tax-sheltered account.

Securities regulators have expressed concern about financial professionals who sell variable annuities, a tax-advantaged investment, to seniors for their IRAs. It makes little sense to put a tax-deferred product in an account that is already tax-deferred.

MoneyTrack Method

You work for yourself when it comes to preparing for your financial future. The company's name is Me, Inc. You're not being disloyal or self-centered; you're simply recognizing that your employer's mission is not to make you financially secure. Nevertheless, most companies make it easy for you to apply the *MoneyTrack* method to retirement savings plans. You can set up an automatic investment program and make regular contributions that will grow and compound over the years in a tax-sheltered account. You'll use our old friend, the dollar cost averaging strategy, to improve your chances of achieving investment success. You'll also be able to take advantage of employee benefits such as an employer's contribution to your retirement savings account.

Make sure you truly understand and fully utilize your employee benefit package. For the longest time, I thought Stevie Nicks was singing about a "one-winged dove." I could never figure out what the song was about and it broke my heart thinking about that one-winged dove. And once I got that song in my head, I'd be humming it all day or singing it with the wrong lyric. As it turned out, the song was called *Edge of Seventeen* and it was a "white-winged dove."

Just as I was confused for years about the white-winged dove, many people go through life with misconceptions about their employee benefits. Fly like a dove, one-winged, white-winged, or whatever, to your human resource department and make sure you're all on the same page. If you're close to retirement, find out how your benefits will change after you leave the company.

You need to get up close and personal with your benefits. Since your 401(k) is your most important benefit, you need to be certain you're getting the biggest bang for your buck. Make sure a chunk of your 401(k) isn't going to a broker, or a brokerette as Jack likes to say. Even your human resource representative might not know what expenses are chipping away at plan assets. Remember that high expenses mean less money in your pocket when it's time to retire and get your pocket watch. To avoid your being disappointed, I'm obliged to tell you that not many companies give pocket watches any more when you retire, unless you're working in a train station.

Keep a close watch on your 401(k) in case someone is raiding the assets for walking around money. Of course, 401(k) thieves usually don't walk much. They're riding in a car that you paid for and can't afford to drive.

You really need to prepare for the day when your employer says someone else can do your job better or someone overseas can do it much cheaper. You should always have an emergency fund of three to six months of living expenses to protect yourself in case of a job loss. It is also helpful to keep your resume and Rolodex up to date, even if you're very content at work and it appears as if they can't get along without you. You should know your next move before you need to make your next move.

Interestingly, a national online survey of 1,334 investors conducted by the Financial Regulatory Authority (FINRA) found that more Americans worry about investment losses than losing their jobs. Only about 50 percent of the group surveyed expressed concern about losing their jobs, while more than 75 percent were anxious about losing money on their investments.

If your job and investments keep you up at night, it's time to implement an action plan that will put you in the best position in case your fears become a reality. There may also be myths and urban legends about investing that keep you up at night and contribute to poor investment decisions. We'll talk about how to overcome those fears and misconceptions in Chapter 8.

CHAPTER 8

Myth Busters

There are hundreds of myths and urban legends that take on a life of their own as the months and years go by. Some of these myths and legends apply to investing, as well as financial and retirement planning. If you believe these myths and urban legends, you might be afraid to invest or you'll make some very bad investment decisions.

My favorite urban legend tells the frightening story of a maniac with a hook who was ready to pounce on two teenagers parked on lovers' lane. According to David Emery's article on About.com "Urban Legends," a teenage boy took his date to a deserted lovers' lane for a make-out session. A news bulletin came on the radio warning that a convicted murderer had escaped from the state insane asylum and was in the vicinity. The girl panicked and demanded to be taken home. When they arrived at her house, dangling from the car door handle was a bloody hook.

According to Emery, this urban legend has been around since the 1950s. The story even found its way into a *Dear Abby* column published on November 8, 1960. The legend has made the rounds over the years, and many people believed or still believe that the event actually occurred. It's likely that parents perpetuated this urban legend to discourage their own teenager from stopping on lovers' lane.

Myths and urban legends about investing don't make for good horror stories around the campfire, unless you go camping with financial services professionals. These myths and legends may discourage you from investing or might cause you to make some very bad financial decisions. If you buy into these myths and legends, you might undermine your retirement and sabotage your portfolio.

These myths affect investors' behavior and whether they'll invest at all. As an example, some experts say there are good months to buy and sell stocks. Or you might hear that October is a questionable time to invest. If you buy into a myth like that, you could interrupt your investment plan. Although there are patterns, trends, and cycles in the market, every month is the right time to invest, provided that you make investing a habit in good times and bad.

Myth #1: Small Investors Shouldn't Invest in the Stock Market

One particular urban legend that bothers me is that it takes a whole lot of money to invest in the stock market. This may be a situation where a myth is based on facts that no longer exist. At one time, investors had few choices other than full-service brokerage firms with expensive fees. In fact, some of these brokerage firms had no use for small investors.

Here's why it's a myth that small investors shouldn't be in the market:

- *Discount and online accounts have lowered the cost of investing.* Today's investors have a multitude of options for investing in the stock market. They can use a discount broker to trade shares at a much lower cost. Investors can open an online account and trade shares inexpensively.
- *The cost of investing in odd lots is small compared to not investing.* The extra cost that is sometimes associated with buying an odd lot may have helped to create the myth that small investors shouldn't invest in the stock market. An odd lot is normally the purchase or sale of less than 100 shares. In contrast, a round lot is 100 shares or a multiple such as 500 shares. If you buy an odd lot, you may sometimes pay in the neighborhood of 12.5 cents more per share to buy or sell your stock. Many brokers do not charge more for buying or selling odd lots. In any event, this extra cost shouldn't discourage you from investing in the stock market. You'll lose a lot more if you delay investing until you can afford to buy 100 shares at a time. Interestingly, some stock analysts look at odd-lot trading

to determine how small investors are reacting to changes in the market.

- *Mutual funds are ideal for small investors.* Mutual funds permit you to invest in the stock market with a minimal amount of money. Many funds require a minimum investment of only a few hundred dollars. If you agree to invest a specified amount each month, most mutual funds will waive their minimum investment requirement.
- *You can invest directly in stocks without a broker.* As we saw in Chapter 2, many companies offer direct stock purchase plans so you can invest without going through a broker. Once you own shares, you can sign up for dividend reinvestment programs to buy shares of stock, even if you're a small investor.

Jeff Hirsch, a guest on *MoneyTrack,* wrote the book *The Stock Trader's Almanac.* Jeff told us that this myth about small investors just isn't true. Even if you only have a small nest egg, you can still invest in stocks. All it takes is a disciplined approach that you stick to through thick and thin. You should also learn from your mistakes. At least those mistakes will be small ones.

Myth #2: Initial Public Offerings (IPOs) Are Always a Good Investment

Another myth is that initial public offerings (IPOs) are always a good investment. An IPO is the first time shares of stock in a company are offered to the public. You buy into a company before it begins trading publicly and get in on the ground floor. The myth is that you are buying shares for a fraction of what they are worth and you'll make an instant profit.

The second aspect of this myth is that these shares will jump to a very high price once the stock goes public. What sometimes happens is that immediately after a highly anticipated IPO hits the market, the stock jumps up in value. Soon thereafter, demand plummets and the stock price falls. IPOs may fluctuate considerably in value, because there is often limited information about the issuer. Since the stock is being publicly traded for the first time, it is unclear what trading patterns will emerge.

Writing in the Winter 2007 issue of *On Investing,* Jeff Ryan, a Schwab senior equity researcher, wrote that the current market for

IPOs is a far cry from what it was in 1999 when technology stocks were booming. He believes expectations for IPO stocks are overly optimistic. When compared with gains from the S&P 500 index, Ryan wonders if IPO investing is worth the risk.

In his article, Ryan also questions the common belief that "flipping" IPO shares is a successful strategy. *Flipping* as it relates to IPOs is where you sell your shares within a day or week after the IPO goes public. Just as trying to flip a house to make a profit is a risky strategy, flipping an IPO is a strategy that might not be successful.

Even if you're still anxious to take this course of action, you may not be able to get in on a well-publicized IPO when it goes public. Very few average investors have access to IPOs. Usually, they are

Testing Your Gullibility

Securities regulators and government agencies are utilizing an interesting exercise to educate investors about the dangers of IPOs. They posted information and a link to a phony Web site for a fictitious company called McWhortle Enterprises, Inc. The company is described as an established and well-known manufacturer of biological defense mechanisms. The company's defense systems purportedly protect executives living in dangerous areas.

The phony Web site describes McWhortle's new product, a Bio-Hazard Alert Detector. The tiny detector is discussed in glowing terms on the Web site.

After you express an interest in the IPO, you find out for the first time that McWhortle Enterprises does not exist. You've been "punked," or tricked as we used to say, by the SEC, the Federal Trade Commission, the North American Securities Administrators Association, and FINRA, formerly known as the National Association of Securities Dealers. If this company were real, your gullibility might have cost you a great deal of money.

The purpose of the phony Web site is to alert investors about the potential for online fraud and the dangers of investing in pre-IPOs. One place to check out this "new IPO" is by visiting the Office of the Kansas Securities Commissioner at http://www.securities.state.ks.us/onlineinvest.html.

Pre-IPO investing is also extremely risky. You are buying a stake in a company before it actually makes an initial public offering of securities. The offering may be illegal unless the transaction is registered with the SEC or meets an exemption. Quite often, the people promoting fraudulent pre-IPO offerings have attractive Web sites and usually use spam to promote the investment. Their marketing materials are often filled with misrepresentations. In some cases, the company never goes public.

reserved for big investors such as institutions and major clients of a brokerage firm.

Investors hope they are buying shares in the next Google, whose IPO took place in August 2004. Unfortunately, IPOs like Google are the exception, not the rule. Sometimes, IPOs don't even get off the ground, because there is very little interest in a company. In 1993, Wilt Chamberlain Restaurants, Inc. withdrew its IPO of 1.4 million shares after the offering drew a tepid response from investors. At the time, the sports-themed family restaurant had only one location named after the legendary basketball star.

There are no guarantees that an IPO will prosper or even survive. Because of the risks, investing in IPOs may be an unwise choice for investors with little tolerance for risk who want to preserve their nest egg.

A safer way to invest in IPOs is through an aggressive growth fund. The investment objective of an aggressive growth fund is capital appreciation. If you look at the prospectus for an aggressive growth fund, you will see that some of them invest heavily in IPOs. The fund manager, a trained professional, decides which IPOs are worthwhile. You assume less risk because you're investing in many IPOs, not just one that might be a bust.

Myth #3: Investing in the Stock Market Is Gambling

Another well-circulated myth is that investing in the stock market is really just gambling. According to Jeff Hirsch, the difference is that when you invest, you're actually buying something, not just laying chips on the table and watching them disappear. When you buy stock in blue chip companies that have been around for decades, you aren't gambling in any sense of the word.

Investing in mutual funds or index funds that contain many solid investments is a far cry from gambling. Certainly, however, if you invest in a company that has never made money, you are a stock market gambler rather than an investor. *Penny stocks* typically sell for less than a dollar per share, and you are taking a serious risk by investing in them.

Investing in the stock market is gambling if you don't do any research or you're engaged in day trading. As we saw in Chapter 6, day traders hope to make a quick buck by investing in a stock and selling it soon thereafter.

Myth #4: The Stock Market Will Crash When Baby Boomers Retire in Waves

Much has been written about the huge wave of baby boomers retiring in about 2017. According to a U.S. Census Bureau estimate, there are 78 million baby boomers who were born between 1946 and 1964. Professor Jeremy Siegel of the University of Pennsylvania said it is possible that stock prices may fall 40 to 50 percent as retirees liquidate their portfolios. Stock prices will fall, because there will be far more sellers than buyers on Wall Street. Professor Siegel concedes, however, that overseas investors may cushion the blow.

I don't buy into this myth. As life spans increase, some baby boomers can expect to live 30 years or more after retiring. Therefore, prudent retirees will keep at least part of their portfolio in the stock market. These baby boomers won't be liquidating their stock holdings at the exact moment they turn 65.

This particular myth presumes that there is a traditional retirement age when most people turn in their employee ID card. Although many boomers will reach the traditional retirement age between 2017 and 2024, a number of them will keep working. They may work until age 70, 80, or beyond. As such, it is unlikely there will be a fire sale on stocks precipitated by baby boomers selling their securities at the same time.

In fact, if millions of boomers begin selling their stocks, it should bolster the economy rather than deflating the stock market. As baby boomer sell their equities, they will be using the proceeds to buy goods and services. Many companies will benefit from these purchases and their stock prices may go up.

U.S. population growth will also negate the impact of boomers selling their stocks at about the same time. According to the Census Bureau, the U.S. population is expected to be about 309 million in 2010. The population is expected to grow to 420 million by 2050. This upward spurt in population means there will be millions of people waiting to buy the stocks that baby boomers are selling.

Generation X, defined as those born during the 10 years after 1964, is likely to pick up the slack when baby boomers cut back on their stock market investing. Furthermore, each new generation is likely to be a little bit more comfortable with stock market investing. With no traditional pension to fall back on and with higher caps on 401(k) and IRA contributions, it is doubtful that the market will feel abandoned as baby boomers switch to more conservative invest-ments. Baby boomers may also decide to curb their risk by investing in the market as a whole, not just individual stocks.

Myth #5: As You Close in on Retirement, You Need to Shift to Conservative Investments and Sell Your Stocks

It's also a myth that people on the verge of retirement should shift to conservative investments and get out of the stock market. Although there can be a gradual shift to more conservative invest-ments as you close in on retirement, stocks should remain in your portfolio to some degree. With a long life ahead of you, your invest-ments need to keep pace with inflation. Historically, the stock mar-ket has been the best place where you can achieve that growth. Money that you won't need until years down the road can remain in stocks.

Retirees should set aside about three to five years of income in liquid investments. By doing so, they can keep a large portion of their assets in stocks without fear that they will need to sell them when the market is down in value. Having a cash reserve of several years allows you to ride out a bear market and avoid selling stocks for your current living expenses. As an example, if you need $50,000 per year to live on and you receive $20,000 a year in social security benefits, you should have at least $90,000 in liquid invest-ments to cover your living expenses for three years.

In early 2008, the editors of *Consumer Reports* wrote that investing too conservatively during retirement is a huge blunder. According to the publication, annual returns on bonds will barely keep up with inflation. Stocks, by contrast, provide returns over time that are sig-nificantly above inflation. *Consumer Reports* estimated that this blun-der may cost you anywhere from $360,000 to $750,000.

Myth #6: Your Spending Will Decrease in Retirement

When you read about retirement planning, you will be introduced to the myth that retirees' spending decreases after they retire. Unfortunately, that myth can leave you short on money in retire-ment, and that's a scary position to find yourself after you've walked away from a dependable income.

A commonly repeated rule of thumb is that retirees will spend 70 to 80 percent of their preretirement income each year. Many retirees, however, actually spend more each year after they retire. Quite often, retirees are playing golf, eating out, and traveling much more than they ever did while they were working. Living the good life costs money, and a retiree's spending may escalate, rather than decreasing by 10, 20, or 30 percent.

The early years of retirement are referred to as the go-go years. Retirees typically take advantage of their new status by engaging in numerous activities that they've dreamed about all their lives. The later stage of retirement has been referred to as the go-slow period, but there is no guarantee that a retiree's spending will decrease at that point either. The go-slow period is sometimes the time in life when medical and long-term care expenses begin to creep up on you. The end result is that your spending may go up in retirement, especially if inflation is roaring.

Misconceptions about how much you can withdraw from your nest egg can exacerbate the realities of how much you'll spend in retirement. You should try not to withdraw more than 4 percent of your principal, especially in the early years of retirement. A 4 percent withdrawal or less, especially during the initial stages of retirement, makes it far more likely that your principal will be sufficient to keep up with inflation and won't be exhausted any time soon.

Investment pros base withdrawals on Monte Carlo simulations. This mathematical analysis uses algorithms to test various withdrawal scenarios in thousands of market simulations. To see how it works, you would need a chalkboard filled with mathematical equations that only John Nash would understand. Russell Crowe played this brilliant mathematician in the movie *A Beautiful Mind*.

Fortunately, you don't need to do the math yourself. The simulation determines the probability that your nest egg will last for whatever time frame you choose. For example, the simulation might conclude that by withdrawing only 4 percent each year, plus increases for inflation, there is a 90 percent probability that your nest egg will last 30 years.

Jonathan Pond, a guest on *MoneyTrack*, tells his clients that they should expect to live to age 95. To be financially safe, they should base their withdrawals on a 6 percent annualized return on investments. This rate of return is about what you should expect on a portfolio that is a mixture of stocks, bonds and other interest-earning securities. In an article in the February 15, 2008, edition of *Bottom Line Personal,* Jonathan recommended that you withdraw about 4 percent annually in the early years of retirement, which is less than you expect to earn on your investments. By doing this, you don't drain your assets too quickly.

Myth #7: You Can Figure Out Your Asset Allocation with a Simple Rule of Thumb

As we discussed in Chapter 6, your nest egg, be it ever so humble, should be allocated among different asset classes such as stocks and bonds. The asset allocation process attempts to find the right mix of assets in view of your age, investment objectives and risk temperament. Over the years, a number of experts have suggested a shortcut for figuring out how much of your money should be in the various asset classes.

As we discussed in Chapter 6, the often-repeated advice is that you should subtract your age from the number 100 to calculate how much of your money should be in stocks. For example, if you're age 70, 30 percent of your assets should be in stock, since 100 minus 70 is 30. If you're age 20, 80 percent of your assets should be invested in the stock market, since 100 minus 20 equals 80.

Although this rule of thumb is very unscientific, it has a noble purpose. It is a starting point for the diversification process. Unfortunately, it doesn't tell you how each asset class should be broken down. For example, knowing that 80 percent of your money should be in equities doesn't help you to decide what kinds of stocks or stock mutual funds to invest in to achieve true diversity.

The rule of thumb also leaves you wondering where to put the remainder of your portfolio. It doesn't direct you toward other classes that are worth investing in to achieve the diversification of your portfolio that is so important. Even if you know that a portion of your portfolio should be in fixed-income investments like bonds, you still don't know what kind to buy and whether they should be short-term, intermediate or long-term.

A number of financial pros have created a new mythological rule of thumb. They contend that the old rule of thumb is outdated and too conservative. They recommend using a number like 130 or 140 as the basis for your calculation, because of increasing life expectancies and the need to keep your assets growing faster than inflation. With this rule of thumb, the 70-year-old in the previous example should keep 70 percent of his assets in stock or stock mutual funds, since 140 minus 70 is 70. The 20-year-old should keep 120 percent of his money in stock, since 140 minus 20 equals 120. Professor Nash will have to explain that equation to me. Better yet, I'm available if Russell Crowe wants to explain how that calculation works.

Using a higher number like 130 or 140 keeps older investors more heavily invested in the stock market. Although I agree that older investors shouldn't be so quick to abandon equities as they age, keeping 70 percent of your assets in stocks at age 70 seems to be very dangerous.

Debunking the Myths

Rather than relying on myths, there are time-tested investing principles that will serve you well. The key to growing wealth is recognizing that money grows faster in the stock market over time than in any other investment, including real estate.

Janet Bodnar of *Kiplinger's Personal Finance* told us that the publication chose dollar cost averaging as the best investment strategy there is. All you need to do is open an investment account with a brokerage firm or a mutual fund and invest a regular amount every single month. In many cases, you can invest as little as $50 per month. The money is automatically debited from your checking account each month.

As we saw in Chapter 2, here is why the dollar cost averaging strategy is lauded by the investment pros.

- *You avoid investing at the market's peak.* With dollar cost averaging, your investment buys more shares of a stock or mutual fund when the price is low and fewer shares when the price is high. Over time, the strategy facilitates the purchase of shares without having to time the market. The strategy is preferable to investing a large amount of money at one time when shares may be at their peak. Dollar cost averaging removes the emotional component from investing and helps us resist the urge to try to time the market. You avoid overinvesting at the top of the market.
- *Dollar cost averaging reduces the psychological pain of investing.* Quite often, when an investment goes down, we're afraid to buy more shares. In fact, that is the best time to invest, since

you get more shares for your money. Conversely, most of us are inclined to buy more shares when the value of our investment is going up, but that's usually a bad idea.

- *The strategy protects you from yourself.* In some respects, dollar cost averaging is a counterintuitive process. Your intuition may tell you to stop investing when a stock is going down, but that's probably the best time to buy if you're using the dollar cost averaging strategy. The strategy brings discipline to investing and protects you from your own worst instincts. It helps your investment strategy stay on course through ups and downs in the market.

If you're sold on dollar cost averaging, you have a strategy for investing your money but must still decide where to invest it. Instead of swinging for the fences and jumping on a hot stock tip, you can use Morningstar Research (www.morningstar.com) to gather information about mutual funds. Morningstar evaluates mutual funds and provides a rating from one to five stars. Although past performance is no guarantee of future success, you can select a few mutual funds to investigate further. Index funds are also good investments to use in conjunction with the dollar cost averaging strategy.

Jack calls dollar cost averaging the Chia Pet of investing. You leave it alone and allow the strategy to work like magic.

Math Is No Myth

The appeal of dollar cost averaging is that it works so well with investments that are readily available to small investors. When you sign up for your 401(k) plan and make contributions with every paycheck, you are making use of dollar cost averaging. If you start investing in a 401(k) at a young age or any automatic investment program for that matter, you take advantage of dollar cost averaging and compounded earnings.

Even if you're investing small amounts, compounding puts your investment into overdrive. The beauty of compounding is that time, time, time is on your side, if you don't mind taking advice from the Rolling Stones. To paraphrase John Lennon, all we are saying is, give this piece (of advice) a chance.

To fully appreciate the benefits of compounding, we asked folks in San Francisco if they would rather have a million dollars now or

Scam Alert

Hyman Taitelman, a feisty former diamond dealer from Queens, New York, told us about an unscrupulous broker who talked him into investing more than a million dollars in an unsuitable investment with way too much risk. The investment also charged excessive fees. The broker convinced Mr. Taitelman to invest in tax-deferred annuities for his retirement accounts. This advice is suspect, because retirement accounts are already tax-deferred and Mr. Taitelman was in his eighties at the time. His attorney, Darren Blum, asked why anyone would need a tax-deferred investment in an investment that's already tax-deferred. Unfortunately, although Mr. Taitelman won his arbitration case, he only got back $60,000.

Another woman we interviewed on *MoneyTrack*, Barbra Leone, bought a variable annuity based on her broker's assurance that it would never go down in value. According to a February 16, 2006 news release from the North American Securities Administrators Association (NASAA), variable annuities may be a trap for investors.

> *Variable annuities are tax-deferred investments that typically place mutual funds inside of an insurance wrapper for tax-deferred potential investment growth. While these products are legitimate investments, regulators are concerned about their popularity in the sales community. Commissions to those who sell variable annuities are very high, which provides incentive for sellers to engage in inappropriate sales. Variable annuities are only suitable for a very small percentage of the investing public and generally are not appropriate for most seniors. The steep penalties for early withdrawals also make variable annuities unsuitable for short-term investors. Be especially wary of any broker who wants to sell you a variable annuity to hold inside a 401(k) or IRA. You are already getting tax-deferred growth in an IRA or a 401(k), and the variable annuity simply adds a layer of cost with no additional tax benefit.*

NASAA has warned that variable annuities are often unsuitable for senior citizens since they have restricted access to invested funds. The high commission paid for selling a variable annuity often motivates the salesperson to ignore whether the product is suitable for the client. Every investment should make sense in relation to your age, your need for unrestricted access to the money, and your risk tolerance.

a penny that doubles every day for a month. A cabbie opted for the million now as did many others we interviewed. If you do the math, however, you'll find out that you're passing up $5.3 million.

Systematic investing produces incredible results. You can see for yourself by using a calculator at one of my favorite Web sites. To find it, hang a left at Funkytown and go to www.Dinkytown.net. For you trivia buffs, Funkytown is the nickname for South Memphis.

Let's say you're 25 years old, which means you were born after the song, *Funkytown,* was recorded in 1980 by the disco band Lipps Inc. If you invest $150 per month until you retire at age 65 and are able to get an 8 percent return on your money, you'll wind up with $486,271. If you're old enough to remember hearing the song on the radio, you'd better start investing now.

MoneyTrack Method

Some of the most popular myths about money and investing can be harmful to your financial health. It's a myth that you can't invest on your own without the help of a professional. You can implement a basic investment strategy on your own that is likely to keep pace with the market as a whole.

There are certain investment strategies that have been proven to work. Dollar cost averaging is one that almost every expert endorses for new investors. A disciplined investment approach helps you to avoid making emotional decisions with your investments or having a knee-jerk reaction to market conditions. Taking advantage of compounded earnings is also close to being a sure thing.

Investing on an ongoing basis is always preferable to handing over money to someone who might be a con artist. An important message of our scam alerts is that investment advisers sometimes put their interests ahead of yours. It's always a good idea to get a second opinion from a knowledgeable and objective person you trust, especially when there's a lot of money at stake.

One of the biggest myths is that you really can't plan for retirement or other financial objectives, because there are too many variables. You figure you'll wing it and make do on whatever you save. You need a plan, even if it's flawed in some respects. Create a monthly budget and see if your projected income will come close to what you need.

Ignoring the myths relating to investing, the stock market, and retirement can help to make your dreams a reality. Systematic investing and thorough planning can help put you on Easy Street someday, whether it's in Funkytown or whatever town you prefer.

Wherever you are, however, stay away from lovers' lane, because I hear there's a maniac on the loose. Worse yet, all those rumors may bring down the value of your property, and that's why we need to look at the pros and cons of investing in real estate.

CHAPTER

9

Let's Get *Real* about Real Estate

Ef there's one thing you can be sure of, it's that investments go in and out of favor. One day, the real estate market is hot and before you know it, home prices fall. It's much like the stock market. Biotechnology stocks are in and then they're out and then they're back in again. Just like the stock market can shift from a bull to a bear market and back again, real estate can shift back and forth from a seller's to a buyer's market. Because investments go in and out of favor, the pros will tell you that your portfolio should include different assets that will react differently to market conditions. In the long run, how you allocate your assets is often more important than where you invest. Owning a home and other real estate investments can add diversity to any portfolio.

Your Home Is Your Biggest Investment

For most people, their home is their biggest investment. But sometimes, however, it can be the worst investment you'll ever make.

In the January 28, 2008, issue of *InvestmentNews,* investment adviser, Bert Whitehead, told the story about his new clients, a couple in their forties who earned about $250,000 between them and had $750,000 in investments. The couple and their two children moved to a new city and bought a home for about $1 million.

Unfortunately, the couple violated what Whitehead called the number one rule for homeowners: "Don't buy a new home until you sell the old one." Their prior home was appraised at $750,000

135

two years earlier. The monthly mortgage payment was $4,000 on the new home and $2,500 on the old one.

Aside from having to make two mortgage payments, the couple didn't realize how much their new property tax bill would be. The yearly property taxes on the new home were $12,000. Homeowners insurance was also much higher than they expected. Their utility and landscaping bills were also much higher than they anticipated. At the same time, the couple watched as the value of their old home decreased by 5 to 10 percent each year.

When real estate prices are declining, Whitehead observed that some people resist the economic inevitability that they might need to cut their losses. If they are reluctant to drop the price of the old house below what comparable homes are selling for in their old neighborhood, the couple risks another long, dry spell without an offer. By the time they're ready to drop the price, the market might deteriorate further and the home still won't sell.

What happens with real estate sellers is that they sometimes get anchored to what they feel is the fair market value of their home. If an appraiser tells them their home is worth $750,000, the homeowner becomes fixated on that amount. Two years later, they believe the home is still worth $750,000, if not more. They tend to ignore the realities of the marketplace. By the time they accept that grim reality, they've missed the opportunity to sell at a better price.

To help sellers understand their desperate situation, Whitehead will assist them with calculating the carrying costs on the old home. He helps them to recognize that if they don't act quickly, dropping the price later may be too little, too late. Whitehead works with them to devise a strategy to prevent the situation from getting worse.

The conduct of investors sometimes resembles real estate sellers. They, too, get fixated on what their stock once sold for and expect shares to return to that level at some point. Because they're anchored to a previous high for that stock, they won't part with their shares as their value goes down. They naïvely believe that the stock will return to that high level and they will miss out on the opportunity to sell their shares at a profit. They hang onto this belief, even if the company's financial picture is dismal.

Similarly, real estate sellers are often reluctant to sell their homes in a declining market, because their profit isn't as high as they're expecting. If they wait too long, however, these sellers may wind up losing money. Whether you're selling real estate or stock, making a profit that's below your expectation isn't a worst case scenario. Losing money is far worse than making a smaller profit than you expected.

Evaluating Your Home as an Investment

If your home has gone up significantly in value, you may be a millionaire—on paper. Unfortunately, being a millionaire on paper doesn't always translate into paper money or a check for a million dollars.

Although your home may be your largest asset, it isn't part of your investment portfolio. The home you own may make you feel like a million bucks, but it isn't like other investment assets. In fact, home ownership may seem like an anchor if the housing market is slumping. It's been found that when home prices go down, people feel less wealthy and tend to spend less, even though they have the same amount of money in their wallet.

Wall Street Journal columnist Jonathan Clements explained why your home isn't like other investments like stocks and stock mutual funds. The article, "Why Your Nest Egg Is Not Your Nest Egg," points out that you don't know the price of your home until you sell. Even though you can imagine your house selling for some fantastic amount, it's not like stocks that you can sell with the click of your mouse.

Clements also observed that if you compare your house to a mutual fund, it has a huge expense ratio. Each year, you're paying 3 to 3.5 percent of your home's value for maintenance costs, property taxes, homeowners insurance, and other expenses. You also owe utilities and mortgage payments. If your house is vacant because you've moved elsewhere and can't sell it, you are still paying that steep expense ratio.

According to Clements, trading stocks looks cheap when compared to buying and selling real estate. When you buy a home, you usually owe money to lawyers, home inspectors, furniture movers, and the bank. Selling costs include more movers, lawyers and realtors whose commissions might be 5 or 6 percent of the home's selling price.

When you buy and sell stocks, you pay minimal amounts for brokerage fees, especially if you use an online broker. If you buy or sell shares of a no-load mutual fund, you avoid trading costs.

Although your home may go up in value, there is no immediate payout and you don't receive dividends as you might with many stocks. The average dividend yield for U.S. stocks is 2 percent.

Even though your home is different from other assets in your portfolio, some conventional investment rules still apply. Just as you don't want to invest too much in any one stock or asset class, you shouldn't have too much of your money tied up in your home. Years ago, many experts advised that you should overextend yourself in order to buy a bigger and nicer home. The advice presumed that your income will keep going up and that home prices would also go up. The presumption was that you had better buy the home now, because a red-hot housing market will soon put it out of your price range.

When you buy more house than you need, you are signing up for higher expenses such as homeowners insurance and property taxes. In the end, you might cause yourself to be "house poor," which means too much of your income is being spent on your home and related expenses. Even if you find a banker who is willing to give you a mortgage, you're buying a house you can't afford. The concept of buying a more expensive home than you can afford is a particularly bad idea as you near retirement and your children are leaving the nest.

Whether your nest egg is invested in stocks or a home or both, you can never bank on those eggs being a certain price at the point when you're ready to sell them. Stocks and real estate inevitably go through good times and bad. The key, as always, is to utilize an asset allocation strategy and keep your portfolio diversified. You also need to build liquidity into your portfolio, so you can withstand difficult economic times and won't need to sell those assets at any price to make ends meet.

Home Equity Loans: The Good, the Bad, and the Ugly

On top of the financial problems that Whitehead's clients were having, they also had a home equity loan. Depending on with whom you speak, home equity loans can be a godsend or a one-way ticket to financial hell.

Proponents of home equity loans argue that they allow you to tap the appreciation in your real estate holdings. The problem, however, is that your appreciation hasn't been realized yet, even though someone is willing to give you a home equity loan on that amount. When it's time to sell your home, your loans may exceed the selling price.

Your friendly neighborhood banker will extol the virtues of home equity loans. They're billed as a great way to secure your financial future. Your interest is usually tax-deductible and you can tap the equity in the home to help secure your financial future in ways such as the following:

- You can use the loan to pay off your high-interest credit card debt.
- You can use it to help finance your child's education.
- You can use it to make home improvements and add value to your current home.

Unfortunately, home improvements do not necessarily increase the value of your home by as much as you're paying the contractor. You may get the same price for your home that you would have gotten without the home improvement.

There are other pitfalls with home equity loans. If you borrow money against your home to pay off your credit card debt, you'll be in big trouble if you go on a buying spree with the plastic in your purse or wallet and run up your bills again. Similarly, some investors have borrowed against their home to invest in the stock market. They risk, however, that their stock market returns won't make up for what they're paying in interest. In fact, they may lose money on their investments and owe interest on their home equity loan as well.

Flipping and Flipping Out over Real Estate

Real estate flipping is the process of buying property and selling it soon thereafter with the goal of making a profit. Unfortunately, as we've said so many times on *MoneyTrack*, investing is a long-term proposition. Just like day trading, flipping real estate can leave you without a roof over your head.

When the real estate market was booming, people were flipping out over how much their home was worth. Caught up in a frenzy, thousands of investors were ready to plunk down money on houses and condos with the expectation of selling them soon thereafter. Everybody you met was making money by flipping homes and making more money than they ever did in the stock market. As the real estate market ground to a halt in many areas, however, flipping those homes and condos became almost impossible. Investors were stuck with real estate they couldn't afford and could not unload at any price. They also flipped out when they received their property tax bills, which don't necessarily fall as quickly as real estate prices.

On *MoneyTrack,* we met Casey Serin, a young man who got caught up in the real estate frenzy. At the time we talked to Casey, he was about $1.6 to $1.8 million in debt. The former Web site designer got a bad case of real estate fever in 2004. He began attending real estate seminars and boot camps to learn about flipping houses. After spending about $15,000 on courses and training, Casey went on a buying spree. He turned a $30,000 profit on the first house he flipped.

Casey then bought eight houses in eight months, and probably spent too much for most of them. As the real estate market slowed down, Casey had no hope of selling them and his home-related expenses kept mounting. Casey couldn't meet the mortgage payments, utilities, remodeling expenses, and other bills that were piling up. Instead of profits, Casey faced foreclosure.

We asked Scott Thompson, president of Mortgage Resolution Services, what Casey did wrong. According to Scott, buying houses with zero experience and zero money down is a recipe for disaster. It takes decades and patience to buy and sell property as a full-time career. Many experts say that the name of the game is reducing your exposure.

Casey, and others like him, should remember our discussions of asset allocation. You need to own a number of assets, not eight houses that you hope to flip. Asset allocation is built on the theory that stocks, bonds, real estate, and other investments perform differently under different market conditions. Therefore, it's unlikely that all of your assets will do badly at the same time. In Casey's case, he invested far too much money in one type of asset, real estate. You need to invest in a variety of asset classes such as stock, bonds, and cash investments like money market funds.

I'm convinced that most people invest based on emotions, not logic. When people got caught up in the dot-com boom, novice investors wanted a piece of the action. Logic should have told them that the boom would finally go bust. Similarly, even though all of the experts warned that the real estate bubble might burst, people like Casey got caught up in the excitement and jumped on the bandwagon.

USA Today reporter Noelle Knox wrote about Casey's miscues in an article called "10 Mistakes that Made Flipping a Flop." (Knox's article was posted on October 22, 2006 and can be found at www.usatoday.com/money/economy/housing/2006–10–22-young-flipper-usat_x.htm.) Casey's rise and fall, according to Knox, is a tale that offers 10 moral and financial lessons. Here are the mistakes Casey made:

1. Using "liar loans," which he got by misstating his income
2. Overpaying for the real estate
3. Having insufficient cash
4. Quitting his day job
5. Hiring an unlicensed contractor
6. Buying property without inspecting it
7. Buying out-of-state property
8. Buying too many properties too soon
9. Underestimating remodeling costs
10. Having a poor exit strategy

Casey read extensively about real estate flipping and attended several seminars. What they don't tell you in the real estate infomercials and seminars is that while you're waiting to flip the property, your outgo is significant for expenses such as:

- Insurance
- Repairs
- Maintenance
- Taxes
- Utilities
- Mortgage expenses
- Tenants who don't pay rent

You also need to watch out for misrepresentations made by real estate seminar companies. The state of Florida reached a settlement with a company that sold seminars and products dealing with how to make a fortune on foreclosures. More than 250 consumers complained that the firm showed them testimonials that were misleading and the company's courses only provided basic information. Advanced courses cost thousands of dollars more. Florida Attorney

General Bill McCollum's January 10, 2008 news release explained how the company made money:

> Consumers complained that the introductory programs and seminars, touted as training that would change careers and lifestyles and give persons financial freedom and independence, covered only very rudimentary information and were used mainly to entice consumers to purchase "more advanced" and significantly more expensive training programs costing thousands of dollars.

Unfortunately, these kinds of programs and seminars can leave you with much less money than you had initially and might lead to foreclosure of the home you already own.

Many real estate get-rich-quick schemes rely on your investing "sweat equity" in the houses you're buying. This is an extremely difficult strategy to execute, especially if you work full time and can barely keep up with the maintenance on your own home. As a wise person once said, it's not an investment if you have to cut the grass and fix the toilet.

Putting on the Ritz with REITS

To build an attractive and well-diversified portfolio, many investment pros recommend real estate investment trusts (REITs). By investing in REITs, you add a different asset class to your portfolio without the risk that you'll be stuck with an investment property that you can't unload at any price.

REITs are bought and sold through brokerage firms, much like stocks and bonds. They invest in all types of real estate:

- Commercial property
- Shopping centers and malls
- Office complexes
- Apartment buildings
- Warehouses
- Hotels and motels

You can even invest in a REIT that owns self-storage properties.

REITs generate their income from rent paid by tenants on the property they own, as well as the capital gains coming from the purchase and sale of properties. Our *MoneyTrack* guest, Jeremy

Glaser, an equity analyst at Morningstar in Chicago, Illinois, told us that REITs are required by law to pay out 90 percent of their taxable income as dividends to investors. If they do, the REIT isn't required to pay federal income tax on that money. The investor, of course, is still obligated to pay taxes on the income. As a practical matter, most REITs pay out 100 percent of their income to investors. Aside from income, the value of your shares may escalate in value.

A REIT may focus on a particular area of the country. This may be a bit more risky if that region goes through tough economic times. For example, if a major employer leaves a particular area, there may be a glut of office space and real estate values will suffer.

REITs offer many advantages to investors who don't want to invest directly in real estate. For example, you may not wish to buy an apartment building, because of the maintenance issues and the hassle of collecting rent. You also might not be able to get a mortgage on the property. Instead of investing directly, you can buy a REIT that invests in apartment complexes and rental communities. If you're short on cash, you can sell your REIT shares. In contrast, if you own an apartment building, it may take months to liquidate your investment.

Nevertheless, you assume risks when you invest in REITs. The REIT may go down in value if dependable tenants are hard to find. If a REIT specializes in one type of property or a particular area of the country, it might be more volatile than one that invests in the broader real estate market. Despite the risks, investing in a REIT may be a good investment for a retiree who needs income or younger investors who want to diversify their portfolio.

Scam Alert

Mortgage fraud is a major problem, especially during a real estate boom. It's not always the consumer who gets cheated. Sometimes banks are victimized by someone who obtains a loan under false pretenses. Unscrupulous mortgage brokers are the intermediaries who try to find the best deal for borrowers. Occasionally, they will overcharge or encourage the borrower to falsify loan documents.

Indiana and other states have cracked down on any person in the process who falsifies documents to get a mortgage, whether it's an appraiser, the borrower, the bank, or a broker. Promises of no-money-down mortgages are often the first sign of a scam. Law enforcement officials, including the FBI, are allocating more of their resources to combat the growing problem of mortgage fraud.

Reverse Mortgage Uses and Abuses

Reverse mortgages are often touted as a way to bolster your lifestyle during retirement or to pay for long-term care. Although a reverse mortgage may be a way to enhance your retirement or to pay for healthcare costs, you need to be on the lookout for marketing abuses and high fees in conjunction with these loans. According to a March 13, 2008 Investor Alert published by the Financial Industry Regulatory Authority (FINRA), fees and costs associated with reverse mortgages may be 4 to 8 percent of the total loan amount.

A reverse mortgage is a loan you take against your home. You do not need to pay back the loan as long as you live in your home. Therefore, you can enjoy the equity you've built up in your home without having to sell it. Whereas some borrowers use a reverse mortgage to pay for necessities, others use the proceeds to fund a dream vacation or make purchases that might otherwise be unaffordable. The loan and fees come due when you die, sell your home, or leave for more than twelve months.

You must usually be age 62 or older to qualify for a reverse mortgage. Since you do not make monthly payments on a reverse mortgage, there are no income requirements to qualify. Because no monthly payments are owed, you cannot lose your home for failing to pay the mortgage. Nevertheless, you must still pay your property taxes and insurance premiums.

The proceeds of a reverse mortgage can be paid to you in a number of different ways. Here are the possibilities:

- A lump sum
- A monthly payment
- A line of credit that you draw upon as needed

You can also combine these payment methods.

Generally, you do not need to pay back the reverse mortgage until you die, sell your home, or move out permanently. As you continue to receive payments from the reverse mortgage, your debt increases and the equity in your home may decrease, unless real estate prices are escalating significantly. If you draw money from the reverse mortgage for a long time, there may be little equity left for your heirs to inherit. Borrowers who take out a reverse mortgage also pay steep fees in conjunction with the loan.

According to a report issued by AARP in December 2007, unscrupulous individuals sometimes encourage older consumers to take out a reverse mortgage to pay for financial products. The individual pushing the reverse mortgage might persuade you to use the proceeds to buy an annuity or a long-term care policy. The person selling an annuity or long-term care policy gets a hefty commission.

Most financial planners recommend reverse mortgages as a last resort. You need to ask yourself why you need a reverse mortgage and if there are any better alternatives. There usually are. Before taking out a reverse mortgage, here are some Web sites you can visit to learn more:

- AARP: www.aarp.org/revmort
- HUD Housing Counseling Clearinghouse: www.hudhcc.org
- National Center for Home Equity Conversion: www.reverse.org
- Consumers Union: www.consumersunion.org

Here are questions you should ask yourself before taking out a reverse mortgage:

- Do I really need it?
- Are there cheaper alternatives, such as a home equity loan?
- Will I be moving soon? The up-front loan costs of a reverse mortgage are steep.
- Am I capable of living in my home for the foreseeable future?
- Do I thoroughly understand how these loans work?
- Will I have a greater need for profits from my home at a later point in my life?

Until you can answer these questions with certainty, you should avoid applying for a reverse mortgage.

If you have no other choice than a reverse mortgage, shop around for the best terms. Before making a decision you can't reverse, ask a knowledgeable friend or relative for assistance in evaluating your options. It should be someone who has your best interest at heart.

Investing in a Vacation Home Is No Day at the Beach

If your home has been a great investment, you might believe that you can't go wrong by buying a second one. Although you certainly can go wrong by investing in a vacation home, here are some reasons why many investors like the idea:

- *Second homes ease the transition to retirement.* Many people view second homes as a means to make the transition into retirement. You might be thinking about buying a second home or a vacation home with the intent of retiring in it. Second homes give you the opportunity to see if you like a particular location. Even if it is too small to live in on a full-time basis, you can stay there temporarily while you're searching for the perfect retirement housing arrangement. You can use the second home for family getaways and rent it whenever you're not there.
- *Second homes can be a great tax shelter.* As long as your debt doesn't exceed $1 million and you're filing a joint return, mortgage interest is generally deductible. The points on the mortgage on a second home aren't deductible in the current year and must be spread over the duration of the loan. You can write off property taxes, no matter how many homes you own and how much you pay. If your adjusted gross income is too high, however, your interest and property tax deductions are limited. You also need to determine if the alternative minimum tax will erode the value of those deductions.

  When you own a rental property, whether it's a vacation home or a duplex that you rent out, you may be entitled to some attractive tax breaks. When you rent the property for 14 days or less, you don't need to report any of the income. If you rent the property for more than 14 days, call your accountant. There are a number of complex rules affecting how much income you must declare on rental property.
- *Second homes will appreciate in value.* As millions of baby boomers retire, the market for vacation homes, according to some experts, will expand enormously. This will lead to rising prices for vacation homes. Nevertheless, when a real estate bubble bursts, home prices go down, no matter how many baby boomers there are.

The Down Side of Owning a Vacation Home

While owning a vacation home may be a dream come true, it won't necessarily be a good investment. In 2007, according to the National Association of Realtors, the median price of a vacation home was $195,000, which was down 2.5 percent from a year earlier. Even if vacation home prices go up, they might not keep pace with the historical growth of investments in the stock market.

For many people, a vacation home is much more than just an investment. It's also an integral part of their dreams for the future. Too many people get caught up in the dream and don't take these factors into consideration.

- *Vacation homes don't always make good full-time dwellings.* If you're buying a second home with the intent of retiring there, keep in mind that it may not be as attractive as a full-time dwelling. It might be too small or otherwise inappropriate as a full-time dwelling. If you choose to live in a condo, carriage home, townhouse, or some other dwelling with shared walls, you might find privacy is a major concern. The situation may remind you of your first apartment, where the walls were paper-thin and you couldn't play the stereo without a neighbor complaining.

- *You may not be used to rules, rules, and more rules.* Condos and homes governed by a homeowners association often have restrictions on how you can use your property. There may be limitations on renting your house and the length of your lease. Normally, you'll need approval from the community for decisions you take for granted, like changing the color of your house or installing a particular kind of mailbox.

- *The costs may be more than you're expecting.* Make sure you understand the true cost of buying a second home. You may be using money that might be invested elsewhere at a potentially higher rate of return. If you're buying in a planned community, there may be costs that you aren't used to paying, such as maintenance fees and special assessments for major expenditures by the homeowners board of directors. Investigate the price of insurance and whether your current carrier even writes policies in the state where you're looking at property. If you underestimate the cost of a vacation home, it can adversely affect other elements of your financial plan.

The Realities of Owning a Vacation Home

Too many people buy a vacation home while caught up in the euphoria of a wonderful and care-free trip. Before making this major financial decision, make sure you look at all of the potential ramifications by asking these questions:

- Will the expense of owning a second home prevent me from contributing as much to my retirement savings plan and IRA?
- Will I use the home enough to justify the cost?
- Will owning a second home restrict my travel to other locations?
- What is the second home's value as a rental unit, and do I want to be a landlord?
- Will I be overwhelmed with friends and relatives seeking a free vacation?
- Do I fully understand the maintenance costs, taxes, and insurance issues associated with that home and the state where it is situated?
- If I plan to retire in this home, is it large enough to live in on a full-time basis?
- What are the tax consequences if I become a permanent resident of that state?
- Will I like living in that area on a full-time basis?

Remember that the town you love to vacation in isn't necessarily a dream come true when you're there all year round. For example, you may not enjoy your home in Florida nearly as much during hurricane season as you do during a balmy winter evening in February.

Make sure you can afford the carrying costs of owning two homes, especially after you retire and you don't have a steady paycheck. If you plan to sell your primary dwelling after retiring, you don't know what the housing market will look like at the time. You may find yourself violating the rule that you shouldn't buy a second home until you've sold the first one.

MoneyTrack Method

Investing in real estate is not a no-lose proposition. Buying a house to live in or flip should not be an impulse purchase. You can't expect to turn a profit quickly. The general consensus is that stocks will outperform real estate returns over the years.

Just as it's difficult to time the market, you are taking a risk when you buy a home. You may be buying when the boom is about to go bust. Make sure you've sold your prior home before signing a contract for the new one. If you do move forward without selling your old house, have a realistic fall-back plan. Many home sellers assume they can rent their old home, but that often isn't an option when the housing market goes haywire. It might not be as easy as you think to rent your old home at a good price, and having a tenant may complicate the selling process.

When buying a home, be realistic about what you can afford. If you set your sights too high, you may wind up with payments that are unaffordable. Even if you can afford the mortgage and other house-related expenses, many new homeowners begin buying accessories and furnishings after they move in, which may lead to credit problems.

You can also cause yourself problems if you don't ascertain how much your closing costs will be. Sometimes, homebuyers borrow money to pay closing costs, even though they assured the bank this wouldn't happen. This extra loan payment can make your financial situation even more precarious. Nevertheless, even though you're short on cash, it is usually a good idea to hire a lawyer to represent your interests at the closing.

Before buying a home, it's imperative that you do your homework. You shouldn't go forward until you are thoroughly informed as to what your expenses will be. The property appraiser's office in your new county should be able to estimate how much you'll be paying in taxes. As part of your due diligence, you should be exploring the neighborhood where you're thinking of buying and can ask about the cost of utilities, lawn care, and even baby sitters. Although there is a great deal of information about real estate on the Web, there is no substitute for having boots on the ground.

There are many headaches associated with buying a house. Real estate expert Ilyce Glink provides a wealth of advice about home-related issues on her Web site www.ThinkGlink.com. Another educational resource is the Motley Fool gang, www.fool.com/homecenter.

Greed can undermine your financial progress, especially if you expect to become a real estate tycoon in your spare time. Usually, get rich quick schemes are just that—schemes. The people who make money by investing in real estate have real-life experience. They are unlikely to become rich by attending a few seminars or reading books. The key is going slow and having a mentor.

Real estate investment trusts (REITs) are an alternative to owning property and may reduce some of the headaches. Like any investment, REITs should represent only a percentage of your assets, and your portfolio should be allocated among different investments.

Owning several houses isn't asset allocation. You wind up with too much of your net worth in one asset class—real estate.

CHAPTER 10

Financial Makeover

With any investment strategy that crashes and burns, whether it's flipping houses or buying Internet stocks that have never earned a dime, you find people searching for a get-rich quick formula. These strategies usually attract investors who are looking for a shortcut but find they are worse off in the end. Instead of getting a financial makeover, these investors make mistakes they might never get over, and there's no do-over.

A *MoneyTrack* makeover strives for long-term results. The *MoneyTrack* method isn't about turning you into an investment pro. It's more concerned with helping you to make the most of your financial situation and to become a more knowledgeable investor. That knowledge will help you to recognize the difference between a sound investment and a scam that will only benefit the person promoting it.

To achieve those goals, most people need a financial makeover. The goal of a financial makeover is to offer realistic advice that you can apply to your own situation. Although it won't make you rich overnight, it can help you to become better off and enhance your financial future. Unlike most makeovers, you'll see the results for years to come.

Meet the Daniels Family

Although we learn from the pros on *MoneyTrack,* we never discuss financial situations in a vacuum. We gave a financial makeover to the Daniels family in Hayward, California. Ken, Rhonda, and their beautiful family were nice enough to let us scour their financial records to see what mistakes they were making. Ken and Rhonda have three children, as well as a cat named Prudence.

When we spent time with the Daniels family, we found that their goals were relatively modest. They wanted to make the transition from renters to homeowners. They aspired to enjoy a comfortable retirement someday. The couple also hoped to have money left over for travel and bingo.

Our job was to help them make those dreams come true. I teamed up with Janet Bodnar, deputy editor of *Kiplinger's Personal Finance* magazine, to make some suggestions. Here are some of the issues we needed to address:

- Ken's income is limited, because he receives permanent disability benefits.
- Ken and Rhonda have different styles of money management.
- Rhonda is more of a spender than Ken.
- Ken keeps a separate account to pay bills.
- They really don't track the family's expenditures.

In response to prodding from us, Rhonda checked with her human resource department and found that she actually has two pensions, a defined benefit plan and a defined contribution plan. The defined benefit plan is the technical name for the traditional pension that is on the wane. The defined contribution plan is the retirement savings plan, which is similar to a 401(k). As a county employee, Rhonda will receive a pension check every month after retiring if she continues working for the government for at least 20 years. Ken will receive a disability pension for the foreseeable future.

Another plus was that Ken and Rhonda's attitudes complement each other. In any relationship, it always helps if one partner is more conservative than the other. The ideal is for a couple to reach a compromise on issues such as spending, investing, and saving.

We suggested that Rhonda invest her $100 per month bingo money in a conservative stock fund through her retirement savings plan at work. She won't need to pay a dime in taxes on her gains until she begins making withdrawals decades from now. Janet and I recommended that they get rid of one car loan, or at least cut their payments. The couple needed to free up some cash and save for a down payment on a home.

Janet gave Ken and Rhonda the gift that keeps on giving, a lifetime subscription to *Kiplinger's Personal Finance* magazine. The publication gives great advice to regular people on how to save and invest.

Credit Makeovers

As we told Rhonda and Ken's story on *MoneyTrack*, we worried that their credit history would keep them from achieving their dream of buying a house. We came to realize that the couple didn't know their credit score. With a little bit of research, we found out that Ken's credit score is well above average and much higher than Rhonda's. Their combined score is about average.

As we saw in Chapter 5, your credit report is available from www.annualcreditreport.com. Under federal law, you have the right to receive a free copy of your credit report once every 12 months. Although your annual credit report is free, you must pay to receive your credit score. Your credit score evaluates the information in your credit report to arrive at a number that lenders use to determine if you qualify for a credit card or loan.

In the February 3, 2008, online edition of the *Pittsburgh Post Gazette*, Caryn Bilotta, the education manager for Consumer Credit Counseling Service, suggested a number of important steps to help you reach your financial goals. When I read the article, I thought about how Rhonda and Ken might benefit from taking these steps.

- Get organized and keep all of your financial papers in one place. After spending a few minutes with Rhonda, it was clear that she was not well organized.
- Start saving 10 percent of your take-home pay. By cutting back on bingo, Rhonda freed up money to save.
- If you can't save or invest 10 percent of your take-home pay, choose an amount you can live with while still meeting your expenses. Gradually increase the amount you're putting aside every few months until you reach 10 percent or more. If you get a raise, bonus, tax refund, or some other windfall, try to save and invest that extra money.
- Create a budget and track your spending. A budget isn't necessarily restrictive. It helps you make the best use of your money.

- Make your purchases in cash or with a debit card instead of using a credit card. By doing this, you have a finite amount of money to spend.

In the end, the couple's biggest problem was not bad credit or a lack of investments. The couple's major hurdle was agreeing on a plan that will get them on the road to financial security. For a couple to reach their goals, they have to be on the same page and work together to reach a common objective.

How Credit Affects Your Ability to Buy a Home

Though Ken and Rhonda's credit history wasn't their biggest problem, yours might be the obstacle standing between you and the goal of owning a home. It might seem so now, but your credit history won't haunt you forever. Although there are ways to improve your credit score over time, you should avoid any company that promises they can "fix" your credit rating.

Here are some solid tips suggested by Freddie Mac, a stockholder-owned corporation established by Congress in 1970 to support home ownership and rental housing, on how to restore your credit:

- Stop spending money you don't have.
- Make a budget if you don't have one and stick to it.
- Make at least the minimum payments you owe in a timely manner.
- Work to pay off your accounts. Pay off the accounts first that were turned over to a collection agency.
- Try to pay off any accounts with small balances and avoid opening new ones. Limit your credit wherever possible.
- Bankruptcy should be a last resort, because it will increase your interest rates and stay on your credit record for anywhere from 7 to 10 years.

Freddie Mac also recommends that you seek assistance from a legitimate credit counselor, but be wary of debt consolidation programs and organizations that say they can "repair" your credit report. You can find more advice from this Freddie Mac at: www. freddiemac.com/corporate/buyown/english/preparing/credit_ and_homeownership/restoring_credit.html.

Scam Alert

The Federal Trade Commission (FTC) has had its hands full with phony credit repair clinics that bilk consumers. These rip-offs have bilked millions of dollars from folks who can ill-afford these losses. On *MoneyTrack*, we interviewed Sarah Foge, who hired a debt manager to manage her finances. The payments she gave to the debt manager were never sent to her creditors. Sarah was $20,000 in the hole when she hired a debt manager and was $60,000 in the red at the time of our interview.

An honest credit counselor will explore realistic ways to resolve your money problems and help you to develop a spending plan. The FTC advises that a reputable credit counseling organization will give you advice on how to manage your money and debts and will help you to develop a budget. Here are some ways to tell if the credit counseling organization is on the up-and-up:

- *You should ask what services are offered and whether they will help you develop a plan for getting out of debt.* Be on guard for credit counseling agencies that give all clients the same one-size-fits-all plan rather than counseling them individually.
- *Ask the organization for a quote in writing regarding initial fees and ongoing fees.* A typical fee will be in the neighborhood of $50 to start with and less than that in monthly fees.
- *Once you've developed a list of potential credit counselors, you should conduct due diligence.* Investigate the agency through your state's attorney general, the Better Business Bureau, and a local consumer protection agency.

You can also call the National Foundation for Credit Counseling, www.nfcc.org, at 800–388–2227. Credit counseling may show up in your credit report, but it won't affect your credit score. A lender decides if credit counseling makes you a better or worse risk.

Debt negotiation programs are different from credit counseling. These programs may have a negative impact on your credit report for years to come. Although a debt negotiation firm may say that it is a nonprofit organization, this may not be true, and it doesn't necessarily mean it has your best interest at heart.

Be skeptical of any claims and promises they make. There is no guarantee that your credit card company and your other lenders will accept partial payment of your debt.

The FTC recommends that you steer clear of any debt negotiation companies that do the following:

- Guarantee they can remove your debt or that you'll pay pennies on the dollar
- Require substantial monthly service fees
- Demand that you stop communicating with your creditors and refrain from making payments to them
- Promise that their system will have no impact on your credit report
- Stipulate that payments be made to the company, not your creditors
- Claim you won't get sued by your creditors

More fiscal fitness tips from the FTC can be found at www.ftc.gov/bcp/conline/pubs/credit/fiscal.shtm.

If you do sign up with a debt negotiation company as Sarah did, and we recommend that you don't, check with the Office of the Attorney General in your state. There may be a statute that regulates these companies. As with credit counselors, you should also check with the Better Business Bureau and a local consumer protection agency.

Savings Makeover

As part of any financial makeover, you also need to change your attitudes about money. Too many people view saving money as the financial equivalent of dieting. They have difficulty sticking with it and quickly resume bad money-management habits.

There's a well-run restaurant chain called Sweet Tomatoes. As you enter the restaurant, you're handed a cafeteria tray and one or more large dinner plates. As you slide your tray toward the cashier, you fill your plate with salad, tuna fish, pasta, croutons, cheese, and top it all with dressing. I picture customers getting on a scale later that day and saying, "I can't understand why I gain weight. All I had for lunch was salad."

Many of us apply the same logic to saving and investing. We spend money all day, whether it's at the vending machine or the mall. At the end of the day, we can't understand why we don't have any money left to save and invest. As part of your financial makeover, you need to rethink your approach to spending money. Here are six rules to consider adopting.

Rule #1: Having a Busy Schedule Is No Excuse for Wasting Money

Busy people often justify expenditures by saying they're too busy to shop around for the best price on goods and services. They rationalize that they're only losing a few dollars here and there and their time is worth far more than that. More often than not, the amount they're losing is significant.

Let's say you hate to clean and spend $75 for someone to clean your house once each week. If you're in the 25 percent tax bracket, you have to earn $100 to pay the person who cleans for you. Over the course of a month, you'll need to earn about $400 to pay for cleaning help. Although you may be very busy, expenditures like this may keep you from reaching your financial goals.

According to the savings calculator at www.dinkytown.net, investing $400 per month may grow to $365,936 after 25 years. This calculation presumes that you start with a balance of zero dollars and are able to achieve an 8 percent annual rate of return.

Perhaps there are other chores around the house that you can do yourself, even though you're busy. Get out in the fresh air and cut the grass. Maybe you can wash your own car for a change and put the money toward an investment. If you're a wee bit handy, handle a few minor plumbing problems yourself or do some painting. You might even find it to be therapeutic. Nevertheless, the corollary of this rule is that if your do-it-yourself projects do major damage, it's better to hire a professional.

Many people say they are too busy to eat at home. Eating out too often can break your budget, even if you make a good income. Even casual restaurants and fast-food joints can be extremely expensive. Over the course of a year, you might spend several thousand dollars or more on restaurant meals. The editor of the E-letter, *Living on a Dime,* www.livingonadime.com, estimated that you can save $2,000 to $4,000 per year by eating at home. Her family limits their dining out to birthdays and anniversaries. When you do eat out, you can cut your cost by skipping an appetizer or dessert. Trust me. Your waistline will thank you.

Rule #2: You're Not Above Using Coupons and Asking for Discounts

A hard-working young man in Delray Beach, Florida, was asked if he ever uses coupons. The man recoiled at the thought of using coupons, especially on a date. Having previously worked in a restaurant, the man equated coupons with the elderly people who used coupons at the restaurant where he worked or who came for the early-bird special. Most of them, he said, were extremely bad tippers.

Even if you never worked in a restaurant, you may feel the same way. Some young people can't stand the thought of using coupons, because it makes them feel like their parents and grandparents. In their mind, there's a stigma attached to using coupons to get a discount.

Even older people sometimes resist using coupons or asking for discounts. When you hit age 50, you're permitted to join AARP. Your AARP card entitles you to discounts on products and services. I know a few people who won't use their AARP card, because they don't want to admit their age.

Rule #3: Don't Buy Your Groceries Where You Buy Gas

Every day, you spend money unconsciously that could be saved. You pick up a few items at the convenience store where you buy gas and pay much more than you would at a supermarket. More than likely, these were impulse purchases that you didn't really need. I've noticed more often that when I pay at the pump, I don't get the receipt I requested. I'm convinced that the gas station wants you to come inside for your receipt, so you'll make a few of those impulse purchases like an overpriced candy bar.

A gas station might also be the place where you're buying one or more lottery tickets every day. Playing the lottery now and then might be an inexpensive form of entertainment, but it's not the ticket to financial security. Walking out of a gas station with a fistful of lottery tickets is wasting money that you might apply to a real investment. If your employer contributes 50 cents for every dollar you invest in the company's retirement savings plan, your $10-per-week lottery habit just cost you another $5. You also are losing the tax savings you might have gotten by contributing more to your 401(k), as well as the growth on that investment over the next 25 years or longer.

If you drive over again to the financial calculators at www.dinkytown.net, you'll be shocked to find out what your lottery habit costs you. Assuming a $60 per month contribution to a retirement savings plan ($40 plus $20 from your employer, your savings could add up to $54,890 after 25 years. This estimate presumes you started with nothing and made 8 percent annually on your investment.

Rule #4: The Vending Machine Isn't a Restaurant

If you appreciate irony, here's a scenario to contemplate: Employees are standing around a vending machine at work, complaining that they don't have any money to save and invest. Meanwhile, they've pumped a few bucks into the machine, which is a morning and afternoon ritual. Pumping quarters or dollar bills into a vending machine can be as bad for your financial health as putting money into a slot machine. I have a theory that even the vending machine feels guilty at times, and that's why it keeps spitting out your dollar bill, even though you've ironed out all the creases.

If you can't get through the day without vending machine snacks, buy them in bulk at Costco or Sam's Club and keep them in your desk. Just don't eat them all in one day. While you're shopping at a warehouse club, stock up on some of the nonperishables that you use regularly. Because of high fuel prices, filling up your grocery cart is much more expensive than it used to be, so cut corners wherever you can.

Rule #5: It's Not a Bargain If You Don't Need It

It used to be that you could avoid spending money by skipping a trip to the mall. Now sales come into your living room or wherever you're watching TV or working on the computer. As you click the remote, someone will be hawking merchandise on the Home Shopping Network or selling some purportedly fabulous product in an infomercial. Furthermore, although shopping online can also be extremely convenient, it's also an opportunity to buy things you really don't need. In addition, you probably receive e-mails each morning notifying you about new sales and special offers.

One way to curb impulse buying is to consider what each purchase costs in terms of your labor. If you clear $20 per hour, that $100 item takes five hours of your labor to buy. The $200 bangle or gizmo takes 10 hours of your time to pay for. If you keep track, you may be working several days each month just to pay for your impulse purchases. This is money you might easily save and invest.

Rule #6: Don't Spend Money to Get Free Stuff

Retailers are good at getting you to spend more money. Perhaps, you'll get a coupon in the mail from your favorite clothing store that offers $25 off if you spend $200 or more. More often than not, you wind up buying things you don't really want in order to "save"

$25. It happens online, too. The online vendor offers free shipping if you buy a second book or spend a minimum amount of money.

Savings makeovers don't just happen. You must make a conscious effort to resist seemingly insignificant expenditures. You also need to show some self-discipline, which is difficult, whether you're dieting or saving money. It helps to realize that you're not depriving yourself. You're just maximizing your paycheck and putting it to better use.

How Much Money Should I Save?

Although most of us know that we should be saving money, we're never quite sure how much is appropriate, given our financial resources. A popular rule of thumb is that you should be saving 10 percent of your salary to guarantee financial stability during your retirement. You should also be investing those savings.

Dr. Roger G. Ibbotson, founder of Ibbotson Associates in Chicago, www.ibbotson.com, questioned the 10 percent savings figure in the February 1, 2008, issue of *Bottom Line Personal.* Dr. Ibbotson said that this rule of thumb only works if you start saving 10 percent of your salary no later than age 35. If you start later in life, Dr. Ibbotson believes that you must save much more than 10 percent of your salary. According to Dr. Ibbotson, a 50-year-old with no retirement savings who makes $80,000 per year must save roughly 30 percent per year until retirement to keep the same standard of living.

An article in the April 2007 issue of *The Journal of Financial Planning,* made even more disturbing projections. According to that article, if you start saving from scratch at age 50 and you earn $80,000 per year, you will need to save 56.8 percent of your salary to replace 80 percent of your income at retirement. If you're age 40 and earn $80,000, you will "only" need to save 29 percent of your income to replace 80 percent of your income at retirement. And to make matters worse, as we discussed in Chapter 8, it may be a myth that you will only need 80 percent of your preretirement income to maintain your lifestyle after you retire.

Nationally syndicated financial columnist Charles A. Jaffe also questioned the 10 percent rule of thumb in an article published on February 10, 2008, in the *Palm Beach Post.* Jaffe advised that the 10 percent figure is merely a starting point. It ignores several factors such as the return you earn, how long you have to build your nest egg, and your anticipated lifestyle. If all you save is 10 percent, you may be sorely disappointed by what life will be like in retirement.

Despite that bleak news, an important step in your financial makeover is to begin saving now if you haven't already and before it's too late. Your retirement savings plan at work is an ideal investment vehicle, especially if your employer adds to your contribution. Even if you only save 10 percent of your salary, your employer's contribution will help you increase the amount you are saving and investing. No, your employer won't add 46.8 percent to your 10 percent, but hopefully you're closer to age 35 than age 50.

If you are age 50 or older, the tax laws make it easier to increase your level of savings. At age 50, catch-up contributions to your 401(k) and IRA are permitted. As we saw in Chapter 4, in 2008 and 2009, you are permitted to contribute a maximum of $5,000 to an IRA. If you've hit the big 5–0, you can put away an extra $1,000, for a total of $6,000. In 2008, you can contribute a maximum of $15,500 to a 401(k) retirement savings plan. If you are age 50 or older, you can contribute an additional $5,000 to the plan.

Rule of 72

One of the best lessons you can learn as part of your financial makeover is that these seemingly small savings add up to a great deal of money over the years. Although this is the case, we pass up opportunities to save a few dollars here and there. The Rule of 72 shows us how important these small savings can be. It also helps us to realize why we need to do more than just save to reach our financial goals. We also must invest those savings to accelerate their growth.

Many financial institutions bank on the fact that most investors are lax when it comes to money. We shop around for the best interest rate on a CD, but we get lazy when it matures. We let the CD roll over for another term, sometimes without even checking what interest rates are available.

Banks count on our being lazy. They often offer a higher interest rate to new customers than to existing ones. The bank knows that once customers deposit their money, they are likely to forget about it. When the CD is about to renew, customers are less likely to shop around for a better rate. This can be a really bad idea, especially if interest rates have fallen.

The Rule of 72 helps you understand the importance of getting a higher return on your money. This simple mathematical rule helps you to calculate how long it takes for your money to double. Suppose you are getting a 3 percent interest rate on your CD.

To calculate how long it will take for your money to double, you need to divide the number 72 by 3, which is 24 years. If your CD pays 4 percent, your money will double in 18 years, because 72 divided by 4 is 18.

I can hear that heavy sigh as you think about waiting 18 years for your money to double. The Rule of 72 helps to illustrate why it is important to seek out a higher rate of return in the stock market. If you can achieve a higher rate of return in the stock market, your money will double much more quickly. If you are able to get an 8 percent rate of return, your investment nest egg will double in nine years since 72 divided by 8 equals 9. If it doubles again in nine more years, you've accelerated the rate at which your nest egg grows.

Though the Rule of 72 isn't high finance, it can help your finances in the short and long-term. If you start thinking about it now, there's less chance you'll find yourself at age 72 in dire financial straits.

MoneyTrack Method

You can implement the principles of the *MoneyTrack* method, even if saving money isn't high on your list of priorities. As long as you're investing on an ongoing basis in a well-diversified portfolio and aren't using your nest egg as a piggybank, you are likely to achieve your financial goals. On the other hand, if you can never find money to invest and are nowhere close to reaching your financial goals, reducing your outgo will need to become a priority.

As you cut the cost of your lifestyle and develop a more frugal mindset, you need to ensure that you're investing that money and not just saving it. There are many ways to ensure you have money left to save and invest. The most important one is that you should save money off the top, not the remainder. Paying yourself first is accomplished by signing up for savings plans that deduct money before you get your hands on it. 401(k) retirement savings plans put away a percentage of your paycheck before you can spend it. The psychology is that you never miss the money and you learn to live on what's left. In contrast, if you get used to seeing the money in your paycheck, you're more inclined to spend it.

Another psychological trick is to increase your 401(k) contribution when you get a raise. Instead of growing accustomed to seeing more in your paycheck because of the raise, you raise your 401(k) contribution instead. More money comes out and you never miss it. And while you're on the way to the human resource department, please don't stop at the vending machines.

Signing up for automatic investment plans achieves a similar result. The deduction takes place automatically. You don't need to physically shift money to savings.

If you're working toward a goal with a special person in your life, make sure that both of you are ready for a financial makeover. That means both of you are willing to cut your spending and invest more. Terri Cullen of the *Wall Street Journal* suggested that couples consider implementing a $500 rule. If an item costs more than $500, you have to check with your spouse or significant other before buying it. According to Cullen, you can adjust the amount based on your financial situation and other circumstances.

Jeff D. Opdyke used to write a column called "Love and Money" for the *Wall Street Journal.* Each week, he openly discussed financial issues affecting his wife, Amy, and family. In his traditional end-of-the-year column as 2007 wound down, Opdyke mulled over a question his friend asked: "What's the biggest lesson you and Amy have learned since you began writing the column?" In response, Opdyke replied that the couple learned how to talk to each other.

Unfortunately, many couples can't or won't discuss the important financial issues they face. It seems easier to ignore those problems rather than fight about them. As Opdyke said in his column, talking about money doesn't mean fighting about it. "It just means talking," he wrote. Perhaps, that's the most important lesson you and your family can learn this year or in any year.

CHAPTER 11

The American Dream

Although the *MoneyTrack* method is designed to help you invest like a pro, people have different plans for their investments. Some invest with the goal of funding their dream retirement. Others invest so they'll have enough money to send their children to college and graduate school. Many investors are seeking to become financially independent or are hoping to enjoy more of the good things in life. Although an old song says that the best things in life are free, some of them take more money to buy than we have right now, and that's why we invest.

Each of us puts our individual imprint on the American Dream. For some people, however, the American Dream seems to be unattainable. On our *MoneyTrack* program, we spoke with a 53-year-old former officer for the Memphis police department. Ralph Hatley broke his back in the line of duty and is now retired on a pension. He has come to believe that $40,000 to $50,000 per year will not allow a family to live the American Dream, even if there are no children to support. Ralph believes the American Dream is only affordable if you earn $150,000 to $180,000 per year.

Ralph told us that he believes the middle class is disintegrating. With inflation and escalating bills, he doesn't believe a prosperous retirement is possible for middle-income folks like himself. As a former school teacher, my co-host, Jack, empathized with Ralph even more than I did. Jack and Ralph both believe it's extremely difficult to save and invest, especially when there are mouths to feed and bills to pay.

Ralph's vision of retirement isn't what most of us view as lavish. Ralph would like to own a cabin in eastern Tennessee in the Smoky Mountains. Ralph envisions the cabin as a retreat where his entire family can get together.

For each of us, the dream is a bit different. Some of us envision ourselves with a boat, retiring by a lake. Others dream of living on a golf course and playing at least 18 holes every day. Many folks want to travel the globe or spend hours reading. Maybe you just want enough time to do the Jumble.

Jack feels we all have similar dreams. We want to work and enjoy our lives while we're working. We want to take vacations and have a new car every few years. And when we're ready to retire, we hope to have enough money with which to enjoy our version of the good life. Jack recognizes that achieving those dreams isn't easy, especially if you have kids. Life's day-to-day expenditures get in the way, whether it's remodeling your kitchen, paying tuition bills, or helping your children buy their own homes.

A survey of accountants who provide financial planning services in December 2007, found that their clients have three primary concerns:

1. Saving for retirement
2. Cost of healthcare
3. Paying for their children's education

The survey, which was conducted by the American Institute of Certified Public Accountants of New York, shows that you need to invest like a pro to reach several goals, not just one. Furthermore, as you pursue the American Dream, you need to put a financial plan in place that addresses all of those concerns.

Regardless of what your dream is, it takes more than just hoping it will happen. You need a plan to get you from today until retirement. Unless you're single, your plan should incorporate the dreams and aspirations of your spouse or life partner. Ralph and his wife found they weren't always on the same page regarding financial matters. Many couples never get around to discussing retirement or their dreams for the future. Too often, they lead frenzied lives that aren't conducive to sharing dreams. Investing like a pro won't help you reach your financial goals unless you and the special person in your life make the time to define what the American Dream means for you.

Is the American Dream Still Doable?

Many of the typical Americans we've met since launching *MoneyTrack* do not believe they are better off than their parents or grandparents, even though they actually are. Most of us have higher expectations than the people who live in other countries, as well as a sense of entitlement. Although our parents and grandparents may not have owned a television, we can't live without a bigger TV with state-of-the-art features. According to a survey conducted by the Consumer Electronics Association, 29 percent of U.S. households own a television set that is at least 40 inches, and 61 percent of the survey's respondents said they expect to own a set larger than 40 inches if they don't own one already. And after you buy a 40-inch screen, you then need a massive piece of furniture to hold it.

Our cell phone bills are larger than what our parents paid each month on their mortgage. We need the latest gadgets, whether it's an iPhone or a Game Boy for our kids. We want to own a nice home and a car for every member of our household that drives. Many of us lease cars that we could not otherwise afford to drive. Robert Reich, the former secretary of labor, pointed out on our program that some of our parents and grandparents couldn't afford a car yet didn't feel they were deprived.

Too many Americans are mortgaging their future instead of saying no to luxuries they can't afford. Credit card debt is at an all-time high time, and many Americans live paycheck to paycheck. Financial belt-tightening isn't our favorite exercise. In fact, exercise in general seems to rub us the wrong way as most of our belts get tighter.

Even if we do tighten our belts, it's difficult to make ends meet. Higher education costs keep going up. The price of milk, eggs, fruits, and vegetables seems to be escalating every day. We may spend $50 to fill the tank of our car, even if we don't own a gas-guzzler. Sometimes it seems that even a scaled-back version of the American Dream is beyond our reach.

Do I Need Financial Advice?

Although our goal is to help you invest like a pro so you can reach your personalized version of the American Dream, you may not feel comfortable making your own investment decisions. You might need to consult with a financial services professional. Just as you need to investigate before you invest, you also need to conduct a thorough investigation before hiring someone to help you with your investment decisions.

Although Jack has learned a great deal since we started filming *MoneyTrack*, he prefers working with an investment adviser. A few years ago, Jack met with his accountant and asked for a recommendation. The accountant gave Jack the name of an investment adviser in northern California. Jack sat down with him and made certain they shared the same philosophy about money. He also wanted to be sure that the investment adviser's strategies made sense.

So far, their relationship has worked out well. As long as the adviser's strategies make money, Jack doesn't mind paying extra for his advice, just as he doesn't mind paying a mechanic to keep his car running.

Jack was lucky. His accountant put him in touch with a reputable investment adviser. As we saw in Chapter 3, Ruth Mitchell and her husband weren't as lucky. Their CPA steered them into a bogus investment and stole their $100,000 nest egg.

If you decide you're in need of investment advice, selecting the right person isn't easy. There are many people who claim to have financial expertise, and it's difficult to sort through their credentials. Just because the person is purportedly a wealth manager, money manager, financial planner, or investment counselor, is no assurance that the individual has the requisite experience and knowledge you're expecting. And as we have seen in many scam alerts, the fact that your friends and relatives trust a particular financial adviser is no assurance that the person is honest and competent. Although references from the people you trust are extremely important, they are only the first step in choosing a financial adviser.

How to Choose a Registered Investment Adviser (RIA)

A study by the RAND Corporation of Santa Monica, California, in late 2007 found that there is considerable confusion among investors regarding financial services firms. Quite often, investors do not know the difference between a stockbroker and a registered investment adviser (RIA). Although brokers and RIAs are highly regulated, the obligations they owe to their clients may be quite different. Generally, brokers owe a duty to recommend suitable investments to their clients. RIAs owe a fiduciary duty to act in the best interest of their clients. As fiduciaries, RIAs must make their clients' interests a higher priority than their own.

RIAs must comply with the Investment Advisers Act of 1940, as well as numerous rules and regulations that were enacted to protect their clients. RIAs must provide their clients with Form ADV, which is a disclosure document, at the onset of the relationship. Full disclosure helps to ensure that RIAs are satisfying their fiduciary obligations to clients. The Securities and Exchange Commission (SEC) has proposed amendments that will require RIAs to present this disclosure in a narrative form that is written in plain English.

You can use an advisory firm's Form ADV as a tool for comparing it to other RIAs that you are considering. Form ADV discloses all of the following information and a whole lot more:

- Investment strategies and business practices
- Educational background of key members of the firm
- Business experience of firm members
- Size and types of accounts handled
- Types of services that are available
- Disciplinary history and litigation against the firm, an affiliate or a management person
- Potential conflicts of interest that might affect the firm's recommendations
- Whether the RIA is affiliated with another adviser, a broker-dealer, or an issuer of securities
- Affiliations, participation, or interest in client transactions
- Fees and other expenses clients must pay

If you read Form ADV closely, you'll find out if larger accounts are charged a lower fee or if the fees are negotiable.

Form ADV tells you what types of services the firm offers and helps you decide whether you need them. You might need help only in creating a financial plan that is a roadmap for you to follow. However, you may decide that you want the RIA to manage your portfolio on an ongoing basis and choose which investments to buy and sell.

When you are choosing a financial adviser, credentials and designations are extremely useful. The key, however, is distinguishing meaningful designations from ones that aren't worth the paper they are written on. Securities regulators are cracking down on the use of professional designations that imply that the financial adviser has special expertise or training in advising older investors, unless those credentials are issued by an accredited organization. In an April 1, 2008 press release, the North American Securities Administrators

Association (NASAA) announced its approval of a model rule that prohibits the misleading use of senior and retiree designations and certifications. Karen Tyler, the North Dakota Securities Commissioner and president of NASAA, urged all members of the organization to adopt this model rule within their jurisdictions as quickly as possible. NASAA is the oldest international organization committed to investor protection and consists of securities administrators in all fifty states, as well as the District of Columbia, the U.S. Virgin Islands, Canada, Mexico, and Puerto Rico.

There are a number of well-regarded designations that require considerable time and effort to acquire such as the CFP (certified financial planner). The CPA-PFS designation, which is held by certified public accountants who are personal financial specialists, is also well respected. If you need help managing your portfolio, the chartered financial analyst (CFA) designation means the person has undergone rigorous training in the analysis of stocks and bonds.

You should never engage a financial adviser until you've checked with your state's securities regulators. In addition, you can learn more about an RIA by visiting the SEC's Investment Adviser Public Disclosure Web site at www.adviserinfo.sec.gov/IAPD/Content/IapdMain/iapd_SiteMap.aspx.

How to Choose a Stockbroker

Stockbrokers often give more advice than which stocks to buy or sell. If you plan to rely on a broker for advice, it is helpful to understand the terminology. The brokerage firm is also known as a broker-dealer. Your sales representative at the brokerage firm may also be referred to as a stockbroker, account executive, or registered representative. The sales representative's business card, however, might list the person's title as "financial consultant" or some other descriptive term. In addition, brokerage firms often give great titles to their brokers to bolster their credibility.

The Financial Industry Regulatory Authority (FINRA) oversees the conduct of all securities firms doing business in the United States. According to the FINRA Web site, www.FINRA.org, it is the largest nongovernmental regulator. FINRA rules and regulations are subject to approval by the SEC. FINRA was formerly known as NASD, the National Association of Securities Dealers.

To choose a broker, FINRA recommends that you meet with potential salespeople at several firms. You should ask each sales representative about his or her education, professional background, and experience. It helps to compare that person's credentials to other brokers.

You can investigate the sales representative's disciplinary history online at www.finra.org/InvestorInformation/InvestorProtection/ ChecktheBackgroundofYourInvestmentProfessional/index.htm. You can also call 800–289–9999, a toll-free hotline operated by FINRA. FINRA will provide you with information regarding disciplinary actions taken by criminal authorities and securities regulators. State securities regulators may be able to provide additional information about the sales representative. Always conduct a background check before hiring a broker and avoid any person who pressures you to sign on as a client.

FINRA advises that you ask for and fully understand how the sales representative is paid. Request a copy of the firm's commission schedule. There may also be fees or charges for opening, closing, and maintaining an account. Remember, too, that sales representatives sometimes receive additional compensation for selling proprietary products that are offered by the firm, such as the broker-dealer's own mutual fund.

Pitfalls to Avoid as You Look for Financial Advice

As we have seen in too many Scam Alerts, many people choose the wrong financial adviser. They make their decision based on all of the wrong reasons. Instead of hiring the person who realistically explains the positives and negatives associated with certain investments, they fall for the sales pitch of the individual who promises too much and minimizes the potential risk.

Although you may encounter a host of people who call themselves financial advisers, they may not necessarily provide you with objective information. As an example, insurance agents sometimes bill themselves as financial advisers. Although they may be very knowledgeable and might have your best interest at heart, they normally make their living through commissions, which gives them an incentive to sell certain products such as annuities. An annuity is usually structured to guarantee a lifetime income for you and your spouse or life partner. An annuity may be the right financial product to meet your needs, but you might be better off getting advice from someone who will consider the full gamut of financial solutions. Nevertheless, it's not uncommon for brokers and persons associated with an RIA to possess an insurance license.

A financial adviser might recommend equity indexed annuities (EIAs), also known as fixed indexed annuities. EIAs are a type of annuity where the interest rate on your contributions is linked to a stock market index. There is a guaranteed minimum return, even if the stock market goes down in value.

NASAA has reported that unregistered securities, variable annuities, and EIAs are the most pervasive financial products involved in senior investment fraud. Regulators are particularly concerned because EIAs are extremely difficult to fully understand. Although EIAs are sometimes portrayed by a sales person as an investment, they are typically regulated as an insurance product.

On December 5, 2005, the Kentucky Office of Financial Institutions' Division of Securities issued a release expressed concern over how EIAs are marketed. The release mentioned several objectionable statements that are used to market EIAs:

- Take advantage of market gains while avoiding market losses.
- Grow with the stock market without risk.
- Obtain competitive yield with minimal risk.

Kentucky also objected to marketing materials and statements comparing rates of return or the annuity itself to recognized financial products such as CDs and mutual funds.

The Division of Securities' release also warned that the person marketing EIAs should refrain from offering a full financial review, asset analysis, estate planning, or substantially similar financial services unless they work for a broker-dealer or RIA. All communications regarding EIAs should contain conspicuous language stating that the person is only licensed to sell insurance products.

EIAs have a number of potential drawbacks, including the following:

- Surrender charges may be incurred if too much money is withdrawn before a certain time frame has elapsed, which might be as long as 15 years.
- Interest rates are capped and won't necessarily match gains in the stock market.
- Withdrawals of tax-deferred earnings are subject to current income tax.

- An income tax penalty of 10 percent may be imposed if earnings are withdrawn prior to age 59½.
- The method for calculating the gain is extremely complicated and may limit earnings.

For example, if the market goes up 20 percent, it's unlikely that the interest on an EIA will be anywhere near that amount.

Aside from EIAs, be wary of life insurance that is marketed as a retirement plan. In the 1990s, several large insurance companies were sanctioned for misleading consumer with sales pitches and marketing materials that misrepresented life insurance as a retirement plan.

Creating Your Own Version of the American Dream

Each of us has our own version of the American Dream. Whereas Ralph dreamed of a vacation home in the Smoky Mountains, other people want to live near the ocean. Researchers are finding that many people want to stay right where they are after retiring. Their dream is to age in the home where they're living now or in a nearby retirement community.

The primary reason folks want to stay put in retirement is because of their ties to family, friends, physicians, and the community. They want to remain close to their children and grandchildren. Retirement communities for active adults are popping up in highly populated areas, so retirees can stay close to the neighborhood where they've lived for most of their life.

Keeping your current house is usually far less expensive than moving across the country and starting over. Aside from moving costs, buying a new or existing home in another town will usually involve significant start-up expenses. When you stay put, there is no need to find new doctors or make new friends.

Your current home may not, however, be conducive to aging in place, especially if you own a two-story house and the steps are becoming more difficult to navigate. Nevertheless, there are ways to remodel your home to accommodate the aging process. Many aging boomers install grab bars in the bathroom, as well as higher toilet seats. If a wheelchair is necessary someday, a contractor can widen the doorway and install a ramp. Switching from door knobs to levers can make life easier for an older resident, as can improved lighting.

In some cases, it makes sense for retirees to downsize to a smaller home on one floor that is easier to maintain. You might be able to use the profit to finance your dream retirement. Your taxes, insurance, and maintenance costs may also be lower.

If you're willing to make major adjustments in your lifestyle, listen to the advice from the authors who have written about the voluntary simplicity movement. Books and publications like *Your Money or Your Life, The Tightwad Gazette,* and *Simple Living: The Journal of Voluntary Simplicity* offer practical advice on how to lead a less stressful life for a lot less money. Some of these books suggest that you can live on less than $10,000 each year.

For most people, however, the cost of living the American Dream lies somewhere between $10,000 and the $150,000 that Ralph says it takes. Most of us aren't expecting to live lavishly in retirement, but we really don't want to downgrade our lifestyle. Although the vast majority of people don't aspire to live a frugal lifestyle, all of us should attempt to get the most bang for our finite number of bucks.

Financing the American Dream

As you apply the *MoneyTrack* method to your financial situation, the goal is that one day you'll have enough money to fund the American Dream that's been playing out in your head. For almost all of us, the funding will come from our ability to save and invest. Too many people believe, however, that their American dream will fund itself— and that's a bad assumption to make. At the risk of bursting your bubble, you can't bank on selling the Great American novel you plan to write to fund your American Dream. Unless James Patterson has asked you to be his co-author, it's unlikely this will happen.

Similarly, if you intend to explore a new career, recognize that even dream jobs can be aggravating and may not be as lucrative as you're expecting. Let's say your dream is to make jewelry and sell it at craft shows across the country. While that may sound like a wonderful idea in the abstract, it might not seem as ideal if a storm closes down the show or your vehicle breaks down on the way. The joy of creating jewelry might be diminished if a few people criticize your jewelry as they pass your booth or negotiate the price of a $10 item. Unless you've been selling your jewelry for years on a part-time basis, you can't expect the profits from your business to finance your American Dream.

No matter what your dream is and how realistic it is, you will need to make adjustments. Many of these changes will be prompted by the fact that real life is much different than a dream. Other changes will become necessary because of financial constraints. Rather than resenting having to make trade-offs, you should expect them to occur. Every dream should have a fall-back plan.

We turned to author and financial planner Jonathan Pond to share his expertise with Ralph and others in pursuit of the American Dream. Jonathan's book, *You Can Do It,* addresses the concerns of people like Ralph. Jonathan believes Ralph has the resources to live his version of the American Dream, especially since he is not expecting a lavish retirement. He has some savings and isn't deeply in debt. The fact that Ralph is entitled to a traditional pension puts him way ahead of most Americans who must rely on 401(k)s and other defined contribution plans to finance their retirement.

Our guest Michelle Singletary, and hundreds of other financial experts, are big fans of using automatic investing to invest in mutual funds. As we know, mutual funds give you the ability to invest and build a diversified portfolio that reduces your risk. You can put your investments on automatic pilot. Michelle joked that automatic investing is the best thing since curling irons that shut off automatically, so you don't burn down your house.

Target Date Retirement Funds

Jonathan called our attention to target date retirement funds. These are mutual funds whose portfolios are geared toward your estimated retirement date. As you move closer to that date, your portfolio is automatically shifted from higher-risk investments to more conservative ones. Target date retirement funds go by a number of different names, including lifestyle funds or life-cycle funds.

Many retirement savings plans will offer a wide choice of target date retirement funds. A large employer offers these target date retirement funds to its employees:

- 2010
- 2015
- 2020
- 2025
- 2030
- 2035
- 2040
- 2045

More than likely, the plan will soon offer a target date retirement fund for employees who will retire in the year 2050 or later.

The rap against target date retirement funds is that some charge very high fees. Jonathan also believes that some of them tend to become too conservative as you near your retirement date. Even when you retire at age 65, you need investments that will sustain your American Dream for 30 years or longer.

To see how they work, it helps to look at the Fidelity Freedom 2035 Fund. It is one of 12 funds offered by mutual fund giant, Fidelity Investments. This particular one is suitable for individuals who plan to retire around the year 2035. The portfolio consists of domestic equity funds, international equity funds, quality fixed-income investments, high-yield fixed income investments, and short-term investments. Right now, roughly two-thirds of the fund's assets are invested in domestic equity funds. As 2035 approaches, more of your money will be allocated toward quality fixed-income investments.

Target date retirement funds differ in many ways, so it pays to read the prospectus. Fees are a very important consideration. The mix of investments may also differ. Even if the target is the same year, one fund might keep more money in the stock market as your retirement date gets closer.

Obviously, there are a wide range of financial options worth considering as you work toward the goal of financing your American Dream. The absolutely wrong option is waiting too long to get started.

Envisioning Your Ideal Lifestyle

Although many people engage in retirement planning from a financial perspective, they neglect to plan what their life will be like. Aside from financial planning, you must envision your dream retirement. Here are some of the steps you should take:

- *Set aside some time to dream and plan.* Perhaps, you're overwhelmed with work and feel you don't have nearly enough time to formulate your version of the American Dream. Although you may dream about retirement, you might rationalize that it is years away and there will be time later to plan. You need to set aside time now to hone in on what your ideal lifestyle is and how it can be achieved.
- *Write down how you want to spend your days in retirement.* After leaving the work force, some retirees become bored or lose their sense of purpose. Instead of savoring the freedom to

do what they want, these retirees find it very difficult to make the transition to what should be a carefree existence. Picture what a typical day, week, and month will be like and whether your daily activities will be emotionally satisfying.

- *Sit down with your spouse or life partner.* Perhaps, you're one of those people who never have time to sit down with their spouse or life partner to discuss these issues. Your spouse or life partner might have a totally different vision of retirement. In fact, your significant other might not even want to retire—ever. The two of you need to make time to discuss your plans for life after work, even if you're relatively young. The data you gain from these discussions have a bearing on the financial decisions you make today. Make a date to discuss this topic over dinner at your favorite restaurant, so you won't be distracted and neither of you has to cook.

- *Plan a field trip to the library.* The *MoneyTrack* team conducts many educational sessions at public libraries across the country, and these events remind us that the answers to life's questions can't all be answered with a Google search. Surrounded by books, magazines, and newspapers, libraries are the perfect spot to think and plan the next stage of your journey through life. There are no distractions like Chloe mooching food.

Planning the Next Stage of Your Life at the Library

I run into too many people who haven't been to the library in years. A library can be the ideal place to think about the endless possibilities that exist for us when we're not consumed by making a living. Set aside a few hours in an evening or on the weekend to go from shelf to shelf in search of ideas and inspiration for your own American Dream.

You'll find magazines and books that discuss hobbies and activities you want to purse. You can learn about exotic places where you want to travel to someday. You can learn about small businesses that are ideal for retirees. There are resources to help you identify where you want to live your dream retirement.

Warren Bland's book, *Retire in Style,* is a good starting point. In his book, Professor Bland identified 12 criteria that are extremely important to retirees:

1. Landscape
2. Climate
3. Quality of life

4. Cost of living
5. Transportation
6. Retail services
7. Healthcare
8. Community services
9. Cultural activities
10. Recreational activities
11. Work/volunteer opportunities
12. Crime

Professor Bland made a number of suggestions for finding your dream locale and gives readers their homework assignment. He suggested that you visit the locations you're considering for at least three weeks and get a feel for the climate, people, and cost of living. You shouldn't make any rash decisions. If you plan to work, make sure there are job opportunities in your dream locale.

An afternoon at the library can also help you to become a smarter investor. Most libraries will have copies of your local business journal. You'll learn about new companies and the business climate in your area. If you'd like to get started investing in individual stocks, you might want to focus on companies that have headquarters in your city. After all, you probably know more about how well they're doing, because those companies receive more newspaper coverage.

A well-stocked library will have copies of the *Wall Street Journal*, as well as newspapers from around the country. You might read a story or two that impacts investments you are thinking of buying or already own. As an example, you would have found out early on that McDonald's was selling gourmet coffees and cutting into Starbucks' business. If you're serious about investing on your own, business periodicals can help you become an intelligent investor.

Publications like *Kiplinger's Personal Finance* magazine, *Smart Money*, and *Money* magazine can help you to identify promising stocks and mutual funds. You should also check out *Barron's*, *BusinessWeek*, and *Fortune*. Nevertheless, it always pays to do your own research before buying any investment instead of relying entirely on recommendations made in a financial publication. The library is one of the best places you can go to investigate before you invest.

Becoming reacquainted with your library is also a great way to save money. Most libraries will let you reserve best sellers and other books, which beats paying $20 or more for them. You can catch up on magazines you like to read instead of buying them. Many libraries offer free lectures and classes on educational topics, which may be a pleasant alternative to a $9 movie that you walk out on. Some libraries even have a decent selection of DVDs you can check out instead of paying to rent one or going to the movies.

And who knows. If you enjoy your visit to the library, you might dream of the day when you can spend more time there without worrying about being at work tomorrow.

Living the American Dream Somewhere Else

Although it seems a bit ironic, your version of the American Dream might be tied in with living in a foreign country. As you ponder what it is you want out of life, you might decide that you've always wanted to live somewhere else—at least temporarily. Living outside the country might cut the cost of your dream lifestyle.

The book *Cashing in on the American Dream: How to Retire at 35* was published in 1988 and is still one of the most important books on how to retire early. The book was written by Paul Terhorst, a former accountant, who managed to chuck the rat race at a very young age to retire in South America. When last we checked, Terhorst and his wife are still happily retired and are traveling the globe at a dizzying pace. According to Paul's home page, www.geocities.com/thetropics/shores/5315/, the couple has been to Thailand, Panama, and a host of other places. They built a home an hour north of Buenos Aires, but are traveling constantly.

In search of the American Dream, some people leave the country to find an affordable retirement lifestyle. A number of retirees have settled in Mexico, Costa Rica, Panama, and other exotic locales instead of traditional retirement spots such as Florida and Arizona. The cost of living is much lower and residents are able to stretch their retirement nest egg. Retirees escape the high property taxes in states like New Jersey and Florida. In some areas, there is a sizable American contingent, so there is less of a language barrier.

Retiring in a foreign country presents a number of obstacles. In Mexico, for example, foreigners are prohibited from buying property within roughly 62 miles of any Mexican coastline. Property meeting this description must be purchased through a trust that holds title to the property for 100 years.

Spending retirement in a foreign country is an enormous adjustment for most people. It is extremely difficult to be far away from family and friends. There are a number of issues to resolve, such as visas and healthcare. Generally, Medicare does not cover treatment outside the United States. Although there have been reports that people are going to foreign countries such as Thailand and India for less expensive healthcare, paying medical and hospital bills out of your own pocket is not a viable option. If you retire in a foreign country, you need to have a health insurance plan that covers you while you're away from the United States.

According to Ingrid P. John, a CPA, you still owe federal income taxes if you move outside the country. Social Security benefits, pension distributions, and money withdrawn from a 401(k) plan, are still taxable. According to John's article in the March 1, 2008 issue of *Bottom Line Personal,* U.S. citizens are taxed on any income they make throughout the world, including income earned outside the country. There may, however, be treaties and exclusions that reduce your tax liability.

Whatever your dream, you need to work out the details now. It may be the right time to live out a dream you never acted upon when you were younger like joining the Peace Corps. Or as companies develop a presence across the globe, you might look for a job where you'll get paid to work overseas. The possibilities are worth thinking about sooner rather than later.

The Dream of Early Retirement

Although there are some people who love their jobs and want to work forever, if not longer, many workers dream of retiring early. As they sit on a freeway that resembles a parking lot or wait for the train on a frigid platform, these frustrated workers dream of boating down an intracoastal waterway or fishing in a mountain stream. Instead of enjoying the outdoors, they are stuffed in a subway as they hang onto a strap for dear life.

The dream of early retirement has become more difficult to achieve. In fact, many workers, especially those with little savings and investments, expect to work long beyond their full retirement age, which might be as old as 67. Although many of us want to explore new careers in retirement or work part time to keep active, this is a far cry from being forced to get a job due to economic circumstances.

A bear market can force you to put your dream of early retirement on hold. The bear market of 2000 through 2002 and the bursting of the technology bubble wreaked havoc on investors' portfolios. It forced many workers to postpone or even cancel their plans for early retirement. It even caused some retirees to return to the work force.

Escalating healthcare costs have also turned the dream of early retirement into a nightmare. The cost of healthcare has risen at twice the rate of inflation over the past decade. Consequently, many workers stay in the work force for the sole purpose of keeping their health insurance coverage.

The dream of early retirement isn't out of reach if you start early. As we have stressed so often, becoming an investor at an early age helps you reach seemingly unattainable goals. Investments you make at a young age compound over the years. In contrast, it's very difficult to build an early retirement nest egg if you start in your forties. You would need to save and invest a large percentage of your paycheck.

Most people aren't willing to cut corners now to achieve a dream that may be decades away. Nevertheless, a working couple that is serious about early retirement might attempt to spend one paycheck and bank the other. Clearly, that's a problem if both incomes are needed to pay fixed expenses like a mortgage, taxes, and insurance. At a minimum, they might both raise their 401(k) contributions to the maximum amount permitted.

Whether you're residing in a one- or two-income household, living on less gives you more money to save and invest. It also reduces the amount of income you'll need to sustain yourself after leaving the work force. When you lower your income requirements, you reduce the size of the nest egg you'll need for early retirement.

One unknown variable facing early retirees is calculating how much their new lifestyle will cost. If you plan to stay in the house where you're living now, you will have a leg up on folks who have no idea where they will be living and how much it will cost. If your early retirement dream is focused on a particular area, make a realistic estimate of how much it will cost to live there.

When planning for early retirement, it is useful to distinguish between the years before and after age 59½. Age 59½ is the age when you can usually tap retirement savings plans like a 401(k) or an IRA without restriction. Your retirement savings plans at work, as well as your IRAs, can be viewed as the money you're investing for the traditional stage of retirement, which is age 59½ or later—or much later, depending on how conscientious you are about investing. Many workers would be thrilled to know they had the financial resources to retire at age 59½.

It is imperative that you secure the second stage of retirement first. Your goal is to fund a pot of money from which you can draw enough to meet your living costs, plus a cushion for inflation and unexpected expenses. Social Security will be available to supplement your income beginning at age 62 at the earliest. Once the second stage of your retirement is funded, you can start dreaming about moving up your early retirement date even sooner.

As you dream about life after work, you must look for a health insurance plan that is not tied to your current job. COBRA is only a temporary solution to tide you over until you're eligible

Testing Whether Early Retirement Is Right for You

As you prepare for early retirement, test the water and give your plan a dry run to use two clichés that seem to be inherently contradictory. There are some steps you can take to see if early retirement will work for you such as:

- *Instead of taking a traditional vacation, spend an extended period doing all of the activities that are part of your early retirement dream.* Find out if the lifestyle bores you. If you're bored after a few weeks or a month, you need to rethink your plan for early retirement.
- *If you plan to turn a hobby into a business, consider starting your venture now in your free time instead of waiting for retirement.* You might find that making money from the business won't be easy. Furthermore, it might not be nearly as much fun when you introduce the dimension of making a profit and it may seem more like a job. If you do make money, plow your profits into a business-related retirement savings plan like a SEP-IRA. Since this should be found money, you won't miss it if you stash the funds into a retirement savings account.
- Look for a role model who retired at a relatively young age. Find out how that person made the transition to retirement and whether it was a satisfying experience.

The psychologists like to call them baby steps, but they can help you make progress toward your dreams and aspirations.

for Medicare. You should price individual health plans through your local Blue Cross/Blue Shield, as well as other carriers. If you're relatively healthy, the premium may not be as expensive as you think. Make certain the coverage is guaranteed renewable.

You can also look at group plans through any professional or trade group to which you belong. If you plan to turn a business into a hobby after retiring early, investigate plans for the self-employed. Assuming you will make an income from your new business, your health insurance premiums may be deductible.

Tweaking Your Version of the American Dream

There's a saying among boaters that the two happiest days in a man's life are when he buys a boat and when he sells it. This observation points out that the realities of owning a boat sometimes drown out the joy that came with buying it in the first place.

As you strive to make your dream a reality, there will be compromises along the way. If you plan to ignore the old saying about boaters, you may still wish to own one. Instead of a 30-footer, a 20-footer may be more in your price range. One Florida couple dreamed of living on a 40-foot boat and owning a small condo instead of their large home. When the real estate bubble burst, they regrouped and put their plans on hold for now. Nevertheless, they're still enjoying their much smaller vessel.

If you are willing to be flexible, you can tweak your conception of the American Dream and make it more affordable. You are not giving up your dream, just tweaking it a bit. You are making trade-offs, just like most of us do as part of do every day. For example, we can't afford to eat in a certain restaurant every week, so we save it for special occasions. When we buy a house, most of us can't have every feature we want, so we make adjustments.

Suppose your dream is to live by the ocean in a coastal community. You may come to realize that you won't be able to afford even a modest home at the beach. You should be willing to adjust your dream somewhat and move a few miles away from the water where homes are likely to be a bit larger and cheaper. Insurance premiums are also likely to be less expensive. Although you won't hear the ocean as you drift off to sleep, you might be able to find a home on a lake or some other body of water.

Rather than compromise, some people will take their toys and leave the sandbox. They might decide that if they can't get their dream home looking out over the ocean, they'll stay where they are now—12 hours from the ocean. I would argue, however, that having a modified version of your dream is better than not pursuing it at all.

Sometimes, new developments in the real estate market can force changes in your version of the American Dream. Perhaps, you dreamed of living in Las Vegas, as did many retirees, and going for all-you-can-eat buffets every evening. Until the real estate bubble burst in many areas across the country, home prices were up 50 percent in Vegas. If you were looking for a home before the real estate market collapsed, you might not have been able to afford living in Vegas.

By tweaking your dream, you can make it happen. One solution is to postpone your dream for a year or two. You can rent in an area until housing prices come down to earth. In certain areas, moving a county or two away can reduce the cost of your American Dream.

Be careful, however, that you aren't adding to your transportation costs. It might also curtail your ability to find a part-time job if you want one.

After you've realized your version of the American Dream, you should still be prepared to tweak it as circumstances change. Here are some of the factors that may cause you to revise your game plan:

- Your health changes.
- Your expenses rise dramatically.
- Your income decreases.
- Your home-related expenses change.

You will be far better off if you can anticipate these changes, so you're not forced to make adjustments when your back is against the wall.

To illustrate how situations change, whether you're retired or still working, it is helpful to look at the Florida example. Florida was once a very inexpensive place to retire, even for residents with homes close to the ocean. As home values escalated before the real estate bubble burst, however, property taxes rose as well.

Homeowners insurance premiums also rose dramatically, and some carriers stopped writing policies in Florida. Many snowbirds, who are retirees with part-time homes in Florida and in the North, found they could no longer afford to keep both homes. When forced to choose, thousands of them decided to keep their northern homes, which were closer to family and friends.

Although you may not be able to afford two homes, one possible trade-off is renting an apartment in a sunny climate during the cold winter months. Although the rent may be steep, it is likely to be far cheaper than the cost of owning a second home. Remember, too, that you'll be able to invest the money that is tied up in the ownership of a second dwelling. The return on your investment might offset some of the rent.

No matter where you live, you need to be ready to tweak your financial plan as conditions change. You may find that you're withdrawing too much for living expenses and risk exhausting your nest egg. You might need to cut corners and settle on a more affordable version of the American Dream. It might be time to generate a little income with a seasonal job or increase your hours if you're already working. The last thing you should do, however, is look for extra income from an investment opportunity that is too good to be true. You're putting a sign on your back, asking to be scammed.

Scam Alert

It seems like the American Dream for some unscrupulous people is to cheat the rest of us out of our money. In New Mexico, members of a church community made the mistake of trusting a con man. Henry Rivera, a member of the church band, collected $6 million from 45 people to invest in a real estate deal. Because of his church affiliation, church members didn't do their homework.

Rivera claimed he was buying discounted properties and selling them at a profit. The truth was that Rivera didn't buy any property. He pocketed the money members of the congregation gave him. Rivera made interest payments with money from new investors but never paid back any of the principal. He kept the scam going for eight years.

In 1993, people wanted their money back and Rivera ran out of excuses. It took 10 years to track him down in Mexico. In 2006, a jury found him guilty and he was sentenced to 37 years in prison. The victims never got their money back.

The toll on the victims' personal lives was even more damaging. There were suicides and divorces attributed to the crime. Sadly, Rivera also robbed the church members of their faith and trust in their neighbors.

When it comes to money, Gena Wilimitis from the New Mexico Securities Division reminded us that you can't assume your friends know any more than you do. Your state securities division should be your first stop when you're investigating an investment opportunity or a financial services professional. This governmental agency has a database filled with information about individuals who work in the industry and the products that are licensed for sale. If the product or the person selling it is unregistered, a red flag should go up immediately.

The New Mexico Securities Division vigorously pursues all complaints and investigates allegations involving violations of rules and regulations. The Division is authorized to "impose civil penalties, suspend or revoke licenses, bar individuals from associating with licensed broker-dealers or investment advisers, and issue orders to cease and desist from further violation of the law." In appropriate situations, the Division refers cases to local authorities and works with them to prosecute fraud and white collar crimes.

MoneyTrack **Method**

The *MoneyTrack* method is geared toward long-term investors. If you get started at a relatively young age and have the patience to invest throughout the inevitable down periods in the market, you stand a much better chance of achieving whatever the American Dream means to you.

Although dreams aren't much fun if you're too realistic, they usually don't come true unless you get real about the obstacles in your path. When it comes to financing your American Dream, this is no time for naïveté or wishful thinking.

You can't set off to achieve your goals until you really understand what your dream is. It's imperative that you develop a clear picture of what your dream lifestyle and ideal retirement will look like. You have to come up with specifics, not just a nebulous statement like, "I want to walk my dog on the beach every day." Even if you're into long walks on the beach, there are a number of hours in your dream day that must be accounted for and addressed specifically in your plan. Furthermore, some ocean-side communities don't permit dogs on the beach, even if you bring a pooper scooper.

You should enjoy this type of planning, and it's a joint effort if there's someone special in your life. You and your spouse or life partner should make time each week to map out a plan to achieve your financial and life goals.

You need to assess where you are in the quest for your own version of the American Dream. You might be better off than you think. You also need to track how your investments are performing and if you're on target to reach your financial goals.

Even if you hire someone to assist you with your investments, you still need to measure how well you're doing. Look at how your investments are performing after advisory fees and other expenses are deducted. Compare those performance results to a benchmark like the S&P 500. You might realize that after you pay the person who is guiding your investment strategy, the net returns you're receiving are less than what you would have earned in an index fund.

No matter how complicated investing may seem, there are simple strategies you can utilize. Target date retirement mutual funds are one approach. You can choose a fund that is designed for folks who want to retire at about the same time as you.

Invest a little time in educating yourself about investing. Knowing the basics of investing can keep you from making mistakes that you'll regret years from now. A little bit of knowledge can also help you avoid being suckered in by a scam artist.

It doesn't always pay to follow the pack, as we saw in another sad case of affinity fraud. There might be a rat at the head of your pack. Wherever you move, watch out for predators who want to feast on your retirement nest egg. Before making any investments, place a call to the securities regulator in the state where you're living.

Above all, remember that if you don't begin planning your unique American Dream now, you'll wake up one day and it will be too late. Depending on what your dream is, you may need to change direction now and find a new route to achieve your goal.

CHAPTER

12

Changing Lanes

A common misconception about the *MoneyTrack* method is that it will turn you into a stock market wizard who knows exactly when to buy and sell stocks and which ones to invest in or avoid like the plague. In all of our conversations with the investment pros, we learned that stock trading should be left to the people who do it for a living. The rest of us should stick with investments that we can buy and hold throughout most of our journey through life. Despite this advice, many of us still wonder if there is a quicker route to reach our investment goals.

As we sat in traffic during an episode of *MoneyTrack,* we wondered if changing lanes and darting in and out of traffic gets you to your destination any faster. All of us have had the experience where someone cuts us out or is weaving in and out ahead of us. Invariably we catch up to those aggressive drivers when we're all stopped for the same red light, unless of course that person ran it.

On *MoneyTrack* and throughout this book, we've stressed the importance of investing systematically. We've warned viewers and readers that attempting to outguess the market is the equivalent of trying to beat Ken Jennings on *Jeopardy.* Jennings holds the record for the longest winning streak on the syndicated quiz show. He won over $3 million on *Jeopardy,* and that doesn't include the money he's made from books, speeches, and appearances.

With that kind of money, you could hire someone to drive you to your destination. More than likely, however, you'll be depending on your investments to help you reach your financial objectives. With help from the investment pros, we'll try to help you get there more quickly without taking any unnecessary risks or detours.

Will Trading Stocks Get Me to My Goal Sooner?

We asked another expert if trading stocks can help you reach your financial goals more quickly. We posed our question to Dr. Nassim Nicholas Taleb, a mathematician and former Wall Street trader.

Nassim told us that the performance of individual investors is far worse than the market. He recommended that you put your money in as broad a market as you can. By taking that approach, you can be assured that you'll achieve average stock market returns.

In his best-selling book *The Black Swan: The Impact of the Highly Improbable*, Nassim argued that it's destructive for us to believe we possess enough knowledge to make a ton of money trading stocks. There are thousands and thousands of companies, and some will be profitable because they're lucky. The events that cause certain stocks to go up and down everyday are truly random and unpredictable. Not many people realize this, however, because we hear success stories from the lucky winners and you never hear from the people who have lost money.

According to Nassim, there is a difference between investors and traders. Investors are those individuals who trade infrequently and usually fare better than traders who actively buy and sell stocks. Nassim expressed his belief that you're better off staying the course rather than buying and selling stocks. Just as with changing lanes on the freeway, the benefits of stock trading are illusory.

Nassim suggested a different course of action to our viewers. He advised that you should stay the course in high-quality investments where you can spread the risk. If you have the urge to trade stocks, take that risk with a small amount of money and don't view it as investing.

Emotional investors are prone to making big mistakes. To avoid costly mistakes, it is imperative that you identify and eliminate impulse decisions. You need to remove the emotional component from your investment decisions.

When Should I Switch Lanes with My Investment Vehicles?

As Kenny Rogers sang in "The Gambler," you've got to know when to hold 'em and know when to fold 'em. Unfortunately, it's not always that easy when you're making decisions about investments.

Isaiah in Washington, D.C., asked us about some mutual funds he owned. One never seems to go up, Isaiah complained, even when the market is moving upward. In a nutshell, Isaiah wanted to know when it's time to unload a vehicle—an investment vehicle that is. Isaiah had bought a super aggressive fund that invests in smaller companies.

Deciding when it's time to sell an investment is very difficult. Manny Schiffres of *Kiplinger's Personal Finance* magazine told us that investors shouldn't switch funds without a good and valid reason. They should also have a different investment vehicle in mind that accomplishes the same objectives.

Ask yourself why you bought this mutual fund in the first place. The facts supporting your rationale for buying the investment may have changed. There are many reasons why you may wish to change investments:

- The reason you bought it no longer exists.
- You bought the fund because a particular manager was running it and that individual has left the company.
- The fund has gotten to be too big. When a mutual fund attracts new investors, it now has far more money to invest and it becomes much more difficult to find suitable investments. As the mutual fund gains capital from new investors, it loses some of the flexibility that is needed to find suitable investment opportunities.
- The fund is not performing as well as its peers. A mutual fund's peers are other funds in the same category.

Morningstar (www.morningstar.com), a research company in Chicago, can help you compare the performance of mutual funds against their peers.

When making comparisons, it helps to know a fund's alpha. Alpha isn't a fraternity or an Italian sports car that you hope to buy with the profits from your investments. A fund's alpha tells you how your mutual fund is performing when compared to its peers. The alpha indicates whether the fund's actual return has exceeded its expected return. This number helps you gauge how well the fund is performing.

A fund's anticipated return depends on a number of factors such as the types of securities it owns. For example, when a fund takes the risk of investing in small company stocks, the expected return is relatively high. The fund's actual return, however, depends on whether the people running it made shrewd decisions regarding which securities to buy and sell.

A fund's alpha will be a positive number if its actual return exceeds the expected return. If the fund underachieved and the actual number falls short of its expected return, its alpha will be a negative number.

You can compare a fund's alpha with other mutual funds on Web sites like Morningstar.com. If a fund's alpha is consistently positive, it is more likely to be a strong performer, although past performance does not assure you of favorable results down the road. If a fund's alpha is consistently negative, it may be time to consider ending your relationship.

Because selling a fund may have tax repercussions, you should consult with your tax advisor before unloading it. One possibility is for you to sit tight on your current investment in the fund. You should consider putting your future investments in a different mutual fund.

When Your Circumstances Dictate Changing Investments

On an episode of the classic TV sitcom *Seinfeld*, George and Jerry discussed how to break up with someone. One technique was the "It's not you, it's me" plan. The goal of their strategy was to purportedly blame themselves for the breakup.

It may very well be you who needs to sever your relationship with a mutual fund and the reasons may have nothing to do with the fund's performance. Here are a few of the possibilities:

- Your financial circumstances change.
- Your risk tolerance changes.
- Your time horizon changes and you will need the money sooner or later than anticipated.

If you've reached the point when it's time to withdraw money from your investment nest egg, it may be a good idea to tap the mutual fund that isn't performing as well as others in which you're invested. In that instance, you can blame both yourself and the mutual fund for the break-up.

Using the Stars to Screen Mutual Funds

With thousands of mutual funds to choose from, a good starting point is to check their ratings from Morningstar. The research company evaluates mutual funds and stocks using a very straightforward rating system. Morningstar's ratings range from one star, the lowest, to five stars, the highest.

Whereas fund analysts look forward to predict a mutual fund's performance, Morningstar's ratings look backward. Although fund analysts' ratings may be somewhat subjective, Morningstar's ratings only use quantitative measures to evaluate performance.

Morningstar's star ratings rank mutual funds based on their relative performance over the last 3, 5, and 10 years. Each mutual fund is ranked within its category. The others in that category are the fund's peers. Here is how Morningstar's rankings are broken down:

- Five stars: Top 10 percent in that category
- Four stars: The next 22.5 percent in that category
- Three stars: The middle 35 percent
- Two stars: The next 22.5 percent
- One star: The bottom 10 percent

Even if a fund receives five stars, there is no guarantee that it will perform well in years to come.

Many financial services firms offer their own ratings of stocks and mutual funds. For example, Schwab Equity Ratings identifies stocks the company believes will outperform or underperform the market over the next 12 months. The guidance is available to all Schwab clients. Schwab offers statistics claiming that by investing in stocks with A ratings, an investor could have earned more than the return of the S&P 500. The ratings range from A to F.

Which Lane Gets Me to Where I Want to Go?

The reason most of us switch lanes is because we think the other one will take us faster to where we want to go. The problem is, however, that we don't always know which lane is the right one to get us to our destination.

Just as you need a road map or Mapquest.com to find certain destinations, you need guidance on how to reach your financial objectives. Unfortunately, there are a number of routes that you can take to get you there. If you hope to retire in a few years, or even 40 years from now, you need to map out your trip now. Although the route won't be the same for everyone and you will probably need to make adjustments along the way, you can at least head off in the right direction. As long as you head in the right direction, you'll be far better off than if you haven't left the driveway yet.

Most big cities have an HOV (high-occupancy vehicle) lane for cars with more than one occupant. I keep warning Jack that having Chloe in the car doesn't count. The HOV lane usually has less traffic and will take you more quickly to your destination. At different stages of your life, there are HOV lanes that can help you reach your financial goals. Although no financial route is the same for everyone and there may be potholes along the way, there are general directions you can follow at various stages of your life.

HOV Lane for Your Twenties and Thirties

If you start saving and investing for retirement while you're in your twenties and thirties, you will be traveling in the HOV lane and will have a huge head start on reaching your destination. It might even enable you to retire at a relatively young age. Here are some tips for putting your investments on cruise control.

> **Sign Up Today for Retirement Savings Plans:** You should sign up today for your employer's retirement savings plan, even if you expect to hit the road for another job in the coming months or years. Aside from the tax savings, you'll be surprised by how much you can put away, especially if your employer matches some or all of your contributions. In addition, depending upon your income, you may be eligible for the retirement savings contributions tax credit. Even better, by investing in your twenties and thirties, you take advantage of the time value of money that we discussed in Chapter 1.
>
> If you work for yourself or have a side business, you shouldn't plow all of your profits back into the business. You can take advantage of retirement savings vehicles for the self-employed, including a SIMPLE-IRA and a SEP-IRA. Even a one-person firm can set up a 401(k) retirement savings plan.

Don't Cash Out if You Leave: If you leave your employer, resist the temptation to spend the amount you've put away. You'll pay taxes on the money, along with a premature distribution penalty of 10 percent. The editors of *Consumer Reports* have called this one of the million-dollar blunders. It's not just the money you're losing in taxes right now. The real loss is the earnings you're losing over the years in a tax-sheltered retirement account.

When you leave your employer, you have several options. By law, you are permitted to keep your retirement savings plan with your current employer, assuming you have more than $5,000. Another option is to transfer that 401(k) to your new employer's plan. You might also roll over the funds in your retirement savings plan to an Individual Retirement Account. According to the Employee Benefit Research Institute, the average rollover in 2006 was $334,176. If that number seems high, remember that rollovers typically occur at the end of an employee's career.

Any Contribution Is Better than Nothing: Don't worry about contributing the maximum amount to your retirement savings plan. You should make a contribution, even if you can only afford to put away 1 or 2 percent of your salary.

Invest Like a Pro for the Next Few Decades: Since you're a long way from your destination, you're much better off with equity investments. Make sure your portfolio includes a variety of equity investments and not just company stock.

Become a Habitual Investor: Although employers don't use waterboarding to force you to save for your retirement, you can force yourself to invest. When you sign up for your employer's retirement savings plan, money is saved and invested automatically every payday. You can also arrange for money to be deducted from your checking account to fund an IRA. Once you sign up, mutual fund companies will automatically debit your bank account and deposit the proceeds into the investment you've chosen.

The biggest advantage to starting your retirement journey at a young age is that you have a long time horizon. Starting early gives you a huge head start, especially if you choose equity investments like stocks. Investing on a regular basis helps to curb stock market risks. Historically, investments in the stock market have produced the highest rates of return.

Consider a Roth IRA: Aside from retirement savings plans through your job, Roth IRAs can give your investments a smooth ride while keeping you sheltered from taxes. Although your contribution does not reduce your current taxable income, all of your earnings over the years may be withdrawn tax-free someday. Usually, that someday is age 59½, but there are ways to withdraw your money before then. You can always withdraw your contributions, but not the earnings, without a penalty or taxes. First-time home-buyers may withdraw up to $10,000 in earnings without paying a penalty. You will, however, pay taxes on the withdrawal and that undermines the value of opening a Roth IRA.

HOV Lane for Your Forties and Fifties

When you reach your forties and fifties, you need to be absolutely certain that you're still in the HOV lane to retirement and haven't taken a wrong turn. It's important to find out where you are now by calculating your net worth. You should estimate how much income you'll need to live on after retiring.

Most people depend on Social Security for some of that income. As you get closer to retirement, your Social Security benefits statement becomes much more meaningful. Here's why:

- Your projected benefit will be much more accurate, because your earnings picture is much clearer. Social Security benefits are based on your 35 highest years of earnings.
- The value of your Social Security benefit in today's dollars is also more accurate, because there are fewer years until you need the money. You're in a much better position to assess your income needs and how inflation will affect your benefit.

If you're age 25 or older, updated benefits statements usually arrive about three months before your birthday. When yours arrives, make certain the earnings credited to your account are correct. If you have questions, you can contact Social Security by calling 800–772–1213 or visiting www.ssa.gov.

Don't plan your retirement party yet for age 65. As we saw in Chapter 4, if you were born in 1960 or later, you'll need to wait until age 67 to collect your full Social Security check. If you were born between 1943 and 1954, you must wait until age 66 to collect full benefits. If you were born between 1955 and 1959, your full retirement age is a particular month between age 66 and 67.

Many interactive Web sites can assist you with your retirement planning. As a starting point, use the American Savings Education Council's Ballpark Estimate which helps you calculate how much savings you'll need to live comfortably in retirement. It can be found at www.choosetosave.org/ballpark/index.cfm?fa=interactive. It is still one of the easiest planning tools to use.

If you haven't done so already, examine your spending habits. Maybe your spending is disproportionate to your income. Over the course of a month, track how much you're spending from large expenditures to the most seemingly insignificant purchase. You may make the shocking discovery that your outgo is larger than your income.

If you haven't started saving for retirement yet, you need to step on the gas. As we saw in Chapter 4, you can contribute up to $15,500 into a 401(k) retirement savings plan in 2008. If you are age 50 or older, you can contribute an extra $5,000 to the plan.

In 2008 and 2009, you are permitted to contribute a maximum of $5,000 to an IRA. If you're over age 50, you can put away an extra $1,000 for a total of $6,000. If you cannot contribute the maximum amount, increase your contribution to any retirement savings plan for which you're eligible.

To stay in the HOV lane, you must continue investing, even if you're saving or paying for a child's education. Money put away in IRAs and retirement savings plans is less likely to hurt your child's prospects for getting financial aid.

Even if you are in your forties or fifties, it is still going to be a while until you need to begin withdrawing money, so a large percentage of your investments should be in the stock market. Your risk tolerance and the amount of time you have until retirement are key factors in determining your mix of investments.

If you're uncomfortable determining your own mix of investments, consider investing in a target date retirement fund. These funds offer a professionally managed and diversified portfolio, based on your risk tolerance, age, and investment objectives. They are also referred to as life-cycle or lifestyle funds. Be careful, however, because the fees are sometimes quite high, which can reduce the return on your investment.

HOV Lane for Your Sixties

Whether you're anxious to retire or not, you should be well on your way to funding your dream retirement by age 60. If you haven't made much progress, it's imperative that you contribute the maximum allowable amount to any retirement savings plan that is available to you. You can also pick up the pace by investing any bonuses, cash gifts, or windfalls that come your way. If you reside in a two-income household, consider banking one of those paychecks and saving the other.

Although you're getting older, a portion of your investment portfolio should still be in stocks. Stock market investments will help your portfolio to keep pace with inflation. Financial planner Jonathan Pond tells his clients that they should invest based on the assumption that they will live until age 95. To maintain your lifestyle for 30 more years or more, some of your money should still be invested in stocks.

With retirement on the horizon, you should be making a gradual shift to more conservative investments. One option is a balanced fund that invests in a mixture of stocks and bonds. In addition, many retirement savings plans offer stable value funds to participants, which grow in value but also protect your principal.

Even though some of your portfolio should be in the stock market, you need to implement a plan so you aren't forced to liquidate holdings for living expenses. Many financial planners recommend to older clients that they keep three to five years of living expenses in cash investments like a money market fund, so they're not put in the position of liquidating stock holdings when the market is in a slump.

A perk of getting older is that age 59½ is the lucky day when you can access your retirement savings accounts like IRAs without a penalty. Before making withdrawals, however, it's imperative that you take care to avoid running out of money. As a general rule, you should try to avoid withdrawals of more than 4 percent of your nest egg per year. If your portfolio is invested too conservatively and is only generating a modest income, you might need to withdraw even less.

You should also choose the right time to collect Social Security. Although you may begin receiving benefits as early as age 62, your monthly check will be permanently reduced based on your full retirement age. In addition, until you reach your full retirement age, your Social Security benefits will be reduced if you work part time and earn more than the maximum amount allowed.

Fixed annuities are one way to avoid outliving your money. You can structure a payout in retirement to provide income for life for yourself and your spouse or life partner. As we saw in Chapter 11, however, watch out for salespeople who market variable annuities and equity indexed annuities, because the fees may be quite steep and the products are very complicated. In addition, most annuities will charge surrender fees if you cash out before a designated date, which might be as long as 15 years.

By the time you reach your sixties, you should know where you will be living after retiring. Once that decision is made, you'll have a pretty good idea how much your retirement lifestyle will cost. Add up your anticipated income and outgo to determine if you have enough money with which to retire. Use all of your fingers and toes, as well as a calculator, to add up your anticipated expenses and try to be as specific as possible when you're crunching the numbers. Don't rely on rules of thumb that say your retirement expenses will be 70 to 80 percent of your current spending.

As you decide where and when to retire, think about what you plan to do with your free time. Your decision about where to live should take those post-retirement activities into consideration. Also, if you dream about pursuing a post-retirement career, make sure that type of work is feasible in the area where you're moving. Aim high but try to be realistic about what your career choices are.

By age 60, you should make your decision as to whether to buy a long-term care insurance policy from a reputable company. As you make this decision, keep in mind that Medicare and Medicare supplemental policies provide little coverage for long-term care expenses. Without a policy to cover the rising cost of long-term care, you may be forced to rely on your personal wealth or turn to Medicaid to pay these expenses. To qualify for Medicaid, you are usually required to exhaust most of your assets, although your spouse is protected to some degree.

Scam Alert

Nicholas Guarino was a con artist who preyed on Kansas investors. Guarino conned them into a bogus scheme to make money trading futures contracts. A futures contract is an agreement to buy or sell a certain commodity or financial instrument at some point in the future at a previously-agreed-on price. For example, you might buy an oil futures contract. Approximately 350 people complained to the Kansas attorney general's office following their dealings with Guarino.

Guarino used the Internet, a newsletter, and his radio program to lure unsuspecting investors. Guarino convinced them that he was hated on Wall Street because he knew too much. He promised returns of 100 to 200 percent. He and his company, Wall Street Underground, Inc., defrauded and deceived customers regarding their can't-miss trading system.

The U.S. District Court in Kansas ordered Guarino and his company to pay $2.4 million in restitution to victims and fined them $7 million. Most of the money, however, was never recovered. The Commodity Futures Trading Commission searched three continents looking for Guarino but couldn't find him.

Investing in commodities, futures contracts, and options is for extremely sophisticated investors. As the old joke goes, how do you make a small fortune trading options? You start with a large one. Don't feel bad if you don't get it. I had to explain the joke to Jack.

It is also important that you don't feel bad or embarrassed if you're being take advantage of by a con man or you've been scammed. On *MoneyTrack*, we met a number of investors, especially older ones, who were too embarrassed to admit they made the mistake of trusting someone who shouldn't have been trusted. Reporting problems immediately to the office of the attorney general in your state and securities regulators gives you a much better chance of getting back your money and keeps others from being scammed.

Chris Biggs is Mr. Big when it comes to protecting Kansas investors. Chris is the Kansas Securities Commissioner. In a press release dated January 28, 2008, Chris warned investors to use common sense before investing. According to Chris, "Get-rich-quick promises are usually signs of investment fraud." During difficult economic times, bogus investments run rampant. His office has a toll-free number, 800–40-SCAMS, that enables state residents to check out someone touting a get-rich-quick investment.

HOV Lane for Your Retirement Years

When you retire, you can leave the HOV lane and cruise life's highway at a more leisurely pace. Make sure to use your turn signal, but for goodness' sake, please shut it off after changing lanes.

Even after you retire, you still need to keep some of your investments in the fast lane during the coming decades. Otherwise, you risk outliving your money. One possibility is fixed annuities that assure you of a certain level of income. There are also mutual funds that pick the right mix of investments to generate income for older investors.

Many retirees are ready to downsize to a smaller and cheaper home at this stage of their life. Assuming your new home costs less than what you made on your former residence, you can use your profits to build up your nest egg and increase your income. You might even enjoy working part time in retirement. Once you reach your full retirement age, you are allowed to earn as much as you want without impacting your Social Security benefits.

Above all, watch out for scam artists who can impact your financial well-being. There are always con artists who hope to downsize your nest egg and make it their own. Though reverse mortgages are touted as a way to increase your income without selling your home, the fees are steep and you need to watch out for con artists who have big plans for the money you draw out of your home.

Changing Your Mindset about Investing

Just as most people can't or won't change their driving habits, many investors can't change their mindset when it comes to investing. As I've found with Chloe, you can't teach an old dog new tricks—or any tricks, for that matter. Try to look introspectively to determine whether it's time to change your attitudes toward saving and investing.

I'm fascinated by the field of behavioral finance. Experts in this field study the interaction of finance and psychology. They have identified psychological obstacles that stand in the way of successful investment decision making.

One obstacle is called availability bias. This is a tendency to judge a situation, as well as the likely outcome, by its similarity to past situations. If you were burned once by investing, you might be reluctant to try again. Ironically, it might have been your strategy, or lack of one, that caused you to fail the first time.

Tied in with availability bias is representativeness heuristic, according to Greg Forsythe who discussed this topic in the Spring and Summer 2007 issues of *On Investing*. Heuristics are rules of thumb that guide our behavior when we're confronted with situations that we've encountered before. These heuristics can lead to serious investment mistakes.

Jeff Ryan of Schwab Equity Ratings expressed his belief in the Winter 2007 issue of *On Investing* that the Initial Public Offering (IPO) market is an example of representativeness heuristic. Many investors developed their perception of the IPO market from the days when high-tech companies were turning ordinary investors into millionaires. The current IPO market is much different and may not be nearly as lucrative.

As they analyze stocks, investors should remember the concept of cognitive dissonance theory from their first course in psychology. When we analyze a situation, we tend to believe information that agrees with our current opinions and discard information that contradicts what we believe to be a fact. To apply this theory to investing, you may make your mind up to invest in a particular stock and then you ignore all of the data that tells you to avoid this particular investment.

In an earlier chapter, we looked at what some psychologists call a *Depression mentality*. Older Americans who grew up during the Great Depression watched as their family's finances fell apart almost overnight. There is a tendency among folks with that mentality to be obsessive about saving. Even after reaching the time in life when they can be more free with their money, they tend to worry about losing everything. As a result, if a loved one has a Depression mentality, he or she might still be watching every penny even into the eighties and nineties.

There is a different kind of depression that can affect your spending. Mark Jewell of the Associated Press reported the results of a study showing that people's spending judgment sometimes goes out the window when they're feeling depressed. A study by researchers from Harvard, Carnegie Mellon, Stanford and the University of Pittsburgh concluded that sadness can trigger a chain of emotions that make people more extravagant. According to the study, subjects were willing to spend more when they were feeling blue, presumably to make themselves feel better.

All of us know people who are shopaholics. They seem to become exhilarated by a trip to the mall or a major shopping spree. Shopping appears to make them feel better about themselves and brightens their mood. Unfortunately, after the thrill of shopping wears off, their mood darkens, especially when they realize how much money they spent during their excursion to the mall.

Some people find it very difficult to delay gratification. When they need something, they need it now. Developing the ability to save and invest means creating a mindset that helps you realize that you're working toward a goal that is far more meaningful than the trinket or gadget that means so much to you right now.

One day, hopefully, you'll get a sense of satisfaction by looking at your portfolio and seeing how far you've come. You'll realize that saving and investing doesn't mean depriving yourself of all the things you want out of life. In fact, it enhances your ability to make your dreams come true.

MoneyTrack Method

Investment decisions are much like the ones we make behind the wheel. They're sometimes nothing more than impulsive and emotional responses. We're not conscious of our behavior. In contrast, smart drivers and investors think rationally and carefully plan each move they make. Because the *MoneyTrack* method encourages investments at regular intervals, no matter what the economic climate is, it removes the emotional component from investing.

Too many people avoid investing because of fear of the unknown and lack of knowledge. Investing should be logical and simple. It is usually greed that pushes investors to take inordinate risks with their money.

When you're driving, you shouldn't be competing with other drivers who pass you by. Similarly, your investments need to be right for you. It shouldn't matter if someone tells you he's making a fortune with his investments or getting a higher rate of return. According to virtually all of the investment pros we interviewed on *MoneyTrack*, you are almost always better off settling for keeping pace with the market by investing in index funds. Exchange-traded funds (ETFs) also tie your investment to an index composed of many securities.

If you prefer the fast track to investing, be prepared for some twists and turns. Avoid turning over the wheel to a supposedly proven trading system that purportedly leaves others in the dust. And even if you think you've mastered a trading system, avoid investing any more than you can afford to lose.

Don't let a scam artist drive your investment portfolio over the guard rail. Never ever let your guard down, and keep your eyes on the road.

If you've been driving a long time, you're probably sure of yourself by now. With a little experience and knowledge, you can also become a confident investor. And just as driving lessons help new drivers, investors will benefit from a few lessons from Warren Buffett.

13

Advice from the Ultimate Investment Pro—Warren Buffett

Our goal on *MoneyTrack* is to teach viewers how to invest with the best of them, and there are none better than Warren Buffett. When I interviewed him on *MoneyTrack*, I came to realize that even the most successful investor in the world relies on a common sense and logical approach that all of us can utilize to some degree. Although we'll never match his success, we can use some of his advice to become better investors.

Investing Doesn't Have to Be Complicated

Warren Buffett is easy to like, because of his humility and ability to discuss investments in plain English. You would never know that you're talking to the richest man in the world. According to an article posted on Forbes.com on March 7, 2008, Warren replaced his good friend and bridge partner, Bill Gates, in the top spot on the list of the world's richest people. Warren's net worth jumped $10 billion to $62 billion based on valuations as of February 11, 2008.

Aside from his net worth, here are some tidbits you might not know about Warren, the most famous stock market investor of our time:

- He formed his first investment partnership with money he collected from friends and family.
- His holding company, Berkshire Hathaway, owns and operates more than 70 businesses with large stakes in companies like

Coca-Cola, American Express, The Washington Post Company, Fruit of the Loom, GEICO, and many others.

- Even though Berkshire Hathaway's profits were down in 2007, its per-share book value increased 11 percent compared to a 5.5 percent increase in the S&P 500s value.
- If you had put $10,000 in Berkshire Hathaway in 1965, you'd have more than $50 million today.

Although almost all of us missed the opportunity to invest in Berkshire Hathaway on the ground floor, we'll set off to find our own investments that might be worth $50 million someday—with a little help from Warren Buffett.

The Secret Millionaire's Club

I visited Warren in his home town of Omaha to learn more about how to invest. Often referred to as the "Oracle of Omaha," Warren bought his home on Farnum Street in 1957 for $32,000 and he still lives there. Warren's childhood helped to shape his entrepreneurial spirit.

Warren has possessed the ability to make money since he was six. He would buy six bottles of Coca-Cola from his grandfather for a quarter. He would then sell them for five cents each and make a nickel. When he lived in Washington, D.C., he delivered newspapers, which helped him to learn about money and human nature. Working also taught him about responsibility. According to Adam Shell's article in the June 5, 2008 edition of *USA Today*, he filed his first tax return at age 13.

Among his many projects, Warren worked on a cartoon to help young people learn about investing called *The Secret Millionaire's Club*. Warren performed a voice-over for the animated character and played himself in the series. The cartoon teaches kids that good investing habits should be learned early. It also helps them to become financially literate. The cartoon also makes the very important point that our behavioral traits affect our ability to invest, whether you're 9 or 90.

Each of the children in *The Secret Millionaire's Club* is a bit different. One of the kids in the cartoon is very rational and is only concerned with facts as they analyze a stock. Another is too afraid he will lose money, so he's always looking at the down side. A third character is the eternal optimist who only sees the positives of every investment. Finally, the fourth character is the risk taker who will invest in almost anything.

Whether in animated form or in person, Warren offers terrific advice on managing your money and becoming a better investor such as:

- Develop the right habits relating to money and that means saving.
- Don't get into debt, because once you do, you're behind the eight ball.
- Giving children a modest allowance is good, as long as there are duties that go along with it.

Warren believes strongly that you think through the investment process and thoroughly analyze the up side and down side before making a decision.

Warren isn't a fan of paying someone to give you investment advice. If you don't have the time or inclination to research every investment you're considering, he recommends investing in a low-cost index fund. You'll get a decent return over 10 or 20 years and you don't need to pick stock market winners to make a profit. You won't be the next Warren Buffett, but you're likely to become a successful investor.

The online edition of *Fortune* magazine reported on June 9, 2008 that Warren puts his money where his mouth is when it comes to index funds. He made a bet with a New York City money management firm that an index fund tied to the S&P 500 will be a better investment over the next ten years than five carefully-selected hedge funds. Warren and the money management firm have each wagered $320,000. Warren bet that after fees, costs, and other expenses are deducted, a low-cost S&P 500 index fund sold by Vanguard will deliver better returns than the five hedge funds chosen by the money management firm.

Buffett-Style Investing

Even though investors like Warren Buffett come around only once in our lifetime, the rest of us can utilize his advice. Be careful, however, when you tell people that your investment style is similar to Warren's. It's inevitable that you'll come out on the short end of that comparison.

One of the most famous moments in political history occurred in 1988 during the vice-presidential debate between Lloyd Benson and Dan Quayle. Quayle, who was accused of lacking experience, compared his tenure in Congress with John Kennedy's. In a stunning put-down, Benson observed, "Senator, I served with Jack Kennedy. I knew Jack Kennedy. Jack Kennedy was a friend of mine. Senator, you're no Jack Kennedy."

You might be afraid that if you tell anyone you're investing like Warren Buffett, you'll be on the receiving end of a similar put-down. After hearing about your investments, someone might say, "You, my friend, are no Warren Buffett." Though you'll never achieve his success, you can still try to emulate Warren Buffett's style.

Another guest on our program, Pat Terrion, teaches Buffett-style investing at the University of Connecticut. According to Pat, Warren's approach is to take one company at a time and study it inside and out. You only invest in that stock if it meets your desired criteria. If you don't have the time or inclination to investigate individual companies, you are better off with a broadly diversified index fund. Whereas Warren gets superior returns by investing his way, most of us should be more than satisfied with average stock market returns.

Warren, according to Pat, has urged investors to stay within their circle of competence. In the late 1990s, Warren backed away from the technology sector, because he felt it was beyond him. In 2000, technology stocks plummeted. According to Shell's article, he was called a "dinosaur" for avoiding tech stocks.

If you'd like to imitate Warren with your fun money, Pat suggested three strategies.

1. Invest in a business you understand and use the products everyday.
2. Make sure the business is consistent over time and it will grow.
3. Pick a company that doesn't require that most or all of its capital be reinvested.

Newer companies tend to be expanding constantly. All of their earnings go into growing the business.

CNBC's Web site, www.cnbc.com, has a regular feature called, "Warren Buffett Watch: Keeping Track of America's Billionaire Next Door."

In a November 23, 2007 posting, Morningstar's Paul Larson suggested five simple steps for investing like Warren Buffett. Larson expressed the opinion that a focused and nominally intelligent person can utilize Warren's investment strategy. Assuming you meet those criteria, here are Larson's suggestions for investing like Warren Buffett:

1. Buy businesses, not stocks.
2. Look for companies that are structurally protected from competition, such as a company that has strong patents and brands. This gives them competitive advantages for the long-term or what Warren calls a "wide economic moat."
3. Let a business' intrinsic value be your touchstone and ignore momentum and charts. (Stock charts provide information regarding trading patterns.)
4. You should always buy a company at a discount to its value.
5. Be greedy when others are frightened and be frightened when others are greedy.

In other words, investors should think independently and take a contrarian approach.

In a *U.S. News & World Report* story posted online on July 29, 2007, Paul J. Lim wrote an article called "Six Keys to Investing Buffett Style." The article fleshes out some of Warren's investment strategies. Although Warren is a value investor, Lim wrote that he isn't "afraid to deviate from the classic definition of value investing" that he learned from Benjamin Graham. Unlike Graham, Warren is far more concerned about the quality of the companies he invests in. He'd rather own a comfortable business at a questionable price than a questionable business at comfortable price.

Whereas most value investors spread their risk among hundreds of stock, Warren's billions are concentrated in far fewer companies. Part of his approach is to be patient and when you swing, swing for the fences. Warren's strategy is to keep money in cash until he sees the right investment opportunity.

According to Lim's article, Warren appreciates the importance of not falling in the hole. If you invest a dollar in a stock and it goes down 50 percent, you have 50 cents left. At that point, you need a 100 percent return just to break even.

When Warren analyzes an investment, he looks at return on equity. Return on equity is calculated by dividing a company's net income by its shareholders' equity. Return on equity reveals how efficiently a company's profits are growing.

Warren attempts to identify companies with a good chance of being successful for the next 25 years. As mentioned earlier, Warren shunned the technology sector—because he couldn't predict which companies would have competitive advantages in 18 months.

Deciphering Your Investments

In February 2008, the SEC published proposed amendments to the document (Form ADV) used by investment advisers to disclose their fees, business practices, and potential conflicts of interest. The SEC urged investment advisers to make this disclosure in plain English.

In 1998, the SEC published *A Plain English Handbook* dealing with how to create clear SEC disclosure documents. The Preface to the handbook was written by none other than Warren Buffett. Near the beginning of the Preface to the handbook, which can be found online at http://www.sec.gov/news/extra/handbook.htm, Warren wrote, "For more than forty years, I've studied the documents that public companies file. Too often, I've been unable to decipher just what is being said or, worse yet, had to conclude that nothing was being said." Unfortunately, many of the corporate reports you must sort through to investigate an investment are filled with jargon and don't resemble plain English.

As noted in the Preface to *A Plain English Handbook*, Warren tries to write simply and clearly when working on Berkshire Hathaway's annual report.

> When writing Berkshire Hathaway's annual report, I pretend that I'm talking to my sisters. I have no trouble picturing them: Though highly intelligent, they are not experts in accounting or finance. They will understand plain English but jargon may puzzle them. My goal is simply to give them the information I would wish them to supply me if our positions were reversed. To succeed, I don't need to be Shakespeare; I must, though, have a sincere desire to inform.
>
> No siblings to write to? Borrow mine: Just begin with "Dear Doris and Bertie."

As I found when I interviewed Warren, he is just as plain-spoken in person and tells you what you want to know.

Even though the SEC expects investment advisers and companies to write in plain English, it may not happen any time soon. As we've said before, if you don't understand a company's business plan, you really shouldn't be investing in its stock. Similarly, if an investment advisory firm cannot disclose its fees, business practices and conflicts of interest in plain English, find someone who can achieve that goal.

Develop Your Own Investment Style

A few pages in a book won't teach you how to invest like Warren Buffett. Nevertheless, when you make your first billion, you'll know who to thank. If you want to invest in individual stocks rather than an investment based on an index, you should learn from the pros but develop your own investment style. Here are some elementary tips on how to pick your own stocks and evaluate companies.

Peter Lynch, who built his reputation at Fidelity Investments, advised investors, "Invest in what you know." He suggested that when you walk the mall, keep your eyes open for potential investments. You really can't stop there, however. A great deal of research is required before you make that investment or any investment for that matter.

Once you've invested in a company, you still need to keep tabs on it. Even if you're a buy-and-hold investor who hopes to keep a stock for years, you may see signs that the company isn't what it used to be. Perhaps, you invested in The Sharper Image after one of your trips to the mall. Sadly, in February 2008, the company filed for bankruptcy. According to an article posted on The Motley Fool's Web site, www.motleyfool.com, on February 20, 2008, the handwriting was on the wall for several years prior to the bankruptcy filing. According to the article, The Sharper Image's "gee-whiz gadgetry" had become too expensive and was available at other retailers. On a more personal level, you and your friends might have noticed that you rarely bought there anymore.

Or maybe investment ideas come to you on a full stomach. Have you ever eaten at a great restaurant that's owned by a publicly traded company? Your first instinct might be to invest in that company. While that's a good starting point, stock analysis is much more complicated.

As part of your analysis, you need to look at what other restaurants are owned by the company. For example, Seasons 52 is a relatively new restaurant chain owned by Darden Restaurants, Inc. in Orlando, Florida. The restaurant serves freshly harvested foods that are high in taste and low in calories. The menu changes daily, so the chefs can use whatever fresh foods and vegetables are in season.

As you investigate Darden, you find that the company also owns the Olive Garden, Bahama Breeze, and Red Lobster restaurant chains. Maybe those restaurants aren't your cup of tea and might make you think twice about investing in Darden. Or perhaps you read that Smokey Bones wasn't performing as well as expected and the company got rid of that restaurant chain.

You still must do more than a superficial analysis before investing in a company, whether it's Darden or any stock. As you begin your research, you should investigate the company's opportunities for growth. Whereas Seasons 52 only has restaurants in a few states, there may be an oversaturation of Olive Garden and Red Lobster restaurants. To increase its earnings per share, a company like Darden must open up new restaurants to increase profitability. Many companies, however, overexpand and hurt their profits.

You should also analyze how the company will fare during anticipated economic conditions. If a recession is expected and consumers are feeling anxious about the economy, they might stop eating out as much. If a once-a-week trip to the Olive Garden becomes once a month, the company's profits will be damaged.

Acquisitions also impact a company's opportunities for increasing profits. Darden has acquired the Longhorn Steakhouse chain, as well as The Capital Grille, which is a more upscale restaurant.

When inflation is roaring, restaurateurs face rising food prices and energy costs. Not all of these expenses can be passed on to consumers, especially if they are tightening their belts which they usually do during tough economic times or after having the all-you-can-eat pasta bowl at the Olive Garden. On the one hand, higher menu prices often motivate consumers to change their dining habits and they might never come back again. On the other hand, if a restaurant bites the bullet and holds the line on prices or offers specials to attract customers, profit margins might shrink.

Whereas Warren looks for companies that have a long-term competitive advantage, restaurants face stiff competition from national chains and local favorites. As part of your analysis, you might poll your friends and relatives to figure out their restaurant of choice, whether it's one of Darden's or another chain like Chili's or Applebee's.

Scam Alert

Warren Buffett believes that to become a successful investor, you need to get in the habit of saving money, not borrowing it. To invest in a home, however, most of us do need to borrow money. And if you're really desperate for a loan, you may become the victim of mortgage fraud.

Mortgage fraud is one of the hottest scams in the country. On *MoneyTrack,* we talked with several people who found out about mortgage fraud first-hand. They lost money on what is known as an *advanced fee loan.*

Advanced fee loans victimize people who can least afford the losses. Typically, you are approved for a loan without even completing an application. To get the loan, however, you must pay a "processing fee," "servicing fee," or a "security deposit." You might even be told that you're required to pay insurance on the loan before you get it or that some of the fees will be refunded if you pay your loan back on time.

One of the people we talked to was told that she would have to wire the scammer $1,900 in three installments as a security deposit. Another lost $3,000 to a company that didn't even exist. A third told us about his experience with Philip Butler, a friendly and seemingly trustworthy individual in Frankford, Indiana.

As we found out, Butler was anything but honest. He met clients at restaurants and other public places. There was no office where they might track him down. Before the authorities caught up with him, he had made off with over $2 million in advance fees for bogus loans. Butler was eventually arrested in 2006 on multiple counts of fraud while acting as a loan broker.

In 2006, 4.5 million Americans lost money to advance fee loan schemes, and that number may be underreported. Some victims were probably too embarrassed to admit their mistake. Don't let your desperation for a loan cloud your judgment and cause you to overlook the warning signs that you are about to be scammed.

The Senate Committee on Aging has heard testimony regarding mortgage fraud aimed primarily at seniors. In addition, the January/February, 2008 issue of *AARP Magazine* warned people about mortgage rescue scams. Scammers offer to take over the homeowner's mortgage, promising that the family will be permitted to stay in their house. Homeowners unwittingly sign over the deed without realizing they will soon be out on the street.

There are trends in the restaurant industry that change frequently. One year consumers want healthy dining. Soon thereafter, they favor a restaurant where the portions might feed a defensive lineman for the New York Giants.

All of these factors and more might influence your decision whether to invest in Darden or any company. Once you've identified a few stocks that intrigue you, your next step is to see what technical analysis of the investment is available from the people who do this for a living. Web sites like MSN Money, moneycentral.msn.com/home.asp, can provide you with analysts' recommendations regarding a particular stock. The analysts' ratings will range from strongly recommending that you buy the stock to the other extreme that encourages you to sell shares you already own.

Analyzing Stocks Like a Pro

Many investment pros buy and sell securities based on fundamental analysis. This analysis differs from pro to pro, and there are a number of different approaches. As we touched on already, value investors seek to buy a company that is worth more than they are paying. Value investing is based on the assumption that if you compare a company's stock price to its value, you can tell if it's overpriced or underpriced.

To make this analysis, value investors will look at factors such as these:

- Price-earnings ratio
- Sales
- Dividends
- Book value

A company's book value is the sum of its assets over and above its liabilities that shareholders would receive if the company were liquidated.

Fundamental analysis for a growth investor might focus on different factors:

- The business model
- Growth rate
- Potential for capital appreciation
- Market potential for new products

Some experts do not believe in fundamental analysis. Their belief is that all of the major players use fundamental analysis, so there is no advantage to using it.

Many investment pros rely on quantitative analysis to analyze stocks. They are focusing on numbers, not the quality of the underlying business. Advocates of this approach evaluate securities based on measurable factors such as profit margins, revenues, earnings and market share. Most of our readers do not have the time or tools to analyze individual stocks. Brokerage firms make analysts' reports available to customers. There is no guarantee, however, that the analysis is on target. Even the best analysts pick winners and losers. You will also find that many people question the objectivity and

Avoiding Advance Fee Loan Shark Attacks

To help others avoid becoming a statistic, the New York attorney general's office has posted this warning about advance fee loan sharks on its Web site, www.oag.state.ny.us/consumer/tips/loan_sharks.html:

Don't pay for a promise. It's illegal for companies doing business by phone to promise you a loan and ask you to pay for it before they deliver.

Advance Fees for a loan are illegal. Ignore any offer that guarantees you a loan for a fee paid in advance. Legitimate lenders never "guarantee" or say that you will receive a loan before you apply, especially if you have a damaged credit history or no credit record at all.

Watch those fees! State law limits the total fee a loan broker can assess (after loan approval) to 0.5 percent of a nonmortgage loan. If anyone tries to charge you more, report it to the Attorney General's office.

Never give your credit card, bank account numbers, or social security number, whether it be asked for over the telephone, by e-mail, or any other means unless you are familiar with the company and know why the information is necessary.

If you don't have the offer in hand—or confirmed in writing—and you are asked to pay, don't do it! It's fraud, and it's illegal!

If you have credit or debt problems or concerns about your personal finances, you may want to contact your local nonprofit credit counseling agency for assistance. To do so, contact the National Foundation for Consumer Credit at 800-388–2227 or www.nfcc.org or the Association of Independent Consumer Credit Counseling Agencies at 703-934–6118 or www.aiccca.org.

wisdom of stock analysts. Furthermore, by the time the information reaches you, it might be old news and the stock will already have gone up or down. As Warren wrote in the 1992 Annual Report of Berkshire Hathaway, "The only value of stock forecasters is to make fortune-tellers look good."

IMHO, you are far better off with index funds that allow you to invest in a cross-section of the market, rather than buying and selling individual stocks. If you have some fun money to invest that might otherwise be spent on eating out, you can speculate on a stock or two. OTOH, you could eat out more and rationalize that you're investigating restaurant company stocks. BTW, don't you just hate people who use acronyms like IMHO (in my humble opinion), OTOH (on the other hand) or BTW (by the way)? I spend half my day trying to figure out what those acronyms mean. It's time I could spend analyzing stocks.

MoneyTrack Method

Unfortunately, in one chapter, it's difficult to more than touch on Warren Buffett's investment strategies. Despite his everyman persona, it's not that simple to invest like Warren Buffett who may be the shrewdest investor who has ever lived. All of us would settle for just a modicum of his investment talent. If you're a Warren Buffett wannabe, limit your home-run swings to money you can afford to lose.

Investigate before you invest or borrow money. Before signing on the dotted line, contact the attorney general in your state and your state securities regulator.

Get in the habit of saving and investing money, not borrowing it. If you don't have the time to dig deeply into a company's financial prospects, limit your investing to index funds and exchange-traded funds (ETFs) in lieu of individual stocks. If you're not satisfied with being a passive investor, you can seek out actively managed mutual funds with the hope of achieving a higher rate of return. If you're patient and persistent, one day you might start your own millionaire's club.

14

CHAPTER

Kids and Money

DON'T KID YOURSELF

One key component of the *MoneyTrack* method is encouraging people to begin investing at a young age. These skills will serve them well throughout their lives. Furthermore, investments made at a young age can grow by an astounding amount over the years. Unfortunately, children don't always listen to their parents and other adults, whether they're giving advice about investing or almost any important issue.

Mark Twain recognized that fact of life and made this wry observation:

> When I was a boy of fourteen, my father was so ignorant I could hardly stand to have the old man around. But when I got to be twenty-one, I was astonished at how much he had learned in seven years. (Mark Twain, "Old Times on the Mississippi" *Atlantic Monthly*, 1874)

Depending on their age, your own children may feel the same way about you, especially if you try to teach them about money.

Parental Influence on Investor Attitudes

My father taught me about money management in high school, and that may be why I became a stockbroker. Unfortunately, I didn't start saving and investing seriously until after college. I lost several years' worth of compounded earnings due to this delay.

My co-host, Jack, is the father of two wonderful boys. Unfortunately, Jack complains that they're not learning much about finances in the real world. Jack wishes someone had sat down with him as a youngster to talk about money. If he had invested $100 per year in the stock market at a very young age, he would have an extra $95,000 today. The next generation won't have any excuse for not beginning to invest at a young age, especially if they watch Warren Buffett's animated series or *MoneyTrack*.

Maybe you had a paper route growing up, cut lawns, or worked in your neighborhood's Baskin-Robbins. Your children, by contrast, may be too busy with soccer and after-school activities to even help around the house. Their cell phone bill may be more than you spent in a month as a child.

Before we go on a rant about how much easier kids have it today, let's look at what they're facing. When you went to college, it might have been $500 a term and you didn't need to borrow money. Today, according to statistics from the College Board, the average yearly in-state tuition for a public college is $13,589. For a private school, the average tuition is $32,307. More than likely, young people will leave college saddled with debt.

Although you may not be able to impart money management advice on your children, you can make sure that they understand the basics of investing. To torture the famous Chinese saying, give a kid a fish and he'll eat for a day. Teach a kid to invest and he'll have enough money for pizza throughout college and graduate school.

Unfortunately, some parents fear investing, and their children are brought up with that same attitude. Although these children may grow up to be good savers, they may not know a thing about investing and might be afraid to take any risks with their money. This is a mistake that can haunt families for generations to come.

Teach Your Children Well

Surprisingly, many of our parents and grandparents know the value of a dollar, even though they never took a personal finance course in high school. Thanks to people like Laura Levine, children have a better shot at achieving financial literacy.

When we interviewed Laura Levine, she told us about the work of the Jump$tart Coalition for Personal Financial Literacy. Each year, the Jump$tart Coalition tests more than 5,500 high school seniors across 37 states to measure their overall knowledge of personal finance. The average score at the time of our interview was slightly over 50 percent. Having recently been elected to the Board of The California Jump$tart Coalition, I hope to help improve those statistics.

Surprisingly, Laura found that students who take a personal finance course don't do appreciably better. Parental involvement is instrumental in helping children to become financially literate.

Personal finance encompasses much more than investing. Among other things, it's knowledge about the following:

- Creating a budget and sticking to it
- Credit and debit cards
- Checking accounts
- Car insurance, health insurance, and other policies
- Wills and trusts
- Taxes
- Retirement planning
- Home ownership

Investing is tied in closely with all of these topics. The Jump$tart Coalition's Web address is: www.jumpstart.org/.

Teaching Children about Credit

It is imperative that children learn about credit, especially before they head off to college. Debit cards and prepaid credit cards can help teach kids about the responsible use of credit. A drawback, however, is that the companies that issue these cards often charge high fees. Furthermore, these cards do not build a credit history for the child.

When purchases are made with a debit card, money is deducted immediately from the cardholder's savings or checking account. The card won't work when the account is empty.

Prepaid credit cards are not tied to a bank account. Parents choose how much credit to extend on the card. They can reload the prepaid credit card as needed or at regular intervals. Prepaid credit cards allow parents to monitor their child's expenditures. There are even ways to block purchases at certain merchants.

When children get older, they may be ready for a real credit card. One possibility is a secured credit card where payment is linked to a bank account in case the child misses a payment. Another possible solution is a joint credit card account with the parent, preferably one that has a low credit limit. Another option is adding the child to one of the parent's credit cards. This gives the parent true oversight over the child's expenditures.

In conjunction with the *MoneyTrack* series, Jack and I have given talks at numerous high schools across the country about financial matters. These events are arranged by securities regulators in an effort to help kids learn early about investing. In October 2007, we gave a talk about investing to students at Hershey High School in Hershey, Pennsylvania. During the short intervals when we weren't eating chocolate, we tried to impress upon them that investing is a sure-fire way to build wealth, especially if you start early.

For many students, it was the first time they ever heard about compounded interest and how it can make you wealthy some day. Based on our experience, kids will get the message. Next time though, we'll take more money for candy and will make sure we don't have chocolate in our teeth.

Damon Williams, Investment Guru in Training

As we saw in Chapter 13, Warren Buffett got started early as an entrepreneur. On *MoneyTrack*, we met an outstanding young man who got started very early as an investor, thanks to his mother. Even at a young age, he was investing like a pro. Before buying any investment, he does a considerable amount of homework, which is a characteristic we find in successful investors.

Fourteen-year-old Damon Williams had a portfolio valued at $50,000 at the time we interviewed him. Unlike most teenagers, Damon listened to his mother who went through difficult financial times at age 19. His mother, April, taught him to be an owner, not a lender. When you buy stock, you become an owner of the company and may achieve a greater return on your investment. When you put money in a savings account, you are lending funds to the bank at a very low interest rate.

Before investing in a stock, Damon does a great deal of research. Using the Internet, he thoroughly researches the companies he's thinking about investing in and examines variables such as these:

- Price-earnings ratio
- Return on equity
- Earnings per share
- Dividend yields

Damon looks for a company that has had dividend growth over at least the last five years. He hunts for companies where he expects dividends to grow by at least 15 percent per year.

He also invests in companies that match his interests. As someone who loves basketball and sneakers, Damon bought Nike stock and owned 54 shares at the time we interviewed him. Once he buys a stock, Damon tends to be a buy-and-hold investor. He also buys tennis shoes as an investment. Damon told us that he buys about 10 pairs of Nikes each year.

To get kids interested in investing, parents should encourage them to buy stock in brands they use every day, whether it's an iPod, the cereal they eat every morning, or a particular cell phone. Nevertheless, just because you like the brand doesn't mean it's a good company in which to invest. Most conglomerates have dozens of subsidiaries, and some of them may not be doing as well.

As we saw in Chapter 13, your fondness for food can whet your appetite for investing in a particular stock. Since Jack never met a doughnut he didn't like, he once regretted not investing in KrispyKreme. Although KrispyKreme went up in value for a long time, it has since fallen on hard times.

On the subject of food, a senior in high school and her mother asked us a question while having a snack at Mother Fool's Coffeehouse located on the east side of Madison, Wisconsin. Mother Fool's is known for its organic coffee and all-vegan pastries. When Clarissa asked us how to get started as an investor, we turned to one of her peers for an answer—Damon.

Damon advised Clarissa to find some good companies and invest the $1,000 she received as a gift from her grandmother. If those companies go up in value by 10 percent, she might have $140,000 by the time she's ready to retire, even if she doesn't invest another dime. If Clarissa can invest $25 per month in addition to that $1,000, she'll have over a half million dollars in 40 years. Damon's calculations are based on historical stock market growth. Naturally, there will be periods when stocks lose money, but your long-term prospects for making money are excellent.

Investment adviser Ric Edelman, agreed with Damon's assessment. He cautioned, however, that money Clarissa needs for college should be invested in money market funds, bank accounts, and certificates of deposit (CDs). Money that Clarissa is saving for her long-term future can be invested in stocks and stock mutual funds.

On his Web site, www.ricedelman.com, Ric suggested that younger children might be interested in investing in a company known for its theme parks. In addition, music or clothing companies might spark a teenager's interest in investing.

Making Allowances for Children

Every family has a different approach when it comes to allowances. As we saw in Chapter 13, Warren Buffett believes that children should receive modest allowances, as long as there are duties that go along with them. Some families dole out allowances to their children and require nothing in exchange for this weekly stipend. In many families, children are compensated separately for performing certain chores around the house. Other families expect the child to perform specified household duties as a *quid pro quo* for receiving an allowance.

Allowances can teach children how to manage or mismanage money. An allowance can teach a child how to live within a budget and develop spending priorities. In addition, children learn how to save and delay gratification. You might also show your child how important it is to invest a portion of that allowance and set aside some amount for charity.

You send children the wrong message by giving them an allowance and then coughing up more money each time they run short of cash. When you do this, children get the message that money actually does grow on trees and you'll bail them out every time they're financially strapped. They might keep coming back for more, even after reaching adulthood.

Allowances can be a source of disagreement between parents and children. Kids might complain that they're not getting as much allowance as their friends or they'll constantly be nagging for an advance or increase. This trait will serve them well when they get a job and begin complaining that they're not making as much as a coworker.

Seriously, while no particular approach is right for every family, there are some generally accepted rules regarding allowances. Many experts view age six as a good time to begin giving an allowance to a child. Some child psychologists believe that even three-year-olds are ready to learn about money, even if they're too young for an allowance.

You should sit down and discuss the size of the allowance with your child. In setting an amount, everyone should agree on what expenses will be paid out of the child's allowance and what payments you'll continue to make. For example, you might continue to buy your child's clothes, but movies, trips to the video arcade, and incidental expenses at the mall will come out of the allowance.

After deciding how much will be paid, agree on a regular payday each week. Always pay the designated amount on time and avoid moving payday up in response to whining.

You should also indicate what chores, if any, are expected in exchange for the allowance. Before sitting down with your child, draw up a list of tasks that are appropriate for someone that age. Make sure your child knows that no allowance will be paid if these chores aren't completed on time, and stick to your guns if the work isn't done.

The size of the allowance depends on the rules of the program you establish and your child's day-to-day expenses. According to a 2005 study by the research firm, Yankelovich, allowances for 6- to 11-year-olds range from $5 to $9 per week. For 12- to 17-year-olds, allowances are in the $20 to $49 per week range. Nevertheless, the study found that less than 60 percent of kids between 6 and 17 receive any allowance.

In the end, it's up to you to determine whether or not your child will get an allowance and how much it will be. You also make the final determination as to whether there will be strings attached to any allowance you give. Janet Bodnar, author of Kiplinger's *Dollars & Sense for Kids,* has written that allowances teach children money management skills. Nevertheless, she does not believe that allowances should be tied to performing chores around the house. They should, however, be tied to financial chores like paying for their own collectibles and entertainment.

As you develop a family policy regarding allowances, keep in mind what we learned from the best-seller *The Millionaire Next Door.* The book's authors interviewed millionaires and found that although they could easily afford to overindulge their children, they chose not to do so. The goal of many millionaires interviewed was to teach their children to become self-reliant at a young age.

The term *affluenza* has been used to describe a so-called financial illness that strikes children in affluent families. These kids have higher expectations than children from families that are less well-off. Until there is a vaccination for affluenza, I would teach children about money management and help them to realize that even wealthy families must avoid spending too much. Even the rich must live within a budget.

Financial Lessons We Learn from Gift Giving

In Jeff Opdyke's "Love and Money" column in the *Wall Street Journal,* the columnist discussed a dilemma he was having. Opdyke and his wife wanted to give their children a vacation as their major Christmas gift. Although the children agreed that this would be their gift, Opdyke was worried that they would be disappointed on Christmas morning. In subsequent columns, Opdyke discussed e-mail he received from readers expressing opinions as to whether he would be Scrooge or overindulgent by giving the children additional gifts on Christmas morning.

No matter what your opinion is, we can all hopefully agree that gift giving can be used to teach children about money management. Children should be able to comprehend that they can't have everything they want. Parents should teach children that family funds are limited and they must prioritize their spending.

Major events like a bar mitzvah or bat mitzvah, confirmations, and graduations, give parents the opportunity to teach children about the balance between saving and spending. In some families, the child is only allowed to spend a portion of the money that he or she receives and must save the rest. Occasions like this are perfect for getting children started in an investment program.

Aside from learning about investing, children are never too young to learn about being philanthropic. Parents can encourage their children to think about people who are less fortunate than they are. Perhaps, some of those unwanted gifts or a bit of that money can be used to brighten the future of a child whose life isn't as easy as your offspring's.

Learning about Investing from Grandparents

It is not just parents who help children learn about investing. Grandparents can get their grandchildren started on the road to financial security and financial literacy. According to a survey by Grandparents.com and Focalyst, a data company, grandparents spend about $50 billion per year on their grandchildren; $25 billion of that total goes toward investments.

Some grandparents open custodial accounts for their grandchildren, so they can begin investing in stocks and mutual funds. In each state, these custodial accounts are subject to a statute called the Uniform Gift to Minors Act (UGMA) or the Uniform Transfers to Minors Act (UTMA). Depending on what state you're in, minors can usually get their hands on these custodial accounts from age 18 to 21.

The big advantage of investing in a child's name is that the tax bite is less severe initially. The "kiddie tax" refers to the tax on investment income of dependent children. Originally, the kiddie tax was designed to prevent wealthy families from shifting unearned income to their children under the age of 14. In 2005, that age was changed to 18. Effective January 1, 2008, the kiddie tax applies to children age 18 and younger and to dependent college students who are under the age of 24. Any unearned income in excess of $1,700 is taxed at the parents' rate.

The down side of investing in the child's name is that the minor takes control of the investment at the specified age and might not use the money for college or anything worthwhile—or at least worthwhile in the parent's eyes. Savings in the child's name also have an impact on financial aid calculations.

Many of these grandparents fund Section 529 educational savings plans. These plans can help families cope with the rapidly rising cost of higher education.

Section 529 Plans

If you still haven't recovered from our discussions of 401(k) retirement savings plans, you may not be ready to learn about another provision of the Internal Revenue Code—Section 529. Section 529 gives tax breaks for contributions to college savings plans. These plans also help you shelter the earnings in the account from taxes. Although Section 529 plans are authorized by the federal tax code, they are run by the states, usually the treasurer's office. The state sets a maximum contribution limit that must meet the requirements of Section 529(b)(7).

Section 529 plans are designed to encourage early and consistent savings. One of the primary benefits is the tax break you get. All money in a Section 529 plan is sheltered from federal and state income taxes. All withdrawals used for qualified higher education expenses are not taxed by the federal government. These withdrawals may also be exempt from state income taxes.

Most plans allow you to make minimal monthly contributions. In some states, you can contribute as little as $15. In certain states, you can contribute $300,000 or more to a Section 529 plan. Contributions can be made through automatic bank transfers or payroll deduction.

There are two broad categories of plans authorized by Section 529, prepaid tuition and college savings plans. The prepaid tuition plan makes it possible for you to prepay all or part of the beneficiary's tuition at an eligible college or university. After making the payment, all or a fixed percentage of the beneficiary's tuition costs are prepaid, regardless of how much the price goes up over the years. To take full advantage of the prepaid tuition plan, the beneficiary must attend the type of college or university on which the prepayment is based. The prepaid tuition plan may not achieve your goals if your beneficiary chooses a more expensive college.

College savings plans give parents and grandparents more flexibility in putting away money for a child's education. According to the SEC's online publication, "An Introduction to 529 Plans," an account is set up for the child that will be used later to pay for eligible college expenses. The publication explains:

> An account holder may typically choose among several investment options for his or her contributions, which the college savings plan invests on behalf of the account holder. Investment options often include stock mutual funds, bond mutual funds, and money market funds, as well as, age-based portfolios that automatically shift toward more conservative investments as the beneficiary gets closer to college age. Withdrawals from college savings plans can generally be used at any college or university. Investments in college savings plans that invest in mutual funds are not guaranteed by state governments and are not federally insured.

The age-based approach invests contributions according to the child or grandchild's current age and when he or she is likely to attend college. Most age-based portfolios utilize growth investments like stocks while the child is young and shift to more conservative investments as college draws near. For example, the age-based portfolio for a 12-year-old might be 60 percent in stock and 40 percent in fixed-income investments. When the child is 16, the portfolio will shift to a smaller percentage of the assets in stock. Depending upon which college savings plan you choose, the age-based portfolio may be more aggressive or conservative.

Certain investment options in a particular plan may ignore the age of the account beneficiary or the year of college enrollment and will focus on the risk temperament of the account owner. The plan may offer a static allocation portfolio, which is also referred to as a fixed allocation portfolio. In a static portfolio, your investment allocation remains fixed until you initiate a change. For example, you

Coverdell Education Savings Account

Section 529 plans are not the only way to save for a child or grandchild's education. The Coverdell Education Savings Account (ESA) is the more recent version of what used to be the Education IRA. It was named after Paul Coverdell, the late senator from Georgia, who was a strong advocate of these accounts. Assuming you meet the income requirements, the ESA permits you to contribute up to $2,000 per year. Unlike an IRA, you don't need to have earned income to make a contribution.

Like the Section 529 plan, the ESA offers enormous tax benefits. Earnings grow in a tax-sheltered account. Qualified withdrawals are tax-free. Funds may be withdrawn to pay for primary and secondary school expenses, not just college and graduate school bills.

ESAs afford you with more control over your investment portfolio. You have your choice of investments, not just the portfolio selected by the college savings plan manager.

might choose a portfolio that will always be 100 percent invested in stocks. Another option might be a more conservative static portfolio that always invests 50 percent of your money in stocks and 50 percent in bonds.

With a typical prepaid tuition plan, the beneficiary may still need money for room and board, books, and other expenditures. In contrast, the college savings plan might grow large enough to pay for all qualified higher education expenses, but only if your investment portfolio does well.

Although Section 529 plans are a great way to save for a child's education, those contributions might eat into the money you should be saving for your retirement. They might also affect your child's eligibility for financial aid.

Savings Bonds Used for Educational Purposes

Savings bonds can be used to put away money for a child's education, but there are many restrictions. First of all, you can't put savings bonds in a child or young adult's name and hope to take advantage of the tax benefits. The bond owner must be at least 24 years of age at the issue date of the bond in order to get tax-free interest. The tax break works better for parents who own the bonds. If your income is too high at the time of redemption, however, you won't qualify for a tax break.

Scam Alert

Even if their college board scores are exceptional, smart students can be conned just like the rest of us. Bijal Chhadva was sucked into a pyramid scheme. In 2005, Bijal had just graduated from a college in Tampa, Florida. A sharp and savvy kid, Bijal possessed a degree in computer engineering.

He learned about an investment from a stranger that was purportedly the opportunity of a lifetime. With pyramid schemes, the only way you make money is by recruiting other salespeople. The schemes force participants to constantly bring in new people. Their money is passed on to the small number of people at the top of the pyramid scheme. Although Bijal lost thousands of dollars of his own money funding the business venture, he learned a very valuable lesson about scams.

Illegal pyramid schemes are sometimes difficult to distinguish from legal multi-level marketing plans which sell products and services through distributors. According to a Federal Trade Commission (FTC) publication prepared in cooperation with the North American Securities Administrators Association (NASAA), "If a plan offers to pay commissions for recruiting new distributors, watch out! Most states outlaw this practice, which is known as 'pyramiding.' State laws against pyramiding say that a multilevel marketing plan should only pay commissions for retail sales of goods or services, not for recruiting new distributors." The publication can be found at www.ftc.gov/bcp/edu/pubs/consumer/invest/inv12.shtm.

Many young people go off to college knowing very little about investing. It's one of the reasons why Jack and I speak at high schools across the country and warn students about scams. Because they are naïve and face huge expenses, college students are ripe to become victims of investment scams.

The editor of *Bottom Line Personal,* a publication filled with great financial tips, saw this happen to her own daughter. After her college-age daughter received an automated call on her cell phone asking for her credit card number, editor Marjorie Abrams interviewed Audri Lanford of ScamBusters.org (www.ScamBusters.org). Dr. Lanford offered this advice to young adults:

- If it's spam, it's probably a scam.
- Investigate any e-mail or calls from a bank or company asking for verification of your account.
- You shouldn't display your full name in online profiles.
- Avoid e-mail surveys that ask for detailed information.
- When posting your resume online, omit your address and phone number.
- Spammers troll the Internet in search of personal information.

Ms. Abrams' article, which was published on February 1, 2008, took note of various scams circulating on the Internet. For example, you're notified that you've won a prize, but need to pay fees and taxes before collecting. Young people are ripe for scams, because they spend so much time on the Internet and they aren't usually as distrustful as the rest of us.

To qualify for the tax exclusion, there are several additional requirements. The bond must be redeemed to pay for qualified educational expenses including tuition and fees. Surprisingly, the cost of room and board is not a qualified educational expense. Books also do not qualify.

A key point to remember is that the interest on savings bonds is unlikely to keep pace with the escalating cost of college. Even with the tax breaks, the return on savings bonds won't compare to the historical return on stocks.

The Times, They Are a Changing

In the introduction to his book *The Lies About Money*, Ric Edelman reminisced about calling PTAs in the 1980s to offer college planning seminars to parents. One president of a PTA asked why the new financial adviser was calling her, because the children in the school were only 10 years old. She suggested that Ric call the high schools.

Ric, a guest on *MoneyTrack*, wrote this in his 2007 book:

> *Back then, parents of young children never thought about college. The only issue pertaining to college was choosing one, a decision easily avoided until the child was a junior in high school. It never occurred to parents that college costs were skyrocketing and that they'd need many, many years to accumulate sufficient savings. It might be obvious to us now, but in the 1980s, college planning was a revolutionary idea. In fact, it wasn't just revolutionary—it was unheard of.*

Obviously, with the creation of Section 529 plans and ESAs, it is clear that saving and investing for a child's education should begin at birth, not at age 10 or when kids are in high school.

Ric was thrilled to see kids like Damon and Clarissa showing an interest in investing. He told us that when someone like Clarissa has 10 or 15 years until she needs the money, it can be invested in stocks and stock mutual funds. This gives her the opportunity to earn as much as is available in the economic environment. Over the years, it makes an extremely big difference whether your money is making 8 percent a year in the stock market versus 2 percent in a bank account. According to Ric, investing in the market can make a huge difference in your future wealth.

The cost of waiting to begin saving, however, is steep. Based on data from Fidelity Investments, here is the monthly savings needed to save approximately $100,000 in college-related costs:

- Birth: $245/month for 18 years
- Age five: $420 month for 13 years
- Age ten: $915 month for 8 years

You don't want to know how much you'll need to save each month if you get started later than age ten.

Sane Money Advice from the Host of *Mad Money*

Though he seems like a madman on his television program, Jim Cramer is quite rational in real life. Because we interviewed him on the *MoneyTrack* program, I can vouch for his sanity. The host of *Mad Money*, an investment program on CNBC, made a very important point that most parents don't realize: Children should learn how to save *and* invest. Most parents are satisfied if their children understand the value of saving.

In an article for the *Costco Connection* in January 2008, Jim gave advice on how to teach children about money. Jim noted that a great many parents teach their children about the value of saving money and how interest works. They set up a bank account for the child. Jim observed, however, that it's even more important that parents teach them to be investors.

Jim's initial investments were yawners, although it's hard to imagine him being sleepy. His first foray into investing was a passbook savings account. The second was savings bonds. As his television show illustrates, his third investment—stocks—got him excited. Jim believes that by teaching children about stocks, they will get excited about investing. They might even start charting how their stocks are doing.

Getting children interested in the market, according to Jim, teaches kids a much more valuable lesson than opening a bank account. When children are taught about stocks, they learn how much they can make by investing. They might also learn about losing money, which is also important.

In the article, Jim pointed out that the key to making stocks come alive for kids is to get them involved with a company they're familiar with and watch them become excited about its prospects. It's fun for parents too as their child grabs the newspaper to see the closing price of stocks from the day before.

Jim opined that kids as young as six have the capability to learn about stocks and invest. Their investments should be in companies that make the brands the child likes or the movies he or she enjoys. Children will feel they have a stake in the company and parents will be ingraining an interest in the investment process.

MoneyTrack Method

Parents make the biggest impression on how children will handle their own money later in life. Take some time to teach them about money and how to invest like the pros. Give them this book to read, or at least this chapter. Sit down with them and watch *MoneyWatch* from time to time. As we saw with Damon Williams, kids can learn how to invest and analyze stocks better than most adults.

Parents should teach their children about money by setting the right example. If children see their parents squandering money, they are likely to pattern their behavior after them. Whether they're buying groceries, a car, a new television, or a cell phone, parents should explain how they set priorities and teach their children about the monetary factors that influence financial decisions.

Parents should also teach their children about how important it is to use credit responsibly. Credit cards should be used for convenience and not to enable spending more than you can afford. Many older people might want to learn that lesson, too.

The *MoneyTrack* method works best when you start using the principles at a very young age. Your child can take advantage of the time value of money and build a portfolio that will put yours to shame. Even better, a child will come to understand the importance of investing to achieve financial goals.

The dollar cost averaging strategy is ideal for children and young adults. If they begin a systematic investment program and contribute the same amount on a regular basis, children and young adults can take advantage of dollar cost averaging. Their regular contribution buys fewer shares when the price of a stock or mutual fund is high and more shares when they are down in value. Dollar cost averaging has proven to be a time-tested way to build a portfolio, and the average cost-per-share is likely to be favorable.

Whether you're young or old, don't allow yourself to get entangled in a pyramid scheme. In most cases, they're not on the level. Parents can help their children learn to recognize the warning signs of a scam and can teach them our often-repeated *MoneyTrack* advice: Investigate before you invest. If you do, you're far less likely to become the victim of fraud.

CHAPTER

15

Tying Up Some Financial Loose Ends

The *MoneyTrack* method recognizes that investment decisions are often inextricably intertwined with other financial issues. If your finances are a mess or you're in debt up to your ears, investing is the last thing you're thinking about doing. That's why we have addressed personal finance issues, as well as investment topics, throughout this book. Nevertheless, there are still a few additional issues we need to wrap up.

As we tie up these loose ends, we're going to skip the party, and you can thank Chloe for that decision. When we're ready to wrap up the *MoneyTrack* season, we always have a wrap party, and Chloe definitely won't be invited next time. I doubt she even remembers what she did, but our lips are sealed. We can, however, answer questions we received from *MoneyTrack* viewers.

Good Debt versus Bad Debt

We're often asked if there's a difference between good debt and bad debt. Jack believes bad debt is any bill that comes in the mail. My belief is that any debt that isn't mine is good debt. Although the distinction between good debt and bad debt is often subjective, the manner in which you use borrowed money is the most important factor in deciding whether you made a mistake by taking out a loan.

We all know people who hate any kind of debt. The thought of owing people money keeps them up at night. You might compare your debt temperament to the investment temperament topic we've discussed throughout this book. Conservative investors have little tolerance for risk. Similarly, some people have a very conservative debt temperament that makes them shy away from borrowing money. If you have that temperament, you find almost any kind of debt is unpalatable, even a mortgage.

A mortgage can be an example of good and bad debt. If you buy a house and have a modest mortgage with an affordable payment, that loan is likely to be viewed as good debt. The interest on that loan is deductible. Paying off the loan forces you to save, because a portion of your payment is applied toward the principal. Because of inflation, you're paying back the loan with cheaper dollars that aren't worth as much.

In some cases, a mortgage can be bad debt. Many people speculated that real estate would keep going up in value. They were able to obtain interest-only mortgages with little money down. Even though the loans were interest-only, their mortgage payments were well beyond their ability to pay. These borrowers assumed they would "flip" the house and sell it at a huge profit. Unfortunately, when the real estate bubble burst, they could not sell the home and the lender foreclosed on the property.

The issue of whether a mortgage is good or bad debt also comes up in a different context. People will often ask if they should pay off their existing low-interest mortgage or invest the money. In theory, you will get a better return by investing that money judiciously in the stock market rather than paying off your mortgage. There are no guarantees, however, that the investments you choose will make you glad you took a pass on paying off your mortgage.

Some people add money to their mortgage payment each month to pay off the balance more quickly. This strategy can cut years off the amount of time it will take to pay off the mortgage. It can be argued, however, that you should plow that extra money into your retirement savings plan at work, especially if your employer will match some or all of your contribution.

Home equity loans are also touted as good debt. Subject to restrictions, the interest is usually deductible. These loans are often advertised as a way to make home improvements that will increase the value of your home. Unfortunately, many borrowers use home equity loans for more frivolous expenditures, like a television set that's the size of a drive-in movie screen or a vacation to Bora Bora from which you'll bring back very boring digital photos. You are putting your home at risk if your income drops. If the value of your home decreases and you need to sell it, you may not receive enough money to pay off your mortgage and home equity loan.

Aside from all of these mortgage-related issues, you need to address an important psychological consideration: Will you have financial peace of mind after you pay off your mortgage? For some people, paying off their mortgage gives them an enormous sense of financial independence. Assuming they pay their taxes, no one can take their home away from them. If you will derive this sense of satisfaction from paying off your mortgage, it doesn't matter how much money you might make in the stock market by keeping the loan.

The distinction between good and bad debt becomes clearer when you're looking at loans against your credit card. Bad debt is when you borrow money to pay for dinners out, shoes, or any items that go down in value. No one should be paying credit card interest on a filet mignon they ate last year.

You pay an enormous amount of interest on credit card debt. You should do everything in your power to pay off that debt as quickly as possible. Once you pay off that debt, put your credit cards in a drawer and avoid using them for impulse purchases.

Depending on the situation, car loans can be good or bad debt. Having a car loan that takes a huge chunk out of your paycheck and keeps you from investing in a 401(k) is an illustration of extremely bad debt. Even if the payment is affordable, you're borrowing money to buy a depreciating asset. Almost every car depreciates the minute you drive it off the lot. Watch out for car ads that promise you an extremely low interest rate. More than likely, you'll pay more for the car.

You'll also see ads from furniture stores and other merchants, promising no payments until a year or two after your purchase. You'll often pay more for the furniture and will owe a great deal of interest. When you fall for one of those deals, you are mortgaging your future. You have no idea what your financial situation will be when your loan payments begin. You might even hate the furniture by then. Maybe your kids or Jack will have spilled something on the sofa by then or Chloe might decide it's her favorite lounging spot.

You should be careful, too, about borrowing from your 401(k) retirement savings plan, which is usually permitted if you meet certain conditions. Although the interest you pay on the loan is returned to your account, you still might lose a great deal in compounded earnings over the years. If you don't pay the money back on time, the loan is treated as a taxable distribution. Furthermore, you are subject to a 10 percent premature distribution penalty if you're younger than age 59½. If you leave your job for any reason, the loan must be fully repaid or you'll owe taxes and a penalty.

Your debt burden can have a negative impact on your life. A December, 2007 survey of CPAs who offer financial planning advice found that 30 percent of their clients are carrying more credit card debt than five years earlier. The accountants surveyed have observed that clients are increasingly likely to use debt to finance their lifestyles. The participants in the survey blamed excessive discretionary spending for the increase in their clients' level of debt.

The survey, which was reported in the February 4, 2008 issue of *InvestmentNews,* gives evidence that debt is affecting important decisions made by younger clients between the ages of 25 and 34. Many of the CPAs surveyed have clients who forgo buying a home, having children, and saving for retirement, because of their loan obligations.

Student Loans

You may still be paying off your student loans when you go back for your college reunion years from now. Student loans can affect many of the financial and lifestyle decisions you make in life.

As a general rule, a student loan is good debt, since more education means you'll usually make a great deal more money over your lifetime. If you're using that money to get a graduate degree in a field where there hasn't been work since the time of Aristotle, student loans may not be examples of good debt.

The impact of student loans affects borrowers for years to come. Borrowers often get off on the wrong financial foot. Because of their loans, they may need to live at home after college. Unless they get a good job right away, they will have difficulty paying back those loans. Too often, young employees burdened by student loans avoid contributing to retirement savings plans through their employer. Decisions not to invest for retirement can haunt you all of your life.

Student loans can also have an adverse effect on your financial well-being. When you owe thousands in student loans, it's possible you will postpone the purchase of your first home. If you have children, you might not start saving for their education. In fact, you may still be paying off your loans when your children go off to college.

According to the National Consumer Law Center and the Project on Student Debt, five million people take out student loans each year. Borrowers typically graduate with $20,000 in student loans. Student debt grew by 8 percent from 2005 to 2006. At the same time, starting salaries rose by only 4 percent.

Owing thousands of dollars in student loans may affect your choice of careers. You might choose a job that pays more in lieu of one that you really want. One bright spot is the recently enacted College Cost Reduction and Access Act of 2007. The law allows for income-based repayment options. Loans are limited to a fixed percentage of your income. The statute also authorizes loan forgiveness if you work for 10 years in certain jobs in the public sector.

One resource for graduates struggling with loans is the Student Loan Borrower Assistance Web site, www.studentloanborrowerassistance.org. The Web site provides information on repayment options, as well as advice on how to deal with collection agencies.

Renting versus Owning a Home

Another question we get is whether you should buy or rent a home. Once again, the answer may not be the same for everyone, since so much depends on your personal situation. As we saw in Chapter 11, the answer is also tied in with your perspective on the American Dream. For some people, owning a home in a particular area or neighborhood is the essence of the American Dream.

In general, although owning real estate will usually increase your net worth, there is no guarantee that the home you buy will go up in value. Sometimes renting makes more sense than buying a house. As you decide whether it's time to buy a home, you need to truly understand the cost of ownership. These expenses include:

- Up-front expenses such as mortgage origination fees and transfer taxes

- Mortgage payments and private insurance if you have little or no down payment
- Upkeep for your home and major repairs such as a new furnace
- Property taxes
- Homeowners insurance
- Utilities

If you own a condominium or a house in a planned community, there is usually a condo or homeowners association that runs the development. You'll pay monthly maintenance fees to the association to cover the cost of upkeep, such as landscapers. In some cases, the board will assess owners a large amount to pay for major expenditures such as new roofs for the condos or repairs needed because of storm damage. You'll also pay for the upkeep of the clubhouse and other facilities.

Although many people view their home as the best investment they've ever made, home ownership isn't as appealing when the real estate bubble bursts and it's a down market. It's not a given that your home will appreciate in value over the years. Even if it does appreciate, the increase in value might not match the rate of inflation. If you're caught up in a buyer's market, you might not be able to sell the house at almost any price.

If you make a bad deal, you might cause yourself to be "house poor." You may wind up spending so much on home-related expenses that you can't afford to invest in your retirement savings plan or other investments. As a general rule, homeowners should spend no more than 28 percent of their income for housing expenses.

Unfortunately, what sometimes happen is that homebuyers have champagne taste and a beer budget. If they're buying a new home, they keep agreeing to add-ons offered by the builder. All of these add-ons turn an affordable home into one that undermines the family's budget.

Even fixer-uppers can exhaust your budget, especially if the house you bought resembles the home in *The Money Pit*, a 1986 movie starring Tom Hanks. Even if you make most of the repairs yourself, trying to fix up a home can strain your budget to the limit. Aside from elective repairs, you may find yourself coping financially and mentally with major expenditures that can't be put off.

Real estate is, however, a great tax shelter. The interest on your mortgage and property taxes are deductible. Some of your up-front expenses, such as "points," may be deductible. If you sell your home at a profit someday, you may not owe any federal income taxes if this was your primary residence and you lived there for at least two years. If you're single, you can make a profit of up to $250,000 and still won't owe any federal income taxes on the gain. If you're married, you can make a profit of up to $500,000 without paying federal taxes.

Buying a home forces you to save. A portion of each mortgage payment goes toward paying off your principal. In the early years of a mortgage, however, only a small portion of your monthly payment chips away at your principal and most of it is interest. Worse yet, if you signed up for an interest-only mortgage, none of your payment reduces the amount you owe.

Why Renting Is the Right Choice for Some People

Depending on their situation, renting may be the right decision for certain people. Here are some reasons why it makes sense.

Renting Is a Better Option if You Don't Plan to Stay in a Particular Area: Renting may be the right decision if you expect to move within the next few years. Because there are so many up-front costs when buying a home, it may not make sense to buy one if you plan to move in the near future. You might not recover all of those up-front costs. Renting might also be the right choice if your job isn't secure.

Renting Minimizes Unplanned Expenses: When you rent, there should be no unplanned expenditures unless you leave the bathtub running and it overflows into the downstairs tenant's apartment. In contrast, when you own a home, there is always an unexpected bill in the mail. If you're a tenant, it's easier to keep to a budget, because you know what your rent is each month. Of course, when you move, you're probably going to lose some or all of your security deposit, because the rental unit never seems to meet the landlord's expectations.

Renting Gives You Time to Save for a Down Payment: Renting may be the right decision until you can afford to make the down payment on a home. Without a decent down payment, you're less likely to find a mortgage with a favorable interest rate. If you don't have a down payment, one possibility is renting a home with the option to buy it later. With this arrangement, some of your rent is applied to the purchase price of the home.

There are people who argue that the stock market is a better investment than buying a home. Your potential returns, they contend, are much greater with equity investments. These folks claim they will invest the money that would otherwise go toward making their mortgage payments. This might be a viable plan if you invariably invest that money each month. Human nature being what it is, you might not get around to investing that money. Depending on what types of investments you make, this plan might expose you to more risk.

Although there are risks to buying a house, home ownership has traditionally been viewed as a goal that most of us share. You get a roof over your head and there is no landlord watching your every move. If you pay your mortgage faithfully, you will someday own the home free and clear, except for taxes and other expenses.

Of course, you might share the vantage point of the late comedian George Carlin, who said that a house is just a place to keep your stuff. Carlin said, "If you didn't have so much stuff, you wouldn't need a house. You could just walk around all the time." According to Carlin, you sometimes need to move to bigger house, because you don't have enough room for your stuff.

Assuming you view a home as more than just a place to keep your stuff, it's a goal that's worth pursuing. Owning a home with a paid-off mortgage is a major step toward the goal of financial independence.

Update on Corporate Fraud and Corporate Ethics in America

Corporate fraud has adversely affected the investments of millions of Americans. In fact, it has wiped out the assets of countless retirement savings plan participants. Because of corporate fraud, many employees of companies like Enron saw their dreams evaporate.

Many will spend years longer in the work force to make up for the losses they suffered as a result of unethical conduct by certain CEOs, CFOs, and other corporate officers.

Over the years, there have been a number of corporate executives who became synonymous with fraud. Perhaps you remember names like Kenneth Lay and Jeffrey Skilling of Enron, Bernard Ebbers of WorldCom, and John Rigas, the founder of Adelphia. Because of their misconduct, people who worked at those companies suffered greatly as they watched their retirement savings plans and their jobs disappear.

Let's not forget Dennis Kozlowski of Tyco. He made somewhere in the neighborhood of $100 million per year. He used company funds to fly his wife to Sardinia for her fortieth birthday. Guests at the $2 million birthday bash were treated to a performance by Jimmy Buffett and models dressed in togas. Eventually, Kozlowski was convicted of grand larceny, securities fraud, and a number of other charges.

There is hope for the future. The Sarbanes-Oxley Act of 2002 was passed to promote corporate accountability. The act requires companies to implement corporate governance policies and controls to prevent fraud. The law also makes it easier for whistleblowers to report fraud. In addition, the statute gave the SEC the authority for the first time to distribute financial penalties paid by violators of securities laws. Pursuant to the Sarbanes-Oxley Act, billions of dollars have been distributed to investors who suffered financial losses due to securities law violations.

In New Hampshire, veteran CNN financial editor Myron Kandel leads a major initiative focused on corporate governance and investor protection. Myron is spearheading the Initiative for Corporate Responsibility and Investor Protection. Much of the funding for the project came from a $5 million settlement negotiated by the New Hampshire Bureau of Securities Regulation with Tyco International. The initiative also receives funding support from the Investor Protection Trust (IPT), a Washington-based group dedicated to providing independent and objective information required by consumers to make well-informed investment decisions.

The IPT operates its own programs and provides grants to underwrite important educational initiatives. Our *MoneyTrack* program has benefited from those grants.

Socially Responsible Investing

Aside from the investment principles we've discussed throughout this book, you can also inject your ethical principles into your decision making. Socially responsible investing is a strategy that incorporates your values into the already-complicated issue of which investments to buy. Depending on your values, you might invest in certain companies because their products are environmentally friendly or you believe their services will benefit mankind. Conversely, you might avoid investing in companies if their products or services offend you.

Socially responsible investors have a wide range of concerns that may affect which companies they wish to buy:

- Environmental impact
- Animal testing
- Nuclear power
- Weapons systems
- Treatment of employees and labor relations
- Policies on outsourcing

A socially responsible investor might avoid companies involved in selling tobacco products, alcohol, or even gambling. A different socially responsible investor might want nothing to do with a company whose clothes or tennis shoes are made in sweat shops.

Before investing in a company, investors must do a great deal of research. Aside from research regarding a company's financial prospects, a socially responsible investor might look at other factors. For example, an investor might read that as of February 5, 2008, Intel leads in U.S. green energy use, according to the Environmental Protection Agency.

There are many socially responsible mutual funds available to investors. There are funds for investors who are concerned about climate change, human rights, and even corporate governance. The fund's prospectus tells you what social factors and values are considered before making investments. You can find a socially responsible fund that has an investment objective that meets your needs, whether it's income or growth.

There are even investment firms that seek to generate solid returns in a socially responsible way. For more information about socially responsible investing, you can visit Web sites such as www. SocialFunds.com.

Choosing the Right Financial Adviser

Bruce in Mount Airy, Pennsylvania, asked us, "How do you go about choosing the right financial adviser?" Whether you live in the Pocono Mountains or Pocahontas County, Iowa, picking the right financial adviser requires you to do your homework.

Some people get their advice from a stockbroker. There are two categories of brokerage firms, full service and discount. Discount brokers are obviously less expensive than a full-service broker. Generally, you will get more advice from a full-service broker, but it may not be objective. You also can get advice through an independent investment adviser who is registered with the SEC or your state.

Barbara Roper of the Consumer Federation of America recommends fee-only financial advisers. Fee-only financial advisers are compensated entirely from fees paid by the client for advice, plan development, and/or asset management.

In the strictest sense, fee-only financial advisers do not earn commissions or fees from investments and products that are recommended to clients. Their fees are not contingent upon the purchase or sale of a financial product. Fee-only advisers do not receive undisclosed compensation, nor do they participate in arrangements where they receive payment in any form from a brokerage firm. These so-called "soft dollars" are used to compensate advisers for using a particular brokerage firm to execute your securities trades.

A client's payment to a fee-only adviser may take a variety of forms. The fee-only adviser may be compensated with an hourly billing, payment by the project, annual retainer, a percentage of assets under management, or some combination thereof. In many cases, fee-only advisers charge clients a specified amount for a particular service, such as creating a financial plan. A comprehensive financial plan might cost anywhere from $500 to several thousand dollars.

Many clients, however, require more than just financial planning. They may need ongoing assistance to implement the strategies laid out in the financial plan, as well as portfolio management. The fee for managing your portfolio is usually a percentage of assets under management. You will be given a choice between discretionary and nondiscretionary asset management. If you give an investment adviser discretion over your portfolio, he or she can make trades without obtaining your prior approval. If the adviser does not have discretion over your assets, he or she must contact you first before making any trades.

When you hire a financial adviser, make sure you know what services are included and what are outside the scope of your arrangement. Ask which of the following services are provided:

- Specialized problem-solving and analysis of complex financial issues, such as divorce planning
- Retirement planning, pension analysis, and retirement income projections
- Assistance with college funding investment choices
- Cash flow and budget analysis
- Mortgage analysis and refinancing decisions
- Estate planning
- Insurance policy analysis
- Stock option analysis
- Tax planning
- Estate planning

Even if services such as estate planning or tax planning are included, there may be additional charges for preparing tax returns or legal documents. You may need an accountant to prepare the actual forms. Furthermore, only a licensed attorney should be giving legal advice and preparing legal documents.

As we mentioned in Chapter 1, watch out for designations and credentials that may turn out to be meaningless. Securities regulators in states such as Nebraska and Massachusetts have taken steps to ensure that financial professionals don't mislead clients regarding their qualifications. Other states are likely to take similar initiatives, especially now that NASAA has formulated a model rule restricting the use of senior-related designations and certifications.

The Nebraska Department of Banking and Finance, Bureau of Securities, has issued an interpretive opinion regarding the use of designations and certifications in advertising by investment adviser representatives and agents of broker-dealers. The department takes the position that using a certification or designation on business cards, stationery, and in advertisements, creates the impression that the individual has special qualifications in a certain area of finance or financial planning. Nebraska is especially concerned about designations and certifications that incorrectly imply that the financial professional possesses expertise in providing services to senior investors.

In accordance with that interpretive opinion, brokers and investment adviser representatives may only use designations approved by the commissioner. They risk fines or suspension for using unapproved designations. The opinion lists all of the certifications and designations that are acceptable for use in Nebraska at this point in time. You might want to use it for guidance when you're evaluating the credentials of a financial adviser you're thinking of hiring. This interpretive opinion can be found at www.ndbf.org/.

You can find additional information about financial advisers and receive referrals by going to the following Web sites:

- Financial Planning Association: www.fpanet.org
- National Association of Personal Financial Advisors: www.napfa.org
- Garrett Planning Network: www.garrettplanningnetwork.com
- WiserAdvisor: www.wiseradvisor.com

After you have received the names of advisers in your area, interview them and make sure you conduct your own investigation.

Scam Alert

Marine Sergeant Christopher Starks survived two tours in Iraq, but got caught in a payday loan trap. He visited a payday lender for a loan to tide him over until his next paycheck, but wound up paying an exorbitant interest rate that makes credit card interest look cheap.

In some states, such as California, the Department of Corporations regulates payday lenders. Payday loans are an example of predatory lending. Predatory lenders use underhanded lending practices.

According to a Federal Trade Commission (FTC) Consumer Alert, payday loans equal costly cash. These short-term, high-rate loans go by a variety of names:

- Payday loans
- Cash advance loans
- Check advance loans

- Postdated check loans
- Deferred deposit check loans

In Nebraska, payday lenders are referred to as delayed deposit services businesses. On August 29, 2007, the Nebraska Department of Banking and Finance issued a cease-and-desist order against a payday lender that was charging fees in excess of state law and automatically renewed loans on the due date.

Typically, a borrower writes a personal check to the lender for the amount borrowed, plus a fee. The lender gives the borrower the face value of the check, minus the fee. If you extend the loan for another few weeks, you pay an additional fee. The annual percentage rate (APR) for the loan will be exorbitant.

According to an article written by Michelle Singletary that was reprinted in the *Palm Beach Post* on February 18, 2008, members of the military use payday loans three times as much as civilians. When you calculate the fee on an annualized basis, it might be as high as 400 to 1,000 percent. The Defense Department has created a Web site to encourage members of the armed forces to reduce their debt and become better money managers. The Web site is called Military Saves and can be found at www.militarysaves.org.

In its Consumer Alert, the FTC provided this example to explain how the interest on payday loans works against you

Let's say you write a personal check for $115 to borrow $100 for up to 14 days. The check casher or payday lender agrees to hold the check until your next payday. At that time, depending on the particular plan, the lender deposits the check, you redeem the check by paying the $115 in cash, or you roll-over the check by paying a fee to extend the loan for another two weeks. In this example, the cost of the initial loan is a $15 finance charge and 391 percent APR. If you roll-over the loan three times, the finance charge would climb to $60 to borrow $100.

The FTC's advice on this subject can be found at www.ftc.gov/bcp/edu/pubs/consumer/alerts/alt060.shtm.

When you borrow money, you should be scrutinizing the terms. The APR tells you the interest rate you are paying, including loan fees and other costs. Instead of a payday loan, consider borrowing from a credit union. Better yet, even if you are living from paycheck to paycheck, alter your spending so you can make it until payday.

How Not to Choose a Financial Adviser

Even if you become knowledgeable about investing, you may still feel you're in need of professional guidance. Perhaps you lack the time or inclination to thoroughly research your investment options. No matter how little time you have, however, it's still absolutely necessary to investigate the person who will be helping you invest. Otherwise, you may learn about that individual's background for the first time when you're reading your morning newspaper.

In the *South Florida Sun-Sentinel* on February 10, 2008, columnist Harriet Johnson Brackey told readers about an investment adviser who was found guilty of fraud. The story offered a number of important lessons on how not to choose a financial adviser.

The adviser could be heard every day on a Boca Raton business radio channel. Although many business programs seem as if they are offering objective advice from bona fide experts, the hosts often buy time from the station so they can pitch their products and services. According to the SEC, this investment adviser made over $4 million in profits and passed on more than $11 million in losses to his clients. Many of his clients assumed that because he was on the radio, the host of the program was an expert. Listeners also may have inferred that the adviser was ethical.

Even if you hear someone on the radio and presume that they are knowledgeable, Brackey advised that you should still investigate the person's background. The Certified Financial Planner Board of Standards had revoked the radio host's Certified Financial Planner (CFP) designation in 1997 for disciplinary reasons. You can check on a CFP's background and find one in your area by visiting the organization's Web site, www.cfp.net.

Clients might also have investigated the radio host by contacting their state's securities regulator. In this case, the securities regulator is the Florida Department of Banking and Finance. You can also use the Broker Check search engine, which is available on FINRA's Web site, www.FINRA.org. With a little research, Brackey learned that the radio host had several client complaints that could have been found during an online investigation.

Brackey also reported that several clients had suspicions but never trusted their instincts. The client's portfolio would only go up by a small amount, even though the market was up 10 percent. This should cause a ping on your radar.

Aside from your initial due diligence when choosing someone to help you with your finances, you should monitor that person and the firm on an ongoing basis. You may find that other clients have discovered a problem that you're unaware of and have filed complaints.

MoneyTrack Method

Although the *MoneyTrack* method is purposefully basic and can help even unsophisticated investors, some people still want and need the services of a financial adviser. If that person cannot explain his or her investment strategy to you in plain English, you are hiring the wrong person. In a *Dilbert* cartoon published on January 31, 2008, Dogbert the financial planner greets a new client with these words: "Investing is far too complicated for your tiny brain. You are a financial troglodyte!!!" The frightened client asks if he can now get some advice. "No," Dogbert replies. "Our first meeting is just to soften you up."

Some financial professionals want you to believe that investing and financial issues are too complex for ordinary people to understand. As we've discussed throughout this book, investing isn't rocket science, and the basics can be learned by almost anyone. If you do decide you need a financial professional to help you, make sure you find one who will explain what steps should be taken in language you can understand.

The more questions you ask, the more you'll learn about credit and investing. The more you learn, the less likely it is that you will be taken advantage of by unscrupulous individuals.

If there is a textbook example of bad debt, it's payday loans. Payday lenders make loan sharks seem benevolent. You also need to examine your lifestyle if you find yourself in need of payday loans. It's imperative that you find out why you're unable to live within your means.

Like your college transcript, mistakes you made in handling credit can follow you around for years to come. If your credit score is low, paying off your bills in a timely fashion can help you to rehabilitate your credit rating. Your credit rating affects many aspects of your life such as insurance premiums, job prospects, and how much you'll pay for future loans. In fact, your ability to become a successful investor is closely intertwined with your success in managing credit and money.

Conclusion

THERE, WE SAID IT AGAIN

No matter which episode of *MoneyTrack* you watch, stuff happens. Sometimes it's the stuff we can't control. For example, Chloe keeps walking in and out of camera range. Sure, we do have some control over the situation, but doggy day care isn't cheap.

Jack and I learn a great deal as we interview the experts each week. Over the years, we've learned that the experts don't always agree. Nevertheless, we have routinely heard very similar advice coming from the investment pros we interviewed. Here are some of tips we heard from many different investment mavens:

- When it comes to investing, you can never start too early or save too much. You won't find too many people who complain that they saved too much.
- The pros invest aggressively, not recklessly. Unless you possess their expertise, you should be putting your money in investments that will match the return of a particular benchmark. Even the investment pros have difficulty beating the market. Therefore, you should be satisfied trying to match it with investments like index funds. For most investors, it's a match made in heaven.
- Speculative investments are not a substitute for regular and systematic investing. If you find yourself without retirement savings in your fifties, you can't say I have to make up for lost time by investing aggressively. You need to start now and keep investing in good times and bad.

- You can't panic when the stock market heads south, as it will inevitably do from time to time. Peter Lynch said this in his book, *Beating the Street*:

  This exerpt from Lynch's book was published by *Money* magazine on March 1, 1993:

  > *Sixty years later, the crash is still scaring people out of stocks, including people in my generation who weren't even born in 1929. In 39 out of the 40 corrections in modern history, those who sold all their stocks would have been sorry. Stocks came back eventually even from the Big One. A decline in stocks is not a surprising event, it's a recurring event—as normal as frigid air in Minnesota. If you live in a cold climate and your outdoor thermometer drops below zero, you don't think of it as the beginning of the next ice age. You put on your parka, throw salt on the walk and remind yourself that by summertime it will be warm outside. A successful investor has the same relationship with a drop in the market as a Minnesotan has with freezing weather. You know it's coming, and you're ready to ride it out, and when your favorite stocks go down with the rest, you jump at the chance to buy more.*

- As we said during our discussions of dollar cost averaging, a downturn in the market gives you the chance to buy more shares with your regular contribution.
- To ensure that a downturn in the market doesn't wipe you out, you need to diversify, diversify, and diversify some more. At any point in time, certain investments will do well and others won't. You need to have your nest egg spread among different types of assets, not just a few. Diversification is the cure for downturns in the market, not a smooth-talking salesperson who pats you on the hand and seems to be so concerned about your welfare.
- It's difficult enough to save and invest for retirement, so don't pass up any freebies that come your way. If your employer will match even a tiny bit of your contribution to a retirement savings plan, don't say no. If the IRS offers tax breaks to help

you keep more of your income and save more for retirement, you've got to make use of them.

- Even Chloe's sick of hearing this one: Investigate before you invest. There are always scam artists waiting to separate you from your money. Unless you investigate, you'll probably succumb to their charm. Quite often, they will belong to the same organizations as you and might seem like pillars of the community. It makes you long for the good old days when the bad guys twirled their handle-bar mustaches and tied the school marm to the railroad tracks.

- There's an old saying that insurance is sold, not bought. Similarly, don't let someone sell you investments you don't want or need. If a financial professional becomes too insistent and uses a high-pressure sales pitch, it should be readily apparent that the person is going to make a great deal of money from your investment. One goal of investing is for you to make more money than the salesperson. Don't let a salesperson posing as your friend sell you a bill of goods.

Can the *MoneyTrack* Method Work for You?

Unlike the shysters who promise you overnight success, the *MoneyTrack* method is designed to help you improve your finances incrementally. It may be years until you realize that the pros' advice actually does work if you stick with it and become a disciplined investor. In addition, you'll hopefully experience an epiphany one day upon realizing that you've become more sophisticated about investing and can spot a scam artist who's peddling a questionable financial product.

Our goal on the *MoneyTrack* program and in this book is to help you become a little bit smarter about investing. This is also our intent when we speak to consumers at conferences sponsored by state securities regulators or in libraries across the country. These sessions are designed to give people objective information about investing in a comfortable setting. Unlike the so-called educational seminars you see advertised, no one tries to sell you anything. Since we're funded by the nonprofit Investor Protection Trust, we have nothing to sell. However, you won't get a lavish meal like you do at those seminars where someone may be pitching unsuitable investment products.

All we can offer is food for thought. Whether you make $12 per hour like Mr. Earl or a whole lot more, it will go a lot further when you become a smarter investor. No one should go through life being a financial illiterate. During the America Saves campaign, Karen Tyler, North Dakota Securities Commissioner and President of the North American Securities Administrators Association, quoted Ben Franklin's immortal words, "An investment in knowledge pays the best interest."

About the Author

P am Krueger is executive producer, co-host, and creator of the national public television series, *MoneyTrack*. *MoneyTrack*'s mission is to help consumers learn how to invest successfully and protect their investments. *MoneyTrack* has aired on more than 200 PBS stations across the country. Though Pam possesses considerable investment expertise and was a stockbroker for nine years, she acts as a facilitator on the series. Her goal is to track down the most respected experts to find out what really works when it comes to investing, and then introduce those experts to real people from the program.

Pam crisscrosses the country to lead investment-related educational seminars in libraries and at events arranged by the Investor Protection Trust. Pam, a board member of the California Jumpstart Coalition, also conducts financial literacy seminars for students at high schools across the county.

Before *MoneyTrack*, Pam created and produced *NETworth*, a one-hour Public Television special about how to use the Internet to manage your money and invest. She also produced *IPO: Investing Pays Off*, a series of 15 short video stories that introduce young teens to the world of investing, saving, and philanthropy. The series earned a CINE Award and was nominated for an Emmy in 2004. The IPO series is used as a teaching tool by thousands of high schools across the country.

Pam was a co-anchor and segment producer on ABC-TV on San Francisco's Emmy Award–winning program, *Marketplace*, as well as KGO-TV's newscasts. She co-anchored and produced TechTV's *The Money Machine*, during the technology boom in the late 1990s.

Pam was also a reporter for the Emmy Award–winning PBS series, *MoneyMoves*.

Although Pam's home base is Tiburon, California, she spends as much time as possible on Cape Cod where she was born. When Chloe, her six year old Labradoodle, takes a break from appearing on *MoneyTrack,* she and Pam watch financial news programs and Animal Planet, depending on who has the remote.

Index

Egleston Square Library Branch
2044 Columbus Avenue
Roxbury, MA 02119